PHARMACY PRACTICE RESEARCH CASE STUDIES

PHARMACY PRACTICE RESEARCH CASE STUDIES

Edited by

ZAHEER-UD-DIN BABAR
Professor in Medicines and Healthcare
Department of Pharmacy
University of Huddersfield
Huddersfield, United Kingdom

ACADEMIC PRESS
An imprint of Elsevier

ELSEVIER

Academic Press is an imprint of Elsevier
125 London Wall, London EC2Y 5AS, United Kingdom
525 B Street, Suite 1650, San Diego, CA 92101, United States
50 Hampshire Street, 5th Floor, Cambridge, MA 02139, United States
The Boulevard, Langford Lane, Kidlington, Oxford OX5 1GB, United Kingdom

Notices
Knowledge and best practice in this field are constantly changing. As new research and experience broaden our understanding, changes in research methods, professional practices, or medical treatment may become necessary.

Practitioners and researchers must always rely on their own experience and knowledge in evaluating and using any information, methods, compounds, or experiments described herein. In using such information or methods they should be mindful of their own safety and the safety of others, including parties for whom they have a professional responsibility.

To the fullest extent of the law, neither the Publisher nor the authors, contributors, or editors, assume any liability for any injury and/or damage to persons or property as a matter of products liability, negligence or otherwise, or from any use or operation of any methods, products, instructions, or ideas contained in the material herein.

Library of Congress Cataloging-in-Publication Data
A catalog record for this book is available from the Library of Congress

British Library Cataloguing-in-Publication Data
A catalogue record for this book is available from the British Library

ISBN 978-0-12-819378-5

For information on all Academic Press publications
visit our website at https://www.elsevier.com/books-and-journals

Publisher: Andre Gerhard Wolff
Acquisitions Editor: Erin Hill-Parks
Editorial Project Manager: Timothy Bennett
Production Project Manager: Punithavathy Govindaradjane
Cover Designer: Christian Bilbow

Typeset by SPi Global, India

Working together
to grow libraries in
developing countries

www.elsevier.com • www.bookaid.org

To my parents

Contents

Contributors

Palli Valapila Abdulrouf
Department of Pharmacy, Women's Wellness and Research Center, Hamad Medical Corporation, Doha, Qatar

Afif Ahmed
Department of Pharmacy, Women's Wellness and Research Center, Hamad Medical Corporation, Doha, Qatar

Basmah Albabtain
Department of Pharmaceutical Practice, College of Pharmacy, Princess Nourah Bint Abdulrahman University, Riyadh, Saudi Arabia; School of Pharmacy, Institute of Clinical Sciences, University of Birmingham, Birmingham, United Kingdom

Moza AlHail
Department of Pharmacy, Women's Wellness and Research Center, Hamad Medical Corporation, Doha, Qatar

Muna Said Al-Ismail
Department of Clinical Pharmacy and Practice, College of Pharmacy, QU Health, Qatar University, Doha, Qatar

Doua AlSaad
Department of Pharmacy, Women's Wellness and Research Center, Hamad Medical Corporation, Doha, Qatar

Muna AlSaadi
Department of Pharmacy, Women's Wellness and Research Center, Hamad Medical Corporation, Doha, Qatar

Filipa Alves da Costa
Research Institute for Medicines (iMED.ULisboa), Faculty of Pharmacy, University of Lisbon, Lisbon; Centre for Interdisciplinary Research Egas Moniz (CiiEM), University Institute Egas Moniz, Caparica, Portugal

Ahmed Awaisu
Department of Clinical Pharmacy and Practice, College of Pharmacy, QU Health, Qatar University, Doha, Qatar

Zaheer-Ud-Din Babar
Centre for Pharmaceutical Policy and Practice Research, Department of Pharmacy, University of Huddersfield, Huddersfield, United Kingdom

Wasim Baqir
Research and Development, Northumbria Healthcare NHS Foundation Trust, Northumberland; School of Healthcare, Faculty of Medicine and Health, The University of Leeds, Leeds, United Kingdom

Ghada Bawazeer
Clinical Pharmacy Department, College of Pharmacy, King Saud University, Riyadh, Saudi Arabia

Hayley J. Berry
Centre for Pharmacy Postgraduate Education (CPPE), University of Manchester, Manchester, United Kingdom

Fraser N. Birrell
Northumbria Healthcare NHS Foundation Trust, Northumberland, United Kingdom

Ruth Buchan
Community Pharmacy West Yorkshire, Leeds, United Kingdom

Amy Chan
School of Pharmacy, University of Auckland, Auckland, New Zealand

Ejaz Cheema
School of Pharmacy, Institute of Clinical Sciences, University of Birmingham, Birmingham, United Kingdom

Rula Darwish
Department of Pharmaceutics and Pharmaceutical Technology, Faculty of Pharmacy, University of Jordan, Amman, Jordan

Wessam ElKassem
Department of Pharmacy, Women's Wellness and Research Center, Hamad Medical Corporation, Doha, Qatar

Kevin Flint
School of Pharmacy and Medical Sciences, University of Bradford, Bradford, United Kingdom

David Gardner
Department of Psychiatry and College of Pharmacy, Dalhousie University, Halifax, NS, Canada

Hayley C. Gorton
School of Applied Sciences, University of Huddersfield, Huddersfield, United Kingdom

Muhammad Abdul Hadi
School of Pharmacy, Institute of Clinical Sciences, University of Birmingham, Birmingham, United Kingdom

Gil Hardy
Ipanema Research Trust, Auckland, New Zealand

Rabia Hussain
Commonwealth Pharmacists Association, London, United Kingdom; Faculty of Pharmacy, The University of Lahore, Lahore, Pakistan

Sue Jones
School of Pharmacy and Medical Sciences, University of Bradford, Bradford, United Kingdom

Tania L. Jones
Population Health Sciences Institute, Newcastle University, Newcastle-upon-Tyne;
Northumbria Healthcare NHS Foundation Trust, Northumberland, United Kingdom

Saira Khan
School of Pharmacy and Medical Sciences, University of Bradford, Bradford,
United Kingdom

Mohamed Izham Mohamed Ibrahim
Social & Administrative Pharmacy; Research and Graduate Studies—Pharmacy, College of
Pharmacy, QU Health, Qatar University, Doha, Qatar

Ahmed Moursi
Department of Pharmacy, Women's Wellness and Research Center, Hamad Medical
Corporation, Doha, Qatar

Andrea Murphy
College of Pharmacy, School of Nursing, Department of Psychiatry, Dalhousie University,
Halifax, NS, Canada

Claire O'Reilly
Faculty of Medicine and Health, University of Sydney, Sydney, NSW, Australia

Theodoros Papasavvas
Cardiac Rehabilitation Department, Heart Hospital, Hamad Medical Corporation, Doha,
Qatar

Ema Paulino
Farmácia Nuno Álvares, Almada; Ezfy, Lda., Lisboa, Portugal

Teresa Isichei Pounds
PGY1 Pharmacy Residency Program, Pharmacy Clinical Services at the Atlanta Medical
Center, Atlanta; Experiential Education of South University School of Pharmacy, Savannah,
GA, United States

Myroslava Sekh
Clinical Pharmacy, Pharmacotherapy and Medical Standardization, Danylo Halytsky Lviv
National Medical University, Lviv, Ukraine

Saba Shamim
Centre for Pharmaceutical Policy and Practice Research, Department of Pharmacy,
University of Huddersfield, Huddersfield, United Kingdom

Hadar Zaman
School of Pharmacy and Medical Sciences, University of Bradford, Bradford,
United Kingdom

Andriy Zimenkovsky
Clinical Pharmacy, Pharmacotherapy and Medical Standardization, Danylo Halytsky Lviv
National Medical University, Lviv, Ukraine

Preface

Pharmacy practice research is increasing globally. For impactful research, methodical data and studies are needed; however, critics argue that a large number of studies in this field lack robustness. This book sheds light on this issue and provides an overview of pharmacy practice research globally, the methodologies and techniques used, as well as in what setting this research is conducted.

Pharmacy Practice Research Case Studies narrates examples, interventions, and case studies. The topics include pharmacy services, medicines use, medicine compliance, counseling, evaluation of pharmacy services, as well as the use of randomized controlled trials (RCTs).

The chapters are in different thematic categories. Some chapters elaborate on a specific "pharmacy service," while others describe the country's literature on pharmacy practice. However, the research methods used are a central theme in all these chapters.

The first chapter describes clinical pharmacy services in cardiac rehabilitation in Qatar. Cardiac rehabilitation programs reduce cardiovascular morbidity and mortality; however, they are underutilized. This chapter presents a global overview of these programs including their benefits and components. The second chapter provides an overview of the clinical pharmacy service innovation in obstetrics and gynecology settings.

Some chapters provide a global literature review on a specific pharmacy service. These reviews also elaborate on methodologies used in these studies. For example, Chapter 3 provides an overview of the literature on pharmacy practice research in a home care setting. Similarly, Chapter 8 provides an overview of pharmacy practice interventions delivered by pharmacists relating to cardiovascular health.

Several chapters provide a literature review coupled with an additional case study. Chapters 4, 6, and 12 fall into this category. Chapter 4 provides a broad overview of pharmacy practice research in Saudi Arabia. The chapter also outlines a proposal for a community pharmacy-based medication therapy management clinic. Chapter 6 elaborates on pharmacy staff attitudes and experiences related to suicide. Chapter 12 presents a review of the role of community pharmacists in improving pharmacovigilance. A case study is also presented with regard to community pharmacists' experiences and views on pharmacovigilance.

Chapter 4 on Saudi Arabia and Chapter 5 on Ukraine elaborate on country-specific pharmacy practice research. Chapter 7 discusses community pharmacy service development and evaluation for people living with learning disabilities. A mixed-methods service evaluation with an ethnographic approach was used to evaluate the effectiveness of this service.

Chapter 9 considers pharmacy practice and continuing professional development (CPD) in low and middle-income countries (LMICs). Evidence shows that CPD can improve clinical knowledge and improve pharmacists' perceptions of their practice. However, the extent to which CPD is implemented varies widely between countries and health systems. This chapter presents a literature review on CPD as well as case studies on Pakistan and Jordan.

Chapter 10 explores the role of the pharmacist in personalizing pharmaceutical care from UK clinical practice. This is done by conducting a randomized controlled trial. Chapter 11 discusses pharmacy services for safe parenteral nutrition. The case study presents a multidisciplinary team approach that leads to effective and safe nutrition.

The purpose of this book is to present a range of methodologies and techniques used in current pharmacy practice. An analysis of the chapters reveal that several pharmacy practice research methodologies are used in this book. An evaluation by using randomized controlled trials is presented in Chapter 10, while the use of qualitative methods can be seen in Chapters 9 and 12. A mixed-methods approach is used in Chapters 4 and 7, and quantitative research methods in Chapter 6, while a service evaluation is presented in Chapter 1.

This book provides a snapshot of global pharmacy practice research and the methods and techniques used.

I hope that the book will be useful for academics, practitioners, students, and policy makers, as well as all those who are interested in medicines use research.

Zaheer-Ud-Din Babar

Professor in Medicines and Healthcare, Department of Pharmacy, University of Huddersfield, Huddersfield, United Kingdom

CHAPTER 1

Experiences with clinical pharmacy services in a cardiac rehabilitation program in Qatar

Muna Said Al-Ismail[a], Ahmed Awaisu[a], Theodoros Papasavvas[b], and Zaheer-Ud-Din Babar[c]

[a]Department of Clinical Pharmacy and Practice, College of Pharmacy, QU Health, Qatar University, Doha, Qatar
[b]Cardiac Rehabilitation Department, Heart Hospital, Hamad Medical Corporation, Doha, Qatar
[c]Centre for Pharmaceutical Policy and Practice Research, Department of Pharmacy, University of Huddersfield, Huddersfield, United Kingdom

Background

Cardiovascular diseases (CVDs), including, but not restricted to, coronary heart disease (CHD), stroke, heart failure (HF), and peripheral arterial disease, are recognized as the leading cause of mortality globally, accounting for an estimated 17.8 million deaths in 2017 [1]. Of these, CHD and stroke account for around 85% of all CVD-related deaths [1, 2]. By 2030, it is projected that CVD-related deaths will reach around 24 million, mainly from CHD and stroke [3]. Qatar is a member state of the Gulf Cooperation Council (GCC) and is currently undergoing healthcare restructuring and transformation, with several comprehensive strategies being implemented to develop an advanced world-class healthcare system. Nonetheless, Qatar's healthcare system is challenged by very high rates of noncommunicable diseases (NCDs), in particular CVDs, which account for 27% of NCDs mortality [4, 5]. In 2017, CHD was the leading cause of mortality in Qatar, contributing to around two-thirds of the total death rate [6]. Therefore, the effectiveness of and accessibility to secondary prevention health-related programs are vital to decrease the burden of CVDs in Qatar.

Cardiac rehabilitation (CR) is a well-established model of care for secondary prevention, designed to mitigate the great burden of CVDs globally [7]. It is well-established that CR is a cost-effective model of care that has been proven to reduce CV mortality and morbidity by 20% [8, 9]. Accordingly, CR programs are recommended by the American Heart Association (AHA) and the American College of Cardiology (ACC) as beneficial and effective (Class I) in the treatment of patients with CVDs [10].

Pharmacy Practice Research Case Studies
https://doi.org/10.1016/B978-0-12-819378-5.00009-X
1

What is a cardiac rehabilitation program?

As defined by various health organizations:

> CR services are comprehensive, long-term programs involving medical evaluation, prescribed exercise, cardiac risk factor modification, education, and counselling. These programs are designed to limit the physiological and psychological effects of cardiac illness, reduce the risk for sudden death or re-infarction, control cardiac symptoms, stabilize or reverse the atherosclerotic process, and enhance the psychosocial and vocational status of selected patients [10, 11].

CR is designed for patients who have experienced one or more of the following conditions: CHD; recent cardiovascular surgery and intervention (coronary arteries or structural heart disease including heart valves); chronic HF; cardiac transplantation; and pacemaker, implantable cardioverter defibrillator (ICD), and cardiac resynchronization therapy (CRT) recipients [11, 12].

Consensus statements from the AHA, the American Association of Cardiovascular and Pulmonary Rehabilitation (AACVPR), and the Agency for Health Care Policy and Research (AHCPR) recommend that all CR programs should contain specific core components that aim to improve clinical stability and symptoms control, reduce overall CV risk, improve adherence to pharmacological intervention, improve prognosis, and advance quality of life (QoL) [12]. These core components consist of patient assessment with medical control, physical activity counseling, prescription of exercise training, diet/nutritional counseling, weight control management, lipid management, blood pressure (BP) monitoring and management, diabetes management, smoking cessation, vocational support, and psychosocial management [10–12].

Moreover, the AHA and AACVPR recommend that CR programs should provide their services through a multidisciplinary skilled team [12, 13]. The availability of expertise from different professionals can facilitate recovery, identify healthcare needs, and prevent deterioration of the patient's condition [13]. The CR team entails cardiologists, physiotherapists, nurses, psychologists, dieticians, pharmacists, exercise physiologists, occupational therapists, consultant professionals, general practitioners, and social services experts [12, 13]. To assure the continuity of care for patients with CVDs, the services provided in CR programs are delivered through three different phases [14]. Phase I represents an early intervention during the acute stay in the hospital, phase II is an outpatient program of exercise and education, while phase III is a community-based maintenance exercise program with focus on prevention of CV events recurrence and maintaining healthy lifestyle [12–14].

Cardiac rehabilitation programs globally and in Qatar

Although the benefits of CR in reducing mortality [15, 16] and readmissions [9, 17] and in improving QoL [18–20] in patients with heart diseases are well-documented, CR remains largely underutilized. Remarkably, CR is available in only half of the countries in the world and higher-income countries are more likely to provide CR than lower-income countries [21]. For example, CR programs are available in 91% of European countries [22] and in only 17% of African countries [21], indicating that resource constraints may significantly impact CR service establishment and delivery. This is also supported in the literature that describes CR delivery worldwide, in which the major barriers to CR availability and delivery are reported to be lack of human and/or financial resources, and space constraints [23].

Furthermore, it is well-documented that women are less likely to be referred [24] and to enroll [25] in CR than men, and this is reflected in the CR programs worldwide, where only 11.8% of CR centers provide women-only CR services [26]. The global CR program volume (the median number of patients served by a program annually) has a median of 248 patients, but varies significantly across countries. This is also positively influenced by the presence of a systematic referral system, the presence of both public and private healthcare insurance funding and coverage for the CR program, and the availability of alternative CR models (e.g., home-based CR) [21]. Canada and Europe have a median program volume of 250 patients [27] and 300 patients [22], respectively. The median number of exercise sessions that are included in the CR programs worldwide is 24 and varies significantly across countries, as it is positively influenced by country income classification, more involvement of physicians, proximity to other programs, and accepting patients with noncardiac indications [28]. Cardiac rehabilitation programs in the Americas include more sessions (36 sessions) than most other programs in the world [28].

Qatar is one of the Eastern Mediterranean countries that provide CR [29] and it has one program currently running in the country. The CR program in Qatar is situated in the national Heart Hospital under the Hamad Medical Corporation (HMC). The Heart Hospital is a state-of-the-art specialist hospital in Qatar for cardiology and cardiothoracic surgeries. It is made up of a 20-bed coronary care unit, a 12-bed cardiothoracic intensive care unit, a 24-bed surgical high-dependency unit, and a 60-bed ward. The program utilizes best practice from around the world and is consistent with the latest CR guidelines [30]. It includes the following core components: patient assessment, physical activity counseling, exercise training, nutrition counseling, weight control management, lipid management, BP management, smoking cessation, psychosocial management, and evaluation of the program outcomes and establishment of structured follow-up. The multidisciplinary team in Qatar's CR program consists of cardiologists, nurses, physiotherapists, exercise physiologists, dietitians, clinical pharmacists, and occupational therapists. The program offers an average of 24 exercise sessions over 2 months and it had a program volume of 275 patients in 2019. The standard provided model of CR is hospital-based CR, and the program also provides the option for alternative models of CR, including home-based CR and hybrid hospital- and home-based CR, to patients who find them more feasible. The program is publicly funded and is offered with no fee to all patients.

The role of clinical pharmacists in cardiac rehabilitation programs

Clinical pharmacists are specialty-trained practitioners who practice in different healthcare settings, in collaboration with their patients, physicians, nurse practitioners, and other healthcare professionals. Their services and activities are focused on optimizing medication therapy and promoting health, wellness, and disease prevention [31, 32]. Clinical pharmacists' pivotal roles as both team members and as individual practitioners have been extensively documented in the literature and many studies have shown positive clinical, economic, and humanistic outcomes toward patient-directed care in a variety of settings, largely through drug therapy optimization, drug-related problems (DRPs) resolution and prevention, medication reconciliation, and patient education [32, 33].

In the last few decades, there has been increasing prevalence of diseases and aging populations that have necessitated more services from healthcare providers, including pharmacists [34]. As part of their expanded role, clinical pharmacists have been actively participating in various multidisciplinary chronic disease management programs such as hypertension (HTN), diabetes, dyslipidemia, anticoagulation therapy, and others [35–37]. These programs are designed for both patients and clinicians, and are delivered in different healthcare settings including inpatient settings, ambulatory settings, and community pharmacies [38, 39]. The clinical pharmacy services that are provided in these programs generally include, but are not limited to, medication management and review, patient education and counseling, lifestyle modification, medication adherence improvement, and collaborative management with other healthcare professionals [37–40].The value of these services has been demonstrated by improvement in clinical outcomes such as glycated hemoglobin A1c, BP, cholesterol levels, and medication adherence; and enhancement of QoL [38, 39].

As with other chronic diseases, disease management programs for CVDs such as HF and CHD have demonstrated improved outcomes [38, 40–43]. The significance of the clinical pharmacist's services that include medication evaluation, patient education and follow-up, and interventions in CVDs was evident in a prospective randomized controlled trial (RCT) of 181 patients with HF treated at an outpatient clinic [42]. At 6-month follow-up, the patients who received clinical pharmacist interventions had significantly lowered all-cause mortality and HF events compared with the control group (4 vs. 16; $P = .05$). Furthermore, patients in the intervention group were closer to targeted doses of the guideline-directed medical therapy. Likewise, another prospective RCT examined the impact of involving clinical pharmacists in the management of patients with CHD [44]. In addition to the usual care, the experimental group received pharmacist support that included medication review, patient education, lifestyle management, discharge guidance, and telephone follow-up. The patients in the intervention group had more pronounced understanding of their treatment goals, drug regimens, and lifestyle modifications ($P < .01$). Furthermore, medication adherence was significantly higher in the intervention group.

As stated earlier, a CR program is an excellent approach for secondary prevention in patients with CVDs [10]. Although the substantial benefits of the nonpharmacological strategies offered in CR programs such as exercise or healthy diet are well-documented, appropriate medication management and high medication adherence rate are other effective known ways to prevent CV events [40, 43, 45]. Unfortunately, the values of these pharmacological strategies are underreported when discussing CR [46, 47]. Likewise, despite the proven benefits of clinical pharmacists' involvement in the provision of various multidisciplinary disease management programs including CVDs, their participation in CR programs is limited and their role is underutilized [47, 48].

In a recent prospective RCT published in 2017 in Egypt, the impact of a clinical pharmacist-led follow-up program in patients with acute coronary syndrome (ACS) who were enrolled in a phase II CR program was evaluated [49].The outcomes evaluated included DRP occurrence, cardiac physiological risk parameters, QoL, and CHD-related knowledge. Forty ACS patients were randomly assigned to either a control group, who received standard medical care, or an intervention group, who received standard medical care plus clinical pharmacist-provided services. Those services included comprehensive baseline assessment through patient record and patient interview, DRP identification and management, patient educational sessions, and patient adherence assessment through telephone follow-up. After 3-month follow-up, there was a significant difference between the intervention and the control groups in the percentage change of DRPs, patient's adherence score, knowledge score, QoL scores, heart rate (HR), BP, low-density lipoprotein cholesterol (LDL), total cholesterol (TC), and fasting blood glucose (FBG). However, the difference between the two groups in number of patients achieving goals for BP, HR, FBS, and TC was not statistically significant, except for LDL. It is worth noting that the clinical pharmacist recommendations were discussed with the cardiologist to ensure their implementation, and the acceptance rate of total DRP-managing interventions was 96.2%. Although this study has several limitations such as the small sample size, the short study duration, and the high dropout rate, it proved that clinical pharmacist involvement in CR programs can play an important role for patients with ACS.

In a prepost quasiexperimental nonequivalent groups comparison study conducted in Malaysia, the impact of early pharmaceutical care (PC) interventions in phase I and phase II CR programs on health-related QoL (HRQoL) was evaluated in 112 patients diagnosed with ACS [50]. The study had three groups: the modified CR program (MCRP), conventional CR program (CCRP), and control group. Patients in the MCRP group received clinical pharmacy services in addition to the CCRP protocol, while patients in the control group were those not willing to participate in any CR program. In phase I, during the patient's hospital stay, the services provided for the MCRP group included intensive pharmacological and nonpharmacological counseling sessions, and PC interventions that were delivered before discharge. In the outpatient phase II, the clinical pharmacists provided individual and group educational sessions. The sessions involved an interactive counseling about risk factors for CHD, relaxation, treatment plan, drug-related nutrition intake, and medication adherence. Upon 1-year follow-up, patients in the MCRP group had better physical component summary in comparison to the CCRP and control group with mean differences of 11.46 ($P = .008$), 10.96 ($P = .002$), and 6.41 ($P = .006$), respectively. Furthermore, the MCRP group showed statistically significant better social functioning than the CCRP and control group. As for the mental health component, the MCRP patient group showed the highest improvement among the three groups. The CCRP participants also performed much better compared to the control group, but less well than the MRCP patients did. Overall, this study has proven the well-known importance of early CR for patients with ACS. Additionally, in this study the significance of clinical pharmacy services in terms of improving HRQoL was demonstrated. Notably, the MCRP group consistently showed better QoL, was more highly motivated, and benefited most from the CRP. The findings of this study are of immense importance as HRQoL is an independent predictor of mortality and morbidity in patients who are suffering from ACS [51].

In a review done by Simon et al. in 2005, 13 reports were identified, of which six reports were purely descriptive of pharmacists' involvement in CR (all from the United States) and seven were evaluative reports (four from the United States, two from the United Kingdom, and one from Canada) [48]. The main descriptions of the pharmacists' involvement in CR programs included inpatient medication-related educational sessions to both patients and healthcare providers and PC activities provision. Another unique involvement described in the review is the communication of the CR pharmacist with the patients' community pharmacists in order to maintain continuity of service and care. As for the evaluative reports, there is a lack of substantial research. One study found QoL and economic benefits due to the pharmacist involvement in CR, and another study found that health professionals provide most of the medicines information and education required by CR patients. However, these studies were weakened by a lack of meaningful outcome measures. This review has demonstrated that there was insufficient evidence on which to base strong conclusions about the effectiveness of the pharmacist involvement in CR programs. This study has implications for pharmacy practitioners, researchers, and policymakers in CR and emphasizes the importance of the need for more substantial research using a range of methodologies that evaluate the involvement of pharmacists in CR and to shed light on their substantial importance in this crucial secondary prevention healthcare setting.

Previous studies from the West (Canada and United States) have documented evidence of the benefit of pharmacist involvement in CR programs [52, 53]. Alsabbagh et al. conducted an open-label RCT involving patients with ACS who were eligible for a phase II CR program in a community-based hospital in Canada to assess the impact of pharmacist service on patients' adherence to CV medications [52]. The investigators randomized the patients into two groups in which the intervention group received pharmacist service through telephone calls to identify the barriers to optimal utilization or adherence with post-ACS or postrevascularization medications, and to provide tailored patient education when required. The control group received phase II CCRP services only. After 6-month follow-up, there was no difference in the mean adherence to all recently initiated CV medications between the intervention and the control groups (88.8% vs. 89.9%; $P=.73$). In a study conducted in USA in patients with ACS who were enrolled in phase II CR, the impact of pharmacist services including consultations and DRPs resolution was reported [53]. The QoL, economic value, and CR staff members' satisfaction all showed better improvement in patients who received the pharmacist-provided services compared to the control group.

Table 1 provides a summary of different studies that describe pharmacist's involvement in CR program and their reported outcomes.

The role of the clinical pharmacist in cardiac rehabilitation programs: Experience from Qatar

Since 2007, pharmacy practice in Qatar has witnessed a positive transformation and development due to a number of national initiatives, which include accreditation programs of healthcare services, establishment of the first and only national college of pharmacy that is internationally accredited, and a trend toward recruitment of pharmacists with advanced degrees in pharmacy practice (doctor of pharmacy (PharmD), masters in clinical pharmacy, etc.) [54, 55]. This change has resulted in introducing generalized and specialized cognitive pharmacy services in which a variety of patient-centered care has been introduced. However, most of these developments predominantly occur in institutionalized settings in Qatar. Clinical pharmacists are actively involved in inpatient and outpatient settings, especially within HMC's hospitals [55]. The Heart Hospital in Qatar has witnessed more focus on ambulatory and outpatient care in which clinical pharmacists provide services in HF clinics, anticoagulation clinics, and a CR program.

The pharmacy services provided in the CR program of the Heart Hospital are mainly focused in the outpatient phase II program and are run by one full-time employee (FTE), a clinical pharmacist with a PharmD degree who joined the CR program 3 years after its establishment. That clinical pharmacist provides a variety of PC services for all patients who are enrolled in phase II of the CR program. In phase II, patients typically start the program around 4–6 weeks after discharge from the hospital.

Table 1 Summary of pharmacist involvement in different CR programs.

Author (year published)	Year(s) study conducted and location	Study design (number of participants and primary diagnosis)	CR program phase	Type of CR pharmacist service (intervention)[a]	Follow-up duration	Outcome measures	Summary of results
Casper et al. (2018) [49]	2017, Egypt	RCT (40/ACS)	Phase II	Baseline assessment, DRPs identification and resolution, patient education, adherence follow-up	3 months	Clinical outcomes: SBP/DBP, HR, FBG, TC, LDL	The intervention group showed a significant improvement in the percentage change in all clinical outcomes
						Humanistic outcomes: QoL (assessed by SF-36 questionnaire)	The intervention group showed a significant improvement in the scores of all the domains of the SF-36 questionnaire
						Medication adherence (assessed by MMAS-8)	The intervention group had a significant improvement in percentage change in the total score of MMAS-8
						DRPs	The acceptance percentage of total DRPs managing interventions was 96.2%

Continued

Table 1 Summary of pharmacist involvement in different CR programs—cont'd

Author (year published)	Year(s) study conducted and location	Study design (number of participants and primary diagnosis)	CR program phase	Type of CR pharmacist service (intervention)[a]	Follow-up duration	Outcome measures	Summary of results
Anchah et al. (2017) [50]	2008–10, Malaysia	A prepost quasiexperimental nonequivalent study (112/ACS)	Phase I and short-course Phase II	Phase I: MCRP intensive educational sessions and PC interventions Phase II: MCRP individual education sessions, which covers mainly pharmacotherapy, CV risk factors, and drug-related nutrition	12 months	HR QoL (assessed by SF-36 questionnaire)	The patients in the MCRP group had better QoL in terms of the physical component and social functioning in comparison to the patients who received conventional CR services and patients in the control group who were not enrolled in the CR program. The mental component score reported in the MCRP patient group showed the highest improvement among the three groups

| Alsabbagh et al. (2012) [52] | 2009–10, Canada | RCT—open label (95/ACS) | Phase II (eligible for CR, regardless of participation in the CR program) | Telephone-based service to: 1. identify the barriers to optimal utilization or adherence with post-ACS or postvascularization medications 2. provide tailored patient education Family physician contacted, if warranted, to address important issues | 6 months | Mean adherence to CV medications (assessed by MPR using electronic filling) | A total of 129 telephone interactions were performed in the intervention group (median, two calls) There was no difference in the mean adherence to all recently initiated CV medications between the intervention and the control groups (88.8% vs. 89.9%; $P = .73$) |

Continued

Table 1 Summary of pharmacist involvement in different CR programs—cont'd

Author (year published)	Year(s) study conducted and location	Study design (number of participants and primary diagnosis)	CR program phase	Type of CR pharmacist service (intervention)[a]	Follow-up duration	Outcome measures	Summary of results
Kammer (2004) [53]	2000, United States	(27/ACS)	Phase II	Weekly pharmacist face-to-face/telephone interview, which included initial assessment, consultation, and resolving DRPs (in collaboration with the physician)	12 weeks	QoL (assessed by Ferrans and Powers QoL Index—CV III) Economic value (assessed by the CliniTrends software (American Society of Health-System Pharmacists, Bethesda, MD))	The intervention group showed an 11% increase in the overall QoL score and a 14% increase in the health and functioning component of QoL It was estimated that for every dollar spent on medication-related services by a pharmacist, there was a potential to save $13.50

				CR staff members feedback about clinical pharmacy service (assessed by a brief evaluation form)	The staff members expressed predominantly favorable opinions about the pharmacist's services and unanimously supported more pharmacist involvement in the CR in the future

ACS, acute coronary syndrome; CADE-Q, Coronary Artery Disease Education Questionnaire; CV, cardiovascular; DBP, diastolic blood pressure; DRP, drug-related problem; FBG, fasting blood glucose; HR, heart rate; HRQoL, health-related quality of life; LDL, low-density lipoprotein; MCRP, modified cardiac rehabilitation program; MMAS-8, 8-item Morisky Medication Adherence Scale; MPR, medication possession ratio; PC, pharmaceutical care; QoL, quality of life; RCT, randomized controlled trail; SF-36, Short Form-36 Health Survey questions; SBP, systolic blood pressure; TC, total cholesterol.
aServices provided are in addition to conventional CR program services.

This phase encompasses multidisciplinary services and exercise sessions that are based on the program schedule. It consists of educational sessions about disease states, medications, diet, lifestyle modification, and exercise. During this time, the CR team works very closely to optimize patients' clinical and humanistic outcomes. Notably, phase I CR services are provided by the clinical pharmacists during acute care in the medical wards.

The clinical pharmacist's primary responsibilities include the following: ensuring proper drug therapy selection, patient monitoring, comprehensive patient-centered education, delivery of individualized PC to patients to guarantee safe and effective medication use, and ensuring that patients receive continuity of care by referring them to other healthcare providers. In addition, the pharmacist provides a smoking cessation service, attends weekly multidisciplinary meetings to discuss the exercising patients at the program, and provides education to the team.

Description of clinical pharmacy services and activities at the CR program in Qatar

Patient assessment

At scheduled appointments, patients are assessed individually upon their first visit to the CR program. A clinical pharmacist interviews the patient to determine if his/her drug-related needs are achieved and that all his/her medications are appropriately indicated, effective, and safe. For the purpose of this initial assessment, the clinical pharmacist collects patients' information from the electronic medical records and patient interview. The information gathered is saved in a special document, which is developed by the clinical pharmacist based on the PC model, to be used as a reference during all the patient's encounters in his/her CR program. The information includes the patient's demographics, medical conditions, medications list (including prescription and nonprescription), medication adherence, social history, allergies and adverse drug reactions, immunization history, surgical history, laboratory data, diagnostic tests, and vital signs. In addition, the patient's medication experience is assessed by evaluating his/her expectations, concerns, and understanding of his/her medical therapy. Data regarding the patient's diet, exercise, and psychosocial status are discussed with and collected from the dietitian, exercise specialist, and occupational therapist, respectively, who are CR team members. Upon patient assessment, collected data is analyzed, DRPs are identified, and a care plan is developed either to prevent or to resolve the DRPs, if any. The care plan is developed and discussed with the attending CR cardiologist, the patient and his/her care-giver, and other CR team members, wherever appropriate. The care plan is documented and saved in the clinical pharmacist's special document.

Education and counseling

During the initial assessment and when required, the patients are educated and counseled about all their medical therapies and medical conditions. Educational sessions are conducted at the clinical pharmacist's clinic to ensure privacy and to give opportunity for the patient to engage in confidential communication. Educational sessions are tailored to the patient's expectations, concerns, cultural beliefs, knowledge, and health literacy level. The clinical pharmacist provides information orally and by using visual aids. The latter includes the use of medications containers and special educational materials that are developed by the clinical pharmacist. The educational material contains easy-to-understand photos for the most commonly encountered diseases in the CR program. Moreover, according to the patient's health literacy level, internationally approved pictograms are used during the educational sessions, and the patient is provided with an individualized printout of photos of his/her medication boxes along with the instructions to be used by the patient to recall the information or to be shared with any healthcare provider, if needed. The content of the medication education and counseling sessions is based on the American Society of Health-System Pharmacists' recommendations (ASHP) [56]. The content to be discussed is based on the clinical pharmacist's professional judgment according to each patient's individual regimen and care plan. In addition to patient education, the clinical pharmacist provides educational sessions and workshops in the continuous professional development (CPD) program of the CR department, with various healthcare providers as attendees.

Medication adherence assessment and follow-up

Improving and/or maintaining adherence to CV medications within 6 months from the time of enrollment in the program so that the patient has medications at least 80% of the time is one of the clinical pharmacist's shared goal for all patients who attend CR phase II. Medication adherence is assessed by both subjective and objective approaches. The former is by using an open-ended questionnaire that is developed by the clinical pharmacist based on literature review, and the latter by calculating the cumulative medication gap (CMG) [57]. The developed questionnaire aims to identify the common factors of medication nonadherence, which may be socioeconomic, therapy-related, patient-related, and condition-related [58]. The CMG is calculated by using refill data from the Heart Hospital electronic pharmacy system. It represents the proportion of time that the patient did not have his/her medications available. All CMG data are kept in an Excel sheet by the pharmacist so patients can be followed up easily. The clinical pharmacist assesses medication adherence during the initial assessment, 2 months later, and at 6-month follow-up. To improve a patient's medication adherence, if needed, the clinical pharmacist provides tailored services such as providing more educational sessions and educational leaflets, and reminder phone calls. Moreover, the pharmacist might seek inputs from the CR team members including the cardiologist, exercise specialist, and the nurse, especially for patients with complex health conditions.

Follow-up evaluation

Upon scheduled face-to-face interviews or telephone calls, the patients are followed up to determine to what extent the developed care plan is producing the desired effects, achieving goals of therapy, and not resulting in any undesirable outcome. The follow-up evaluation is systematic and ongoing. Upon discharge from CR phase II, the clinical pharmacist keeps following up with the patient, by either scheduled appointments or telephone calls follow-up, until the desired goals of therapy are achieved and to ensure continuity of care. Furthermore, medication adherence is assessed during the follow-up appointments. As with the assessment, the patient and his/ her caregiver and other CR team members are involved in the process, as appropriate. Since the Heart Hospital is a specialty hospital, the clinical pharmacist might communicate with other healthcare providers in other healthcare facilities to ensure proper communication, patient management, and continuity of care.

Smoking cessation clinic

The smoking cessation clinic provides smoking cessation-related services to all patients enrolled in the phase II CR program who smoke. The clinic was developed in collaboration with the CR program manager and a cardiologist. The components included the clinic workflow, behavioral change counseling form, and the potential treatment plan. All patients who smoke are scheduled an appointment in the clinic to be assessed by the clinical pharmacist, and the CR cardiologist when required, who uses the transtheoretical model of health behavior change in deciding upon the plan of care, which could include motivational interviews, tailored education, and medication prescribing [59]. The assessment outcomes are discussed with the CR cardiologist and the patient to agree upon the plan. Patients are regularly followed up during their time in CR phase II to assess their smoking and behavior change status. In cases where medications for smoking cessation such as nicotine replacement therapy or bupropion SR are prescribed, the clinical pharmacist will assess medications safety and efficacy and patients' adherence.

Multidisciplinary interactions

To ensure proper team communication and optimize patients' outcomes, the CR team sets a weekly multidisciplinary meeting to discuss the status of all phase II patients. The meeting consists of CR cardiologists, nurses, dietitians, exercise specialists, occupational therapists, and the clinical pharmacist. During the meeting, the clinical pharmacist shares with the team any remarks and updates regarding all patients so that all the team can be aware of the pharmacist's plan of care; this also allows the team to share inputs.

Documentation

All the above-described services are documented in a special documentation file developed by the clinical pharmacist and kept saved in the clinical pharmacist computer. This helps in the ease of information access and sharing with the CR team. More importantly, all clinial pharmacist-patient encounters are documented in the hospital electronic system under each patient's personal health file so any healthcare provider who provide services for that individual patient can access and follow up the clinical pharmacist's plan of care. The clinical pharmacist documents each patient encounter, including initial assessment, medication counseling and education, smoking cessation-related services, and adherence assessment, using a SOAP format. Furthermore, all clinical pharmacist interventions and ADR reporting are documented in a special format in the electronic system for each individual patient.

Summary of clinical pharmacists interventions

During 2016, the total number of clinical pharmacist interventions in the phase II CR program was 321 and the acceptance rate was 89.4%. The distribution of the most common drug categories involved in DRPs was as follows: CV agents (200), vitamin and nutritional agents (48), gastrointestinal agents (31), and endocrine system and hormonal agents (26).

The distribution of the most common recommendations by the clinical pharmacist was as follows: dosing optimization (20%), need for additional therapy (17%), adherence improvement (9.6%), and discontinuation of therapy with no indication (8.4%).

Evidence-based pharmacy services in cardiac rehabilitation programs and future directions

To meet the fast-growing need for safe and effective uses of medicines, the WHO, the International Pharmaceutical Federation (FIP), and many other pharmacy associations have highlighted the need to expand the clinical services provided by pharmacists in both hospital and community settings, including cognitive pharmacy services in CR programs [60]. Therefore, pharmacy practice has expanded and is currently considered more diverse in terms of scope of practice and practice setting [61]. Community pharmacists are highly accessible to patients and play a significant role in providing care and promoting public health in communities [62, 63]. In addition to the dispensing role, community pharmacists have recently become more involved in cognitive services such as disease management and medication management programs, screening/wellness counseling, and immunization services [63].

However, in the era of evidence-based healthcare, it is insufficient to propose new services and new roles for pharmacy without demonstrating evidence of benefits [64, 65]. Hence, the services must be proven to be cost-effective to the healthcare system, patients, and society. Pharmacy practice research is the gateway to providing such evidence, and can ultimately inform development of new policies and demonstrate the feasibility and value of such services [64–67]. Although the impact of both community and hospital pharmacy services in improving organizational and patient care outcomes has been widely reported in the literature [34], there is paucity of evidence on the value and impact of pharmacist-provided services in CR programs globally. Looking at the Qatar case study highlighted in this chapter, there is a need to conduct audits and robust research studies to prove the evidence of the value of pharmacist services in both inpatient and outpatient CR programs. Well-designed RCTs should perhaps be conducted to document this evidence. In addition, determination of human resource need and capacity building for pharmacy staffing are equally essential parameters for these services to succeed. Finally, conducting rigorous economic evaluations and health technology assessments is also essential in complementing the process of generating evidence that will ensure the justification and the continuity of such services.

Conclusion

Cardiac rehabilitation is a well-established model of care for secondary prevention designed to reduce the burden of CVDs globally. It is well-recognized that CR is a cost-effective model of care that has been proven to reduce CV mortality and morbidity. Clinical pharmacists have been actively participating in various multidisciplinary chronic disease management programs such as HTN, dyslipidemia, and CR, and their roles have been extensively documented in the literature in which many studies have proven their positive clinical, economic, and humanistic outcomes. Nevertheless, clinical pharmacists' participation in CR programs is limited and their role and services are underutilized. Further research is needed to evaluate pharmacists' involvement and to help establish and standardize their services in CR programs.

References

[1] GBD 2017 Causes of Death Collaborators. Global, regional, and national age-sex-specific mortality for 282 causes of death in 195 countries and territories, 1980–2017: a systematic analysis for the Global Burden of Disease Study 2017. Lancet 2018;392(10159):1736–88.

[2] Mozaffarian D, Benjamin EJ, Go AS, Arnett DK, Blaha MJ, Cushman M, et al. Heart disease and stroke statistics-2016 update: a report from the American Heart Association. Circulation 2016;133(4):e38–360.

[3] World Health Organization. Cardiovascular disease. [Internet]. Available from: https://www.who.int/cardiovascular_diseases/about_cvd/en/; 2020. [cited 25 May 2020].

[4] Ministry of Public Health. Qatar National Health Strategy, 2018–2022. [Internet]. Available from: https://www.moph.gov.qa/Admin/Lists/PublicationsAttachments/Attachments/54/NHS.pdf; 2020. [cited 25 May 2020].

[5] World Health Organization. Noncommunicable diseases (NCD) country profiles 2018. [Internet]. Available from: https://www.who.int/nmh/countries/qat_en.pdf?ua=1; 2020. [cited 25 May 2020].

[6] Institute for Health Metrics and Evaluation. Measuring what matters. [Internet]. Available from: http://www.healthdata.org/qatar; 2020. [cited 25 May 2020].

[7] Price KJ, Grodon BA, Bird RS, Benson AC. A review of guidelines for cardiac rehabilitation exercise programmes: is there an international consensus. Eur J Prev Cardiol 2016;23(16):1715–33.

[8] Shields GE, Wells A, Doherty P, Heagerty A, Buck D, Davies LM. Cost-effectiveness of cardiac rehabilitation: a systematic review. Heart 2018;104(17):1403–10.

[9] Anderson L, Oldridge N, Thompson DR, Zwisler AD, Rees K, Martin N, et al. Exercise based cardiac rehabilitation for coronary heart disease. J Am Coll Cardiol 2016;67(1):1–12.

[10] Balady GJ, Williams MA, Philip AA, Bittner V, Comoss P, Foody JM, et al. Core Components of Cardiac Rehabilitation/Secondary Prevention Programs: 2007 update: a scientific statement from the American Heart Association Exercise, Cardiac Rehabilitation, and Prevention Committee, the Council on Clinical Cardiology; The Councils on Cardiovascular Nursing, Epidemiology and Prevention, and Nutrition, Physical Activity, and Metabolism; And the American Association of Cardiovascular and Pulmonary Rehabilitation. Circulation 2007;115(20):2675–82.

[11] Thomas RJ, King M, Karen L, Oldridge N, Pina LI, Spertus J, et al. AACVPR/ACC/AHA 2007 performance measures on cardiac rehabilitation for referral to and delivery of cardiac rehabilitation/secondary prevention services endorsed by the American College of Chest Physicians, American College of Sports Medicine, American Physical Therapy Association, Canadian Association of Cardiac Rehabilitation, European Association for Cardiovascular Prevention and Rehabilitation, Inter-American Heart Foundation, National Association of Clinical Nurse Specialists, Preventive Cardiovascular Nurses Association, and the Society of Thoracic Surgeons. J Am Coll Cardiol 2007;50(14):1400–33.

[12] Piepoli MF, Corra U, Adamopoulos S, Benzer W, Bjarnason W, Cupples M, et al. Secondary prevention in the clinical management of patients with cardiovascular diseases. Core components, standards and outcome measures for referral and delivery: a policy statement from the cardiac rehabilitation section of the European Association for Cardiovascular Prevention & Rehabilitation. Endorsed by the Committee for Practice Guidelines of the European Society of Cardiology. Eur J Prev Cardiol 2014;21(6):664–81.

[13] Woodruffe S, Neubeck L, Clark R, Gray K, Ferry C, Finan J, et al. Australian Cardiovascular Health and Rehabilitation Association (ACRA) core components of cardiovascular disease secondary prevention and cardiac rehabilitation 2014. Heart Lung Circ 2015;24(5):430–41.

[14] American Association of Cardiovascular and Pulmonary Rehabilitation. Guidelines for cardiac rehabilitation and secondary prevention programs. 5th ed. Champaign, IL: Human Kinetics; 2013.

[15] Kabboul NN, Tomlinson G, Francis TA, Grace SL, Chaves G, Rac V, et al. Comparative effectiveness of the core components of cardiac rehabilitation on mortality and morbidity: a systematic review and network meta-analysis. J Clin Med 2018;7(12):E514.

[16] Huang R, Palmer SC, Cao Y, Jiang L, Strippoli G, Li X. Cardiac rehabilitation programs for chronic heart disease: a Bayesian network meta-analysis. Can J Cardiol 2020. S0828-282X(20)30176-8.

[17] Long L, Mordi IR, Bridges C, Sagar V, Davies EJ, Coats AJS, et al. Exercise-based cardiac rehabilitation for adults with heart failure. Cochrane Database Syst Rev 2019;29, CD003331.

[18] Shah NP, Abuhaniyeh A, Ahmed H. Cardiac rehabilitation: current review of the literature and its role in patients with heart failure. Curr Treat Options Cardiovasc Med 2018;20(2):12.

[19] Richardson CR, Franklin B, Moy ML, Jackson EA. Advances in rehabilitation for chronic diseases: improving health outcomes and function. BMJ 2019;365:l2191.

[20] Prabhu NV, Maiya AG, Prabhu NS. Impact of cardiac rehabilitation on functional capacity and physical activity after coronary revascularization: a scientific review. Cardiol Res Pract 2020;2020:1236968.

[21] Turk-Adawi K, Supervia M, Lopez-Jimenez F, Pesah E, Ding R, Britto RR, et al. Cardiac rehabilitation availability and density around the globe. EClinicalMedicine 2019;13:31–45.

[22] Abreu A, Pesah E, Supervia M, Turk-Adawi K, Bjarnason-Wehrens B, Lopez-Jimenez F, et al. Cardiac rehabilitation availability and delivery in Europe: how does it differ by region and compare with other high-income countries? Endorsed by the European Association of Preventive Cardiology. Eur J Prev Cardiol 2019;26(11):1131–46.

[23] Pesah E, Supervia M, Turk-Adawi K, Grace SL. A review of cardiac rehabilitation delivery around the world. Prog Cardiovasc Dis 2017;60(2):267–80.

[24] Colella TJF, Gravely S, Marzolini S, Grace SL, Francis JA, Oh P, et al. Sex bias in referral of women to outpatient cardiac rehabilitation? A meta-analysis. Eur J Prev Cardiol 2015;22(4):423–41.

[25] Cossette S, Maheu-Cadotte M, Mailhot T, Fontaine G, Cournoyer A, Cournoyer C, et al. Sex- and gender-related factors associated with cardiac rehabilitation enrollment: a secondary analysis among systematically referred patients. J Cardiopulm Rehabil Prev 2019;39(4):259–65.

[26] Turk-Adawi K, Supervia M, Lopez-Jimenez F, Adawi AM, Sadeghi M, Grace SL. Women-only cardiac rehabilitation delivery around the world. Heart Lung Circ 2020. S1443-9506(20)30060-3.

[27] Tran M, Pesah E, Turk-Adawi K, Supervia M, Lopez-Jimenez F, Oh P, et al. Cardiac rehabilitation availability and delivery in Canada: how does it compare with other high-income countries? Can J Cardiol 2018;34(10 Suppl. 2):S252–62.

[28] Chaves G, Turk-Adawi K, Supervia M, de Araújo Pio CS, Abu-Jeish A, Mamataz T, et al. Cardiac rehabilitation dose around the world: variation and correlates. Circ Cardiovasc Qual Outcomes 2020;13(1), e005453.

[29] Turk-Adawi K, Supervia M, Pesah E, Lopez-Jimenez F, Afaneh J, El-Heneidy A, et al. Availability and delivery of cardiac rehabilitation in the eastern Mediterranean region: how does it compare globally? Int J Cardiol 2019;285:147–53.

[30] Ambrosetti M, Abreu A, Corrà U, Davos CH, Hansen D, Frederix I, et al. Secondary prevention through comprehensive cardiovascular rehabilitation: from knowledge to implementation. 2020 update. A position paper from the Secondary Prevention and Rehabilitation Section of the European Association of Preventive Cardiology. Eur J Prev Cardiol 2020;30. 2047487320913379.

[31] American College of Clinical Pharmacy. Clinical pharmacy defined. Pharmacotherapy 2008;28(6):816–7.

[32] Jacobi J. Clinical pharmacists: practitioners who are essential members of your clinical care team. Rev Med Clin Condes 2016;27(5):571–7.

[33] Touchette DR, Doloresco F, Suda KJ, Perez A, Turner S, Jalundhwala Y, et al. Economic evaluations of clinical pharmacy services: 2006–2010. Pharmacotherapy 2014;34(8):771–93.

[34] Maqbool M, Dar MA, Rasool S, Mir SA, Bhat AU, Khan M. Clinical pharmacy practice in health care system: a review. Eur J Pharm Med Res 2019;6(4):630–3.

[35] Bajorek B, Lemay KS, Magin P, Roberts C, Armour CL. Implementation and evaluation of a pharmacist-led hypertension management service in primary care: outcomes and methodological challenges. Pharm Pract (Granada) 2016;14(2):723.

[36] Jacobs M, Sherry PS, Taylor LM, Amato M, Tataronis GR, Cushing G. Pharmacist assisted medication program enhancing the regulation of diabetes (PAMPERED) study. J Am Pharm Assoc 2012;52(5):613–21.

[37] Abdulrhim SH, Saleh RA, Hussain MA, Al Raey H, Babiker AH, Kheir N, et al. Impact of a collaborative pharmaceutical care service among patients with diabetes in an ambulatory care setting in Qatar: a multiple time series study. Value Health Reg Issues 2019;19:45–50.

[38] Milfred-LaForest SK, Chow SL, DiDomenico RJ, et al. Clinical pharmacy services in heart failure: an opinion paper from the Heart Failure Society of America and American College of Clinical Pharmacy Cardiology Practice and Research Network. J Card Fail 2013;19(5):354–69.

[39] Bero LA, Mays NB, Barjesteh K, Bond C. Expanding the roles of outpatient pharmacists: effects on health services utilisation, costs, and patient outcomes (review). Cochrane Database Syst Rev 2000;2, CD000336.

[40] Omboni S, Caserini M. Effectiveness of pharmacist's intervention in the management of cardiovascular diseases. Open Heart 2018;5(1), e000687.

[41] Riegel B, Thomason T, Carlson B, Bernasconi B, Clark A, Hoagland P, et al. Implementation of a multidisciplinary disease management program for heart failure patients. Congest Heart Fail 1999;5(4):164–70.

[42] Gattis WA, Hasselblad V, Whellan DJ, O'Connor CM. Reduction in heart failure events by the addition of a clinical pharmacist to the heart failure management team: results of the Pharmacist in Heart Failure Assessment Recommendation and Monitoring (PHARM) study. Arch Intern Med 1999;159(16):1939–45.

[43] Dunn PS, Birtcher KK, Beavers CJ, Baker WL, Brouse SD, Page II RL. The role of the clinical pharmacist in the care of patients with cardiovascular disease. J Am Coll Cardiol 2015;66(19):2129–39.

[44] Zhao SJ, Zhao HW, Qin YH. The impact of clinical pharmacist support on patients receiving multi-drug therapy for coronary heart disease in China. Indian J Pharm Sci 2015;77(3):306–11.

[45] Ho PM, Magid DJ, Shetterly SM, Olson KL, Maddox TM, Peterson PN, et al. Medication nonadherence is associated with a broad range of adverse outcomes in patients with coronary artery disease. Am Heart J 2008;155(4):772–9.

[46] Dudek D, Siudak Z, Solheim S. New model of secondary cardiovascular prevention for patients after acute coronary syndromes in Poland with regard to Norwegian experiences. Kardiol Pol 2016;74(2):101–3.

[47] Supervia M, Turk-Adawi K, Lopez-Jimenez F, Pesah E, Ding R, Britto RR, et al. Nature of cardiac rehabilitation around the globe. EClinicalMedicine 2019;13:46–56.

[48] White S, Anderson C. The involvement of pharmacists in cardiac rehabilitation: a review of the literature. Int J Pharm Pract 2005;13:101–7.

[49] Casper EA, El Wakeel LM, Saleh MA, El-Hamamsy MH. Management of pharmacotherapy-related problems in acute coronary syndrome: role of clinical pharmacist in cardiac rehabilitation unit. Basic Clin Pharmacol Toxicol 2019;125(1):44–53.

[50] Anchah L, Hassali MA, Han Lim MS, Ibrahim MI, Sim KH, Ong TK. Health related quality of life assessment in acute coronary syndrome patients: the effectiveness of early phase I cardiac rehabilitation. Health Qual Life Outcomes 2017;15(1):10.

[51] Brink E, Grankvist G, Karlson BW, Hallberg LR. Health-related quality of life in women and men one year after acute myocardial infarction. Qual Life Res 2005;14(3):749–57.

[52] Alsabbagh MW, Lemstra M, Eurich D, Wilson TW, Robertson P, Blackburn DF. Pharmacist intervention in cardiac rehabilitation: a randomized controlled trial. J Cardiopulm Rehabil Prev 2012;32(6):394–9.

[53] Kammer RT. Pharmacist's role in a cardiac rehabilitation program. Am J Health Syst Pharm 2004;61(15):1593–5.

[54] Wilbur K, El Hajj MS, Kheir N. Pharmacy practice in the Gulf states. In: Babar ZUD, Austin Z, editors. Encyclopedia of pharmacy practice and clinical pharmacy. Massachusetts: Elsevier; 2019. p. 526–34.

[55] Kheir N. Pharmacy practice in Qatar. In: Fathelrahman AI, Ibrahim MI, Wertheimer AI, editors. Pharmacy practice in developing countries: achievements and challenges. Massachusetts: Elsevier; 2016. p. 233–52.

[56] American Society of Health-System Pharmacists. ASHP guidelines on pharmacist-conducted patient education and counseling. Am J Health Syst Pharm 1997;54(4):431–4.

[57] Kripalani S, Schmotzer B, Jacobson TA. Improving Medication Adherence through Graphically Enhanced Interventions in Coronary Heart Disease (IMAGE-CHD): a randomized controlled trial. J Gen Intern Med 2012;27(12):1609–17.

[58] Lee SQ, Raamkumar AS, Li J, Coa Y, Witedwitayanusat K, Chen L, et al. Reasons for primary medication nonadherence: a systematic review and metric analysis. J Manag Care Spec Pharm 2018;24(8):778–94.

[59] Atak N. A transtheoretical review on smoking cessation. Int Q Community Health Educ 2007–2008;28(2):165–74.

[60] Atif M, Razzaq W, Musthaq I, Malik I, Razzaq M, Scahill S, et al. Pharmacy services beyond the basics: a qualitative study to explore perspectives of pharmacists towards basic and enhanced pharmacy services in Pakistan. Int J Environ Res Public Health 2020;17(7):2379.

[61] World Health Organization. Joint FIP/WHO guidelines on good pharmacy practice: standards for quality of pharmacy services; Report. Geneva, Switzerland: World Health Organization; 2011.

[62] Melton LB, Lai Z. Review of community pharmacy services: what is being performed, and where are the opportunities for improvement. Integr Pharm Res Pract 2017;6:79–89.

[63] Yuan C, Ding Y, Zhou K, Huang Y, Xi X. Clinical outcomes of community pharmacy services: a systematic review and meta-analysis. Health Soc Care Community 2019;27(5):e567–87.

[64] Bond C. The need for pharmacy practice research. Int J Pharm Pract 2006;14:1–2.

[65] Babar ZUD. The need for an evidence-based encyclopaedia in health services research in pharmacy. Int J Environ Res Public Health 2020;17(7):2549.

[66] Babar ZU. Economic evaluation of pharmacy services. Elsevier; 2016, ISBN:9780128036594. http://store.elsevier.com/product.jsp?isbn=9780128037003&pagename=search.

[67] Babar ZU. Pharmacy practice research methods. 2nd ed. Springer; April 2020. https://link.springer.com/book/10.1007/978-981-15-2993-1.

CHAPTER 2

Clinical pharmacy service innovation in an obstetrics and gynecology setting: A case study from Qatar

Doua AlSaad[a], Ahmed Awaisu[b], Moza AlHail[a], Afif Ahmed[a], Ahmed Moursi[a], Palli Valapila Abdulrouf[a], Wessam ElKassem[a], and Muna AlSaadi[a]

[a]Department of Pharmacy, Women's Wellness and Research Center, Hamad Medical Corporation, Doha, Qatar
[b]Department of Clinical Pharmacy and Practice, College of Pharmacy, QU Health, Qatar University, Doha, Qatar

Overview of pharmacy services in an obstetrics and gynecology setting

Over the last few decades, hospital pharmacy services have expanded beyond the traditional dispensary roles, to include clinical, research, and administrative roles. Clinical pharmacy as a health science discipline deals with patient care through optimizing medication therapy, and promoting health, wellness, and disease prevention [1, 2]. The American College of Clinical Pharmacy (ACCP) has defined clinical pharmacy as "that area of pharmacy concerned with the science and practice of rational medication use" [1]. The early work of clinical pharmacy emerged in the 1960s and its growth was initially slow [3]. However, in recent years the practice has grown rapidly and been developed largely to cover a wide range of patient care settings and therapeutic areas. For instance, primary healthcare settings, emergency departments, critical care and high dependency units, hospital wards, as well as various specialty and ambulatory care clinics are fortunate to receive clinical pharmacy services [4–8]. Variable patient populations benefit from clinical pharmacy services including patients with diabetes, and respiratory, cardiovascular, oncology, and pediatric diseases [8–12]. The benefits of clinical pharmacy services have been well-documented in the literature and include improving patients' clinical outcomes, reducing length of hospital stay and re-admissions, reducing morbidity and mortality associated with many health conditions, and improving quality of life [13]. Furthermore, the economic impact of clinical pharmacy services has also been reported in the literature [14]. Education and research are also among areas where the clinical pharmacy discipline contributes significantly [2].

In Qatar, clinical pharmacy services were introduced in public hospitals in 2006 [15]. The services were introduced in many hospitals under the Hamad Medical Corporation (HMC) with a wide range of specialties and activities [15–17]. For the Obstetrics and Gynecology (OB/GYNE) Department at Women's Hospital (currently known as Women's Wellness and Research Center, or WWRC), clinical pharmacy services were introduced in 2009. Women's Hospital has extensive obstetric services and is responsible for the vast majority of births in Qatar with more than 17,000 deliveries annually. The hospital has 330 beds, a large outpatient department, an emergency department, 16 labor and delivery suites, and three operating theaters. The Pharmacy Department at Women's Hospital consists of inpatient pharmacy, outpatient pharmacy, intravenous admixture preparation room, and clinical pharmacy services for the OB/GYNE and Neonatal Intensive Care Unit (NICU) Departments. Additionally, the Pharmacy Department also provides a drug information service, quality assurance and medication safety services, and continuing professional development [18].

The literature has extensively described clinical pharmacists' roles and activities for a large number of practice settings. However, literature describing clinical pharmacists' role in obstetrics and gynecology settings is limited. One study revealed a high level of physicians' satisfaction with clinical pharmacy services in an obstetrics teaching clinic. They recommended more routine clinical pharmacy service integration into the prenatal care team [19]. A triage tool specific for obstetric patients was developed by another study aiming to help pharmacists in prioritizing higher-risk patients requiring pharmacist review [20]. The outcomes of clinical pharmacy services in the obstetrics field was evaluated in asthmatic pregnant patients. Overall, pharmacists improved patients' perceived knowledge about asthma, its control, and proper inhaler use techniques [21]. Furthermore, the ACCP Practice and Research Network (PRN) established a group for women's health [22]. The purpose of Women's Health PRN is to provide clinical pharmacists interested in this population with the opportunity for exchange of practice ideas and for collaborative research [22]. However, a standard model for clinical pharmacist services in the OB/GYNE field is still lacking.

The case study describes activities and responsibilities of clinical pharmacy services at an OB/GYNE setting in Qatar. This also highlights the challenges and opportunities in this setting.

Data retrieval process

This case study provides a retrospective review of clinical pharmacy service activities over a 2-year period (2016–17) at Obstetrics and Gynecology Department at Women's Hospital, Qatar. Information related to current services description was retrieved from available resources, HMC website, and pharmacy key informants. Key informants were pharmacists who were working at Women's Hospital Pharmacy Department for at least 5 years at the time of data collection and were holding clinical and/or administrative positions that qualify them to represent the current pharmacy practice at Women's Hospital. Characteristics of the staff were obtained from Women's Hospital pharmacy administration. Data related to clinical pharmacy interventions, medication reconciliation, and patient education were retrieved from the electronic health system used in the hospital (Cerner) by information technology pharmacists. This case study is descriptive in nature. The current work does not involve disclosure of patients' or pharmacists' specific information. Waiver of ethics approval was obtained from HMC's Medical Research Center (MRC-01-18-344).

Manpower resources and characteristics of clinical pharmacy practitioners

The OB/GYNE Department covers morning duty from 07:00 AM to 03:00 PM 5 days a week (Sunday to Thursday), with a total of eight full-time (FTE) clinical pharmacists, including a clinical pharmacy specialist and an assistant director. The clinical pharmacy specialist's assignments are divided between patient care activities and managerial responsibilities, while the assistant director of clinical pharmacy has no direct patient care responsibilities. Table 1 describes the characteristics of clinical pharmacists providing services in the department. The majority of the clinical pharmacists are holders of postgraduate certificates, 37.5% with PharmD and 50% with MSc. Sixty two percent of them have 5 years or more of experience in the obstetrics and gynecology field.

With 242 obstetrics and gynecology beds at the hospital and with an average of six to seven clinical pharmacists available to provide patient care services, the estimated clinical pharmacist to bed ratio is one to 35–40 beds. This ratio is close to the general guidance regarding clinical pharmacists staffing level where bed to pharmacist ratio for obstetrics population is 50 and for gynecology population is 40, assuming minimal

Table 1 Clinical pharmacists characteristics.[a]

Variables	N (%)
Gender	
Female	6 (75)
Highest degree	
BSc	1 (12.5)
PharmD	3 (37.5)
MSc	4 (50)
Years of experience at obstetrics and gynecology	
< 5 years	3 (37.5)
≥ 5 years	5 (62.5)
Years since BSc graduation	
0–10 years	4 (50)
> 10 years	4 (50)
Country where highest degree was received	
Qatar	3 (37.5)
United Kingdom	3 (37.5)
India	1 (12.5)
Iraq	1 (12.5)
Practice position	
Clinical pharmacist	6 (75)
Clinical pharmacy specialist	1 (12.5)
Assistant director of clinical pharmacy services	1 (12.5)

[a]Characteristics description refers to the eight clinical pharmacists who were assigned to the obstetrics and gynecology department during the last quarter of the year 2017.

dispensing and medicine distribution activities by clinical pharmacists [2]. The total number of hospital admissions with a length of stay of 24 hours or more was 24,601, while the total number of hospital discharges with a length of stay of 24 hours or more was 24,574 for the year 2017. The average length of stay of these patients who stayed for 24 hours or more was 2.9 days, reflecting the high turnover nature of the obstetrics and gynecology population.

Staff development involves fulfilling the continuing professional development (CPD) requirements as stated by the Qatar Council for Healthcare Practitioners (QCHP), as well as hospital-based training [23, 24]. Furthermore, clinical pharmacists undertake self-initiated activities for career development including postgraduate certificates and education.

Description of obstetrics and gynecology patient population

Clinical pharmacy services cover antenatal, gynecology, and postnatal wards, as well as two high dependency units. Generally, obstetric patients are young women due to the fertility age, which ranges between menarche and menopause, while the age group of gynecological patients is wider. Level of disease complexity of these patients is variable, with a conservative medication use practice for obstetrics patients to minimize fetal exposure and limit maternal medication use to the needed ones. Many medical conditions known to affect the general population can be encountered in obstetrics patients such as asthma, type 1 and type 2 diabetes mellitus, thyroid diseases, and autoimmune diseases (e.g., systemic lupus erythematosus and multiple sclerosis). On the other hand, physiological changes that commonly occur during pregnancy can induce medical conditions specific for pregnant women like preeclampsia, hyperemesis gravidarum, gestational diabetes, venous thromboembolism disease, and cholestasis of pregnancy.

Clinical pharmacists' role in obstetrics and gynecology

Patient care-related activities present the main role of clinical pharmacists, where they spend most of their daily work schedules. Other activities in which clinical pharmacists participate include educational and research activities.

Patient care activities

Clinical pharmacists play a vital role in the management of these highly specialized populations. They participate in daily multidisciplinary rounds and provide individualized patient care. These patient care activities are accomplished through:

- reviewing medication orders, managing drug-related problems, and optimizing patient therapies as appropriate;
- conducting medication review and participating in medication reconciliation on admission, transfer, and discharge;
- assessing past and present allergies and resolving any related problem;
- monitoring safety parameters of medications including side effects, fetal exposure to medications over the three trimesters of pregnancy, and breastfed infants' exposure to medications though mothers' milk;
- conducting therapeutic drug monitoring (TDM) for narrow therapeutic index drugs;

- answering drug information inquires received from other healthcare providers and providing evidence-based recommendations; and
- educating patients and caregivers about safe and effective use of medications.

Clinical pharmacists document their contribution to patient care as "interventions" on the electronic medical record of the patients. Interventions refer to any action taken by the clinical pharmacist that aims to change or optimize patient therapy or management. A total of 8593 interventions were documented over a 1-year period (January–December 2017), as shown in Table 2. The intervention types are divided into nine categories: appropriateness of therapy, medication reconciliation, patient education,

Table 2 Description of clinical pharmacy interventions over a 1-year period.[a]

Description	Number (percentage)
Total number of interventions	8593
Intervention category/examples of subcategory	
Appropriateness of therapy	**2910 (33.8)**
Additional therapy required	1318 (45.3)
Preventive/prophylaxis	388 (13.4)
Appropriate laboratory recommended	292 (10.0)
Alternative therapy	280 (9.6)
Omitted medication	199 (6.8)
Medication without indication	163 (5.6)
Untreated condition	145 (5.0)
Therapeutic drug therapy	80 (2.8)
Inappropriate duration	36 (1.2)
Discontinue inappropriate lab	9 (0.3)
Medication reconciliation	**2678 (31.2)**
Medication reconciliation	2678 (100)
Patient education	**1774 (20.6)**
Patient education	1712 (96.5)
Compliance assessment	62 (3.5)
Dosing/administration	**665 (7.7)**
Optimum dose	192 (28.8)
IV to PO	139 (20.9)
Optimum administration	107 (16.0)
Dose calculation	89 (13.4)
Wrong dose	47 (7.1)
Formulation selection	45 (6.8)
Wrong frequency	40 (6.0)
Wrong route	3 (0.5)
Optimum diluent	2 (0.3)
Dose rounding	1 (0.2)
Contraindication/safety	**251 (2.9)**
Allergy	98 (39.0)

Table 2 Description of clinical pharmacy interventions over a 1-year period.[a]—cont'd

Description	Number (percentage)
Breastfeeding	63 (25.1)
Adverse drug event[b]	41 (16.3)
Pregnancy	31 (12.4)
Other drug therapy	13 (5.2)
Kidney dysfunction	3 (1.2)
Liver dysfunction	2 (0.8)
Drug information	**222 (2.6)**
Drug information inquiry	222 (100)
Drug interactions	**55 (0.6)**
Drug-drug interaction	37 (67.3)
Drug-disease interaction	17 (30.9)
Drug-food interaction	1 (1.8)
Duplicate therapy	**26 (0.3)**
Patient on same pharmacological class	26 (100)
Nonformulary medication	**12 (0.1)**
Patient own medication	7 (58.3)
Therapeutic substitution	3 (25.0)
Formulary recommendation	2 (16.7)
Clinical importance[c]	
Insignificant/not applicable	49 (0.6)
Minor	807 (9.4)
Moderate	7726 (89.9)
Major	10 (0.1)
Catastrophic	1 (<0.1)
Prescriber response	
Accepted	8102 (94.3)
Corrected prior to contact	31 (0.4)
Modified	35 (0.4)
No response	55 (0.6)
Not accepted	118 (1.4)
Patient discharged before response	23 (0.3)
Pending	229 (2.7)
Intervention time	
<1 min	164 (1.9)
1–5 min	3776 (43.9)
6–15 min	3845 (44.8)
16–30 min	733 (8.5)
>30 min	75 (0.9)

[a] Year of 2017.
[b] The number of the reported adverse drug events over the year was 151 reports, which was not reflected in this intervention form, as an adverse drug event has a separate form for reporting.
[c] A description is provided in Box 1.
IV, intravenous; *PO*, per oral.

dosing/administration, contraindication/safety, drug information, drug interactions, duplicate therapy, and nonformulary medication. Interventions related to the appropriateness of therapy present the largest part of the documented activities (33.8%), while drug interactions, duplicate therapy, and nonformulary-related interventions present the lowest parts, with <0.1% each. Around 90% of the interventions were indicated to be moderate in clinical significance as per clinical pharmacist judgment utilizing a standardized definition (Box 1). Ninety-four percent of clinical pharmacists' interventions were accepted, and the time needed to complete these interventions was between 1 and 15 minutes for the majority of the interventions.

Calculating the number of medication education or reconciliation activities per clinical pharmacist, or the average number of interventions per clinical pharmacist, was challenged by the frequent movement of the staff (e.g., some new staff joined, while others left the service during the year, and the number of staff was not fixed throughout the year), which led to poor representation for the actual number of conducted interventions. Furthermore, clinical pharmacists take the lead in the monitoring of medications safety including side effects and adverse drug reaction (ADR) reporting. A total of 151 ADR reports have been documented by clinical pharmacists over a 1-year period, which were submitted to the patient safety and quality office for further analysis.

Educational activities
Education for healthcare providers and trainees/students
Rational drug use is one of the most significant areas where clinical pharmacists can enhance knowledge and change practice. As healthcare educators, clinical pharmacists at Women's Hospital provide education sessions, and deliver in-service professional development activities for multidisciplinary teams, pharmacy colleagues, as well as pharmacy trainees and students.

OB/GYNE clinical pharmacists have a daily morning report to discuss patient cases, review updated guidelines, and conduct journal club sessions. Clinical pharmacists also deliver educational sessions in the OB/GYNE physicians' morning report. Additionally, they take part in nurses' education such as insulin and heparin administration. Some educational sessions are accredited by QCHP [23], while others are delivered at institutional level.

In addition, clinical pharmacists provide training for new pharmacy staff and for pharmacy trainees under clinical attachment programs. Additionally, they are registered preceptors for the Structured Practical Experiences in Pharmacy (SPEP) for the BSc Pharmacy degree and experiential training

Box 1 Description of the clinical importance of the interventions

Grading level	Description Consequence (C): assume intervention not made Impact (I): direct outcome on patient	Examples
Insignificant/not applicable	(C): No harm or injuries, low financial loss (I): No direct benefit	—
Minor	(C): Minor injuries, minor treatment required (I): Reduce cost, enhance patient care, but are not expected to alter patient stay, clinical outcome, or hospital resource utilization	Drug information, in-service presentation, patient medication education group, medication history, resolution of nonformulary issues, and order clarification
Moderate	(C): Major temporary injury (I): Enhance the effectiveness of drug therapy, prevent exacerbations of medical conditions, reduce patient length of stay, reduce costs, and/or prevent patient harm	Add/discontinue medication, dosing adjustment, allergy clarification, monitoring laboratory orders, pharmacokinetic monitoring, prompting medical follow-up, therapeutic consult, and individual patient education
Major	(C): Major permanent injury, re-admission, morbidity at discharge, potential for significant financial loss (I): Prevent serious drug-related problems or potentially life-threatening complications that may otherwise increase patient length of stay	Adverse drug event detection, and prevention of adverse drug events
Catastrophic	(C): Death and/or large financial loss	—

for Doctor of Pharmacy (PharmD) degree programs at Qatar University College of Pharmacy [25]. They are also registered preceptors for the pharmacy residency program, which is accredited by the American Society of Health-System Pharmacists (ASHP) [26]. Clinical pharmacists contribute to the objective structured clinical examination (OSCE) case preparation and examination of the student. Furthermore, they participate in community outreach activities such as school visits and career fairs. They promote for the field and practice of pharmacy.

Clinical pharmacists are part of the organizing committees for workshops such as "the basics of clinical and translational research workshop" [27], and the scientific committees for conferences, such as the "4th Qatar International Pharmacy Conference," and they are providers for workshops like "the role of healthcare providers in the effective and legal use of drugs in sport."

Education for patients

OB/GYNE clinical pharmacists at our hospital actively provide bedside education for patients. They deliver education verbally and through written materials, and when needed, sample medications are used to help visual medication education. Over a 1-year period (2017), clinical pharmacists have participated in the preparation of more than 60 patient education leaflets, which have been customized to fulfill the needs of the OB/GYNE population. Education is provided for patients' chronic medications, newly introduced medications, and vitamins and supplements used in pregnancy. Counseling takes into consideration the safety aspects for medication use during the three trimesters of pregnancy as well as during the breastfeeding period.

Research and other activities

Research activities are vital to improve practice in any hospital setting and for evidence-based patient care provision. Clinical pharmacists serve as the medication expert of research teams. They can assist in a wide range of research activities including literature search for parts pertinent to medications, study protocol, writing especially for pharmacy-related sections such as pharmacology, pharmacokinetics, adverse effects, and medication adherence monitoring, studied medication preparation, simple randomization treatment schedules generation, study data analysis and organization, and dissemination and implementation of results with consideration of the clinical settings. The obstetrics and gynecology field is challenged by lack of research due to ethical concerns and practicality of conducting clinical trials. Clinical pharmacists have a more apparent role in research, as they contribute significantly to the building of knowledge in this field. Clinical pharmacists in our setting lead case reports writing [28–30], conduct systematic reviews [31, 32], and participate in other research activities according to their research skills [33–36]. An example of a currently ongoing research project is the "provision of anti-D prophylaxis to Rh negative pregnant women at Women's Hospital."

Research projects undergo a rigorous review process by the Medical Research Center, Hamad Medical Corporation, to ensure research projects are conducted in accordance with ethical considerations and the policies of the hospital. Research results dissemination includes not only journal publications, but also conference presentations and departmental seminars. Drug use evaluations (DUEs) are among the studies conducted routinely by clinical pharmacists in our hospital. Findings of these DUEs are communicated through departmental meetings and institutional presentations, as well as through journal publications to disseminate knowledge to other OB/GYNE settings [37–39]. Clinical pharmacists in the OB/GYNE field are also involved in other indirect patient care activities. They participate in clinical practice guidelines development and review for the management of the specialized population of OB/GYNE. Examples of these hospital guidelines at our setting include guidelines/protocols for cholestasis of pregnancy, rubella vaccination, and maternal sepsis. Furthermore, clinical pharmacists review the clinical policies in the hospital, and serve as members of drug/pharmacy-related committees, including Pharmacy and Therapeutics (P&T) committee, hospital Joint Commission International (JCI) steering committee, and MMU committee.

Challenges

Clinical pharmacists in OB/GYNE departments are challenged by the high turnover nature of the patient population. Having high turnover of patients increases the workload for pharmacists, which might indirectly affect the quality of patient care through pharmacists having limited time to deal with each patient and to monitor health outcomes.

On the other hand, the obstetrics population is characterized by having a different level of complexity compared to some other fields of practice and by dealing with patients in a health transition state, antenatal, peripartum, and postpartum. Generally, the population of pregnant women is young, with less chronic medical comorbidity than the elderly. However, medication options in pregnancy are fewer due to safety concerns. The plan of care considers not only the current health status of the pregnant woman, but also the future health status. The management of some medical conditions is affected by the delivery, such as venous thromboembolism treatment, while future breastfeeding plans may affect the selection of some medications such as antidepressants.

Despite having some institutes developing guidelines for managing pregnancy-related disorders such as the Royal College of Obstetricians and Gynecologists (RCOG) and the American College of Obstetricians and Gynecologists (ACOG) [40, 41], answering drug information inquiries sometimes remains a challenge, due to gaps in knowledge in the obstetrics field. Vulnerability of pregnant women, the right of human subject protection by regulations, hesitancy of pregnant women to participate in clinical trials, and reluctance of physicians in using medications for fetal safety considerations are some of the contributing factors for these knowledge gaps.

Moreover, there is a lack in literature of a comprehensive model of clinical pharmacy service in the obstetrics and gynecology field providing a detailed description for the scope of service of clinical pharmacists. Current practice was adapted utilizing clinical pharmacy models from other practice settings, and according to the needs of the healthcare providers and patients at the hospital.

Gaps in current clinical pharmacy services

Activities documentation by clinical pharmacists is still not well-established. Clinical pharmacists chart their interventions using a standardized form, as presented in Table 2. Progress notes documentation in patients' medical files is not a routine practice. Moreover, the documented interventions do not reflect the actual workload of clinical pharmacists; patients might be discharged before the clinical pharmacists' document conducted activities due to time limitation, or clinical pharmacist might prioritize other activities over documenting his/her interventions. Modifying the currently used clinical pharmacy intervention form was planned for further practicality of use while capturing the most important types of patient care activities. Another gap in current practice is that clinical pharmacy services focus mainly on patients admitted to the hospital, with limited activities for outpatient clinics.

Future opportunities and direction

The current case study describes clinical pharmacist work at Women's Hospital, which was in a transition process to a new hospital, Women's Wellness and Research Center (WWRC), where clinical pharmacy activities was planned to be broadened. In addition to the current activities, each clinical pharmacist is assigned to a specific patient ward, where he/she is responsible for reviewing and verifying prescription orders for the patients under his/her care. This ensures that the plan of care for patients is implemented as discussed in the clinical round, and helps clinical pharmacists to master their patients' medications. On the other hand, part of a clinical pharmacists' time is spent in dispensary activities (e.g., prescription verification). The efficiency and practicality of this plan need to be reviewed to capture the advantages and disadvantages for such practice on patient outcomes.

Involvement of clinical pharmacists in the outpatient clinics, e.g., contraceptives and family planning services, or medication safety consultation and education service, could be a future plan.

Conclusions

Providing clinical pharmacy services in the obstetrics and gynecology field was a fruitful initiative at Women's Hospital. Clinical pharmacists contribute to diverse aspects of practice including not only patient care activities, but also education and health promotion, research and quality projects, and administrative tasks. The dynamic nature and complexity level of the obstetrics and gynecology patient population challenge the clinical pharmacists; however, the practice concepts remain the same as in any other clinical setting.

Acknowledgment

The authors would like to thank the clinical pharmacy team at the Obstetrics and Gynecology Department, Women's Hospital for their active contribution in the clinical pharmacy service.

References

[1] American College of Clinical Pharmacy. The definition of clinical pharmacy. Pharmacotherapy 2008;28(6):816–7.
[2] SHPA Standards of Practice for Clinical Pharmacy. SHPA committee of specialty practice in clinical pharmacy. J Pharm Pract Res 2005;35(2):122–46.

[3] Miller RR. History of clinical pharmacy and clinical pharmacology. J Clin Pharmacol 1981;21(4):195–7.

[4] Wanbon R, Lyder C, Villeneuve E, Shalansky S, Manuel L, Harding M. Clinical pharmacy services in Canadian Emergency Departments: a national survey. Can J Hosp Pharm 2015;68(3):191–201.

[5] Ho CK, Mabasa VH, Leung VWY, Malyuk DL, Perrott JL. Assessment of clinical pharmacy interventions in the intensive care unit. Can J Hosp Pharm 2013;66(4):212–8.

[6] Truong H, Kroehl ME, Lewis C, et al. Clinical pharmacists in primary care: provider satisfaction and perceived impact on quality of care provided. SAGE Open Med 2017;5, 2050312117713911.

[7] Mekonnen AB, Yesuf EA, Odegard PS, Wega SS. Implementing ward based clinical pharmacy services in an Ethiopian University Hospital. Pharm Pract 2013;11(1):51–7.

[8] Makeen HA. Clinical pharmacists as medication therapy experts in diabetic clinics in Saudi Arabia – not just a perception but a need. Saudi Pharm J 2017;25(6):939–43.

[9] Wang KY, Chian CF, Lai HR, Tarn YH, Wu CP. Clinical pharmacist counseling improves outcomes for Taiwanese asthma patients. Pharm World Sci 2010;32(6):721–9.

[10] Spence MM, Makarem AF, Reyes SL, Rosa LL, Nguyen C, Oyekan EA, Kiyohara AT. Evaluation of an outpatient pharmacy clinical services program on adherence and clinical outcomes among patients with diabetes and/or coronary artery disease. J Manag Care Spec Pharm 2014;20(10):1036–45.

[11] Gatwood J, Gatwood K, Gabre E, Alexander M. Impact of clinical pharmacists in outpatient oncology practices: a review. Am J Health Syst Pharm 2017;74(19):1549–57.

[12] Zhang C, Zhang L, Huang L, Luo R, Wen J. Clinical pharmacists on medical care of pediatric inpatients: a single-center randomized controlled trial. In: Su Z, editor. PLoS One 2012;7(1):e30856.

[13] Viktil KK, Blix HS. The impact of clinical pharmacists on drug-related problems and clinical outcomes. Basic Clin Pharmacol Toxicol 2008;102(3):275–80.

[14] Schumock GT, Butler MG, Meek PD, Vermeulen LC, Arondekar BV, Bauman JL, 2002 Task Force on Economic Evaluation of Clinical Pharmacy Services of the American College of Clinical Pharmacy. Evidence of the economic benefit of clinical pharmacy services: 1996–2000. Pharmacotherapy 2003;23(1):113–32.

[15] Kheir N, Fahey M. Pharmacy practice in Qatar: challenges and opportunities. South Med Rev 2011;4(2):92–6.

[16] Elewa HF, AbdelSamad O, Elmubark AE, Al-Taweel HM, Mohamed A, Kheir N, Mohamed Ibrahim MI, Awaisu A. The first pharmacist-managed anticoagulation clinic under a collaborative practice agreement in Qatar: clinical and patient-oriented outcomes. J Clin Pharm Ther 2016;41(4):403–8.

[17] Abdelaziz H, Al Anany R, Elmalik A, Saad M, Prabhu K, Al-Tamimi H, Salah SA, Cameron P. Impact of clinical pharmacy services in a short stay unit of a hospital emergency department in Qatar. Int J Clin Pharmacol 2016;38(4):776–9.

[18] Women's Hospital, Hamad Medical Corporation. Available from: https://www.hamad.qa/EN/Hospitals-and-services/Womens-Hospital/Pages/default.aspx. [Accessed 24 October 2017].

[19] Forinash AB, Chamness D, Yancey A, Mathews K, Miller C, Thompson J, Myles T. Physician satisfaction with clinical pharmacist services in an obstetrics and gynecology teaching clinic. J Pharm Technol 2016;32(5):191–5.

[20] Covvey JR, Grant J, Mullen AB. Development of an obstetrics triage tool for clinical pharmacists. J Clin Pharm Ther 2015;40(5):539–44.

[21] Forinash AB, Chamness D, Yancey AM, Koerner J, Mathews K, Miller C, Thompson J, Myles T. Impact of clinical pharmacy on asthma in pregnancy in a maternal-fetal care clinic: a pilot study. J Pharm Technol 2016;32(6):240–4.

[22] Practice and Research Networks (PRN), American College of Clinical Pharmacy (ACCP). Available from: https://www.accp.com/about/prns.aspx; 2020 June.

[23] Qatar Council for Healthcare Practitioners (QCHP). Available from: http://www.qchp.org.qa/; 2016.

[24] Hamad Medical Corporation. Available from: https://www.hamad.qa/; 2018.

[25] College of Pharmacy, Qatar University. Available from: http://www.qu.edu.qa/pharmacy/; 2016.

[26] Pharmacy Residency Programs, American Society of Hospital Pharmacy (ASHP). Available from: https://accred.ashp.org/aps/pages/directory/residencyprogramsearch.aspx; 2008.

[27] Basics of Clinical and Translational Research Workshop. Available from: https://www.hamad.qa/EN/All-Events/CTRW/Pages/welcome.aspx; 2016.

[28] AlSaad D, Alobaidly S, Abdulrouf P, Thomas B, Ahmed A, AlHail M. Misoprostol for miscarriage management in a woman with previous five cesarean deliveries: a case report and literature review. Ther Clin Risk Manag 2017;13:625–7.

[29] ElSalem S, Elawad S, Ahmed A, AlSaadi M, AlHail M. A case of probable piperacillin/tazobactam-induced bone marrow suppression in a pregnant woman. Eur J Hosp Pharm 2017. https://doi.org/10.1136/ejhpharm-2017-001243.

[30] AlSaad D, Abdulrouf PV, Parappil H, Tarannum A, Thomas B. Neonatal outcomes after oral administration of antenatal corticosteroid: a case report. Saudi Pharm J 2015;23(6):716–9.

[31] AlSaad D, Awaisu A, Elsalem S, Abdulrouf PV, Thomas B, AlHail M. Is pyridoxine effective and safe for post-partum lactation inhibition? A systematic review. J Clin Pharm Ther 2017;42:373–82.

[32] AlSaad D, Awaisu A, Benilles A, Saad A. Breastfeeding determinants and barriers in Middle East countries: a systematic review. PROSPERO 2017;, CRD42017054339.

[33] AlSaad D, ElSalem S, Abdulrouf P, Ali A, AlHail M. Perception, interest, and barriers toward continuing pharmacy development program at Woman's Hospital in Qatar. Int J Pharm 2014;4(4):43–9.

[34] Awaisu A, Mottram D, Rahhal A, et al. Knowledge and perceptions of pharmacy students in Qatar on anti-doping in sports and on sports pharmacy in undergraduate curricula. Am J Pharm Educ 2015;79(8):119.

[35] Alsaad T, Qaisuddin M, AlSaad D, Chandra P, AlAbd O, Nasser AA, Janahi M, Pilari A, Morsi H. Central line-associated bloodstream infection in pediatric oncology patients in Qatar: a prospective study. J Appl Hematol 2017;8:49–53.

[36] Wilbur K, Shabana S, Maraghi F, ElMubark A, Kheir N. An evaluation of the translation of continuing education into diabetes public health care by pharmacists. Int J Clin Pharmacol 2017;39(4):774–82.

[37] World Health Organization (WHO). Drug and therapeutic committee: a practical guide to drug use evaluation (drug utilization review). vol. 155. Geneva: World Health Organization; 2003.

[38] ElSalem SA, AlSaad DT, Abdulrouf PV, Ahmed AA, AlHail MS. Misoprostol use in medical evacuation of spontaneous miscarriage: pilot drug use evaluation study at the Women's Hospital in Qatar. Qatar Med J 2016;2016(1):5.

[39] AlSaad D, ElSalem S, Abdulrouf PV, Thomas B, Alsaad T, Ahmad A, AlHail M. A retrospective drug use evaluation of cabergoline for lactation inhibition at a tertiary care teaching hospital in Qatar. Ther Clin Risk Manag 2016;12:155–60.

[40] Royal College of Obstetricians and Gynaecologists (RCOG). Available from: https://www.rcog.org.uk/; 2018.

[41] The American College of Obstetricians and Gynecologists (ACOG). Available from: https://www.acog.org/; 2017.

CHAPTER 3

Pharmacy practice research conducted in the delivery of home care services

Mohamed Izham Mohamed Ibrahim[a,b]
[a]Social & Administrative Pharmacy, College of Pharmacy, QU Health, Qatar University, Doha, Qatar
[b]Research and Graduate Studies—Pharmacy, College of Pharmacy, QU Health, Qatar University, Doha, Qatar

Introduction

Pharmacy practice worldwide is becoming important in many ways and for many reasons. The service ranges from inpatient tertiary hospital care to home care services. Pharmacy practice has moved away from medicine supply toward patient care, and away from a product compounder and supplier toward becoming patient care providers [1]. The main contribution of pharmacists is to focus on medication therapy outcomes and the quality of life of the patient. Among the barriers to good public health are lack of access to quality medical products, poor access to trained healthcare staff and care, an insufficient health workforce, high cost of care, and poor standards of education of healthcare professionals [2]. Additionally, studies are producing evidence of the impact of health services and healthcare practices on society, systems, and policy. The practice and services can be expanded and redesigned in line with evidence of their outcomes—clinical, economic, and humanistic values [3]. Society needs high-quality accessible pharmacy services. Research into pharmacy practice generates evidence that can be classified into different levels of quality, i.e., evidence-based practice, and can be translated into best practices.

Healthcare services refers to any medical or remedial care or service to maintain or improve health through prevention, diagnosis, treatment, recovery, or cure of disease/illness, injury, and other physical and mental impairments in people [4]. These services are delivered by healthcare professionals (e.g., physician, pharmacist, nurse) or allied health professionals (e.g., pharmacy technician, dietician, paramedic). The service delivery spectrum should consider the care from prevention to diagnostic, rehabilitation, and palliative care. It has also been observed that in addition, we should

Pharmacy Practice Research Case Studies
https://doi.org/10.1016/B978-0-12-819378-5.00008-8

41

include self-care, home care, community care, primary care, long-term care, and hospital care [5]. Overall, the purpose is to ensure the society receive integrated healthcare services [5]. The services and care provided should be seamless, safe, accessible, high quality, people-centered, and integrated [5, 6].

What is home-based care?

Home-based care is support services provided in the home of an individual with special needs; these services allow an individual to live safely and well [7]. Home-based care is defined as "an array of services for people of all ages, provided in the home and community setting, that encompasses health promotion, teaching, curative intervention, end-of-life care, support, maintenance, social adaption, integration and support for family caregivers" [8]. The main aim is to achieve the highest quality of life possible. Clients may be people who are aging, people who are chronically ill, those who need further care after they are discharged from hospital, those recovering from surgery, or the disabled. The services range from companion caregivers to healthcare. The OECD, European Union, and WHO [9] definition states: "home-based care comprises medical, ancillary and nursing services that are consumed by patients at their home (regardless of the duration) and involve the provider's physical presence." Home-based care can be further classified into home-based curative care, home-based rehabilitative care, and home-based long-term care. Among others, the services include: activities of daily living (e.g., having a shower, personal hygiene, dressing); transportation to doctor's appointments; housekeeping (e.g., meal preparation, laundry); nursing activities (e.g., taking and recording vital signs, feeding, assisting with medical equipment such as walkers, wheelchairs, and oxygen, changing catheters, treating cuts or wounds); and hospice care (e.g., palliative care for critically ill patients).

What are home healthcare services?

Some individuals need long-term care due to chronic illness or injury, or they require care after surgery. These services and care can be provided at home. The range of home healthcare services can be limitless and wide-ranging, depending on the situation of the individual patient. The home service can include care by a doctor, nursing care, pharmacy care, physio/physical therapy, nutritional support, and medical social services, in addition to the other services mentioned earlier [10].

Medical equipment and medicines can be delivered and administered at the patient's home. Patients might need training on how to take certain medications and using certain therapeutic equipment. Some patients also need home dialysis, respiratory therapy (e.g., oxygen delivery system, nebulizers), intravenous therapy, intravenous admixtures therapy after surgery, total parenteral nutrition for patients who cannot eat by mouth, home self-diagnostics and monitoring equipment (e.g., blood pressure monitor, heart rate meters, blood glucose monitor and test strips, apnea and sleep monitor), home telehealth/telemedicine services or counseling and advice on their medications. Furthermore, many patients are elderly, have multiple chronic diseases, are taking multiple medications, receive medications from multiple prescribers, and are at risk for medication-related problems (e.g., nonadherence, suboptimal therapy, adverse drug events) [11, 12]. Medication discrepancies can put patients at higher risk of adverse drug events.

For such services, pharmacist intervention and pharmaceutical care become important. Pharmacists are able to intervene to review medications (e.g., for specific conditions, high-risk medications), resolve medication-related issues, minimize hospitalizations and need for emergency care services, and promote wellness. A few expected potential benefits from the service include: avoiding traveling to the hospital to collect the patient's repeat medication, not having to waste time waiting at the hospital pharmacy department to collect medications, convenience, and cost-effectiveness for the payer [13].

It is also important for healthcare professionals to have a comprehensive emergency and preparedness plan to minimize the interruption of patient care and health services during threats such as war/conflict, hurricanes, floods, wildfires, tornadoes, and earthquakes. In this context, pharmacists can take the main responsibility concerning medication procurement, supply, and use in the disaster plan. Pharmacists can ensure that home care services are accounted for in the disaster plan.

Home healthcare services are a new focus for the improvement of care for patients in the community. Patients with chronic diseases or the elderly may at times struggle to manage the progression of their health conditions and changes within the therapeutic regimen. Pharmacists have knowledge and capabilities that can enhance the care provided to the patient at home. The American Society of Health-System Pharmacists (ASHP), for example, has established guidelines for pharmacists to define their role and responsibilities in providing pharmaceutical care and services in the home setting [14]. When these services are needed, the patient or family members need to consider the quality, cost, credentials, and license of the agency and personnel who will provide the care [15].

The present and future healthcare system demand cost-effective services. These services can be expanded and redesigned according to the needs of the patients and clients; one way in which this can be done is through quality research. Pharmacy practice research on home healthcare is intended to help answer questions such as the following [16]:

Is the home healthcare practiced in a certain way?

Why should the service be practiced in this way?

How do I expand this service?

Is my service valuable?

Who is benefiting from my service?

In what way are people benefiting?

We need to conduct research utilizing high-quality scientific methods that can create new knowledge, produce ideas on how to change, and improve the service, practice, and policy related to home care.

How large is the market for home care services?

The worldwide home care and self-care market growth from 2009 to 2014 was reported to be around 8.4% [17]. According to Grand View Research [18], the global home healthcare market size in 2019 was estimated at around USD282 billion. Further, the research institute projected growth from 2020 to 2027 to be around 7.9%. The anticipated market growth is due to the increase in the aging population (estimated to rise from 703 million in 2019 to 1.5 billion by 2050), patient preference (e.g., for portability, automation) for value-based healthcare services, increases in accidents and injuries, declining elderly support ratio, technological advancements, and the shift of patients by hospitals and physicians to home care to reduce the high patient inflow [17, 18]. There has been a shift of patients from healthcare institutions to home healthcare due to the advantages experienced by the users, and this trend is expected to continue. Research also indicates a need for trained medical professionals. Among the big players in the global home healthcare market are F. Hoffmann–La Roche AG (Switzerland), Koninklijke Philips N.V. (the Netherlands), A&D Company (Japan), Abbott (United States), Fresenius SE&Co KGaA (Germany), GE Healthcare (United States), and B. Braun Melsungen AG (Germany) [19].

Translating evidence into pharmacy practice

Existing lessons about how to carry out and use research related to home-based healthcare should be widely shared. This section considers evidence obtained from the literature review regarding home care practices, services, and outcomes. It is intended to serve as lessons learned for pharmacists.

Flanagan and Barns [20] investigated the evidence of pharmacists providing home care clinical services. Their studies classified the evidence into different aspects: competency, patients, safety, technology, collaboration, home visits, and autonomy. According to their findings (studies published between 2007 and 2017), 11 countries described pharmacists' home visits in the literature: Australia, Brazil, Canada, Japan, Jordan, the Netherlands, New Zealand, Singapore, Thailand, the United Kingdom, and the United States. The impacts or outcomes of these services at home by pharmacists were unclear. There is a need to refine and establish a clear plan on how the clinical pharmacy services in home care should be implemented/carried out, including identifying what type of patients should be served, what practice model should be implemented, and the best way to perform collaborative care practices. The services should also consider the competency of the health personnel, the use of technology, the safety of health personnel, the kind of activities to be provided, and pharmacist autonomy. According to the study, these elements are important considerations for pharmacists to establish their role and responsibility in providing home clinical services.

Many patients who are taking their medications at home can be classified as high risk and presenting with high complexity. These patients are exposed to medication-related problems. Jennifer et al. [21] compared hospital discharge medication lists to the medications that patients were taking at home. The authors found that discrepancies of medications were common in all studied patients and medication omissions were the most common issue. Myrka et al. [22] highlighted a pharmacist pharmacotherapeutic medication reconciliation service at hospital discharge that continues the support at home in collaboration with the nurses at the time of initiation of care and continuation of care. This service aimed to reduce hospital readmissions and resolve medication-related problems. A study by Reidt et al. [23] indicated that pharmacists provided a positive clinical impact on patients when integrating them into the home healthcare model for hospital discharged patients. Polypharmacy, the complexity of medication regimen (dosing, administration, or instructions), and high-risk medications such as warfarin and antidiabetic medications can cause medication errors or adverse events. These are potential reasons for hospital readmissions. Thus, the geriatric pharmacy home program can overcome these issues [24, 25].

Pharmacists can be involved in ensuring effective medication reconciliation at home. "Medication reconciliation is a process of comparing medications being used by a client to a current list of prescribed medications to verify its accuracy and is a best-practice strategy to reduce medication errors" [26]. This is especially important for patients with chronic illnesses, who might be prescribed medications that the patients already have at home [27]. There is also the possibility of patients having other medication-related problems. Pharmacists can offer medication reconciliation services. The pharmacist can compare medications specified in hospital discharge instructions, those taken before hospitalization, and those now taken by the client, and document action taken to resolve discrepancies [26].

Reidt et al. [11] reported how pharmacists carried out medication reconciliation services in the patient's home. The pharmacist reviews the patient's list of ordered medications and chart notes from other home care clinicians (e.g., nurses, occupational therapists, and physical therapists) before the home visit. While visiting the home, the pharmacist discusses every medication (i.e., prescriptions, nonprescription, OTC, and herbal supplements) with the patient and caregiver to assess their indication, safety, effectiveness, and adherence, including affordability. They reconcile the medications with how the patient is taking medications. At each home visit, the number of conditions, number of medications, number and type of medication-related problems, number of prescriber recommendations made, and outcome of these recommendations are documented. Ware et al. [28] studied the healthcare barriers and needs of Latino children with medical complexity. The authors found that the families experienced difficulty getting medical supplies at home, which might affect the health outcomes. There are several beneficial aspects of the pharmacy home visit program. Pharmacists review each medication according to the patient's needs, ensuring that the medications are effective, avoid side effects, are convenient for patients, and are affordable. Pharmacist interventions can identify medication-related problems and minimize the risk of adverse events.

Triller et al. [29] studied a referral-based, pharmacist-conducted medication management program designed to identify, categorize, and resolve drug-related problems (DRPs) in a home healthcare (HHC) population. A clinical pharmacy service model with policies and procedures was developed to identify patients at high risk of adverse health events resulting from DRPs. The findings indicated that patients were referred for and received clinical pharmacy services. Additionally, pharmacists identified many DRPs and almost two-thirds of pharmacist recommendations were accepted and actions were taken.

According to Mahan et al. [30], medication nonadherence is an important problem among patients who continue to receive care at home. Mahan et al. created a pilot test and tool to assess medication-related problems and found on average 2.3 problems per patient that could cause medication nonadherence. Schain et al. [31] developed a comprehensive evidence-based assessment tool for older adults who are at high risk and could affect their health outcomes. Kalista et al. [32] studied a community pharmacist-provided home health service for heart failure patients. The service was targeted to improve medication adherence and reduce hospital readmissions. The patients were visited and received followed-up phone calls. Medications were reconciled and patients received education about their medication. It was observed that medication adherence improved and hospital readmission rates reduced. Community pharmacists can solely contribute to home care services or collaborate with other health personnel. Moreover, pharmacists can design a quality tool, which can be used to evaluate medication-related problems for home care: a pharmacist-driven pilot home medication therapy management (MTM) program.

Corsi et al. [33] studied the financial impact of the pharmacist-driven pilot home medication therapy management (MTM) program. They identified the types of medication-related problems experienced by the patients. Among patients who received comprehensive medication reviews, many problems relating to their medications were identified, covering various intervention categories. The cost avoided from medication-related problems, i.e., savings with interventions by pharmacists (e.g., MTM), can reach about USD124,000. Pharmacists can provide cost-effective and cost-saving interventions regarding medication-related problems for patients with multiple chronic conditions at home. Pharmacists' interventions can catch errors, saving money and lives.

Pharmacy colleges can play a role in home-based care. Pharmacy students and faculty members can contribute to the home care service by collaborating with other healthcare professionals and agencies. They can contribute, for example, by minimizing the risk of falls among the elderly through collaborative care with other healthcare professionals and review of medication therapy. In other situations, patients who, in the process of transferring from hospitals to home, might experience issues such as complex medical histories, poor health literacy, lack of medication documentation, and medication-related problems, which can cause adverse events. In these instances, pharmacists can assist in managing their medications, providing medical advice, and ensuring proper medication documentation [11, 34, 35]. In another case, a drug information service was set up as a pilot project under a college of pharmacy [12], and several other pharmacy services (e.g., pharmaceutical care, medication review) were initiated. Preliminary findings showed that pharmacist involvement positively affected patient care and outcomes. Academic leaders can identify services and communities in which the college of pharmacy can participate in the delivery of services through students' activities and training, or college of pharmacy educators who have the license (i.e., are allowed) to practice. More opportunities should be explored beyond the routine and traditional services provided at home.

The condition in low- and middle-income countries (LMICs) in relation to home medication management might be more critical for some countries due to inefficiency in the system, health illiteracy of the people, lack of financial support, etc. For example, Kalyango et al. [36] found that home medication management was inappropriate and associated with the perceived severity of the disease. In addition, medication storage was inappropriate and associated with inadequate information about the disease and distance to the health facility (i.e., more than 5 km). Other problems include no medication schedule, inadequate information about the disease, missing appointments for medical review, medication duplication, and expired medicines. In summary, patients with chronic diseases have poor home management of medicines. Patients need to be educated about their disease and handling their medications. Based on the observations, the service in LMICs is relatively less taken up and not effectively provided compared to certain developed countries where the service has been well established. Thus, there is an excellent opportunity for pharmacists in LMICs to expand and extend their services to the patient's home.

One area that is important to ensure seamless care is an efficient medicine supply. According to Smego Jr et al. [37], the hospital pharmacy can be a central point for the preparation and distribution of medications and specialty nursing services. It can provide a cost-effective home treatment program in a resource-limited country.

In the United Kingdom, the NHS provides a home care delivery service to the community [38], which provides medicines and other supplies. The types of medication services provided are home care medicines services for which one or more home care provider are commissioned by a manufacturer of a drug (pharma company), NHS-funded home care services, and low- (e.g., self-administration oral or external use medicines), middle- (e.g., therapy that requires significant clinical support or diagnostic testing), or high-tech (e.g., intravenous infusion) medicines home care service. In these examples, pharmacists can ensure a continuous supply of medications to the clients.

Patient engagement is important to ensure effective home-based care. The pharmacist-patient relationship and communication are also important to ensure positive health outcomes. Miner et al. [39] stressed that patients' understanding of medication information when at home is crucial. Rational and safe use of medication is important and can be achieved if patients are health- and medication-literate. Otherwise, patients will always be in danger. Furthermore, according to Miner et al. [39], medication literacy among Somali older adults was an issue. Techniques, tools, and professional support are in need for diverse and vulnerable non-English-speaking community living in English-speaking countries. It is also important to train future healthcare professionals and to be prepared when serving these ethnic groups.

A study was conducted to evaluate evidence-based home care practices [40]. It looked at the impact on the ability to enhance the home health outcome-based quality improvement in the management of oral medications. According to the author, "evidence-based practices include use of reminder strategies, phone follow-up interventions, repeat patient education about medications at subsequent home care visits, and use of medication simplification strategies for patients receiving multiple medications."

Home-based healthcare: Countries' experience

This section presents examples of developed (i.e., Australia, Canada) and developing (i.e., Malaysia, Qatar) countries that provide home-based services to the community.

Malaysia

The Malaysian government does provide home care and rehabilitation services to patients who have been discharged from hospital and are bedridden [41]. There are also mobile clinics that provide home care for the elderly [42]. Under the Pharmacy Practice and Development Division, Ministry of Health, the Home Medication Review (HMR) by the pharmacist was introduced to monitor and review patients' medication use at home [43]. The first HMR protocol was developed in 2011 [44]. This service aimed to advocate optimal and quality use of medications, and involved medication reconciliation and review of all medications, both prescription and nonprescription items.

Qatar

Hamad Medical Corporation (HMC), Doha, is the main provider of secondary and tertiary healthcare in Qatar. Rumailah Hospital is a member of HMC. It provides quality home healthcare to adults (e.g., falls prevention) and pediatric care services [45].

HMC has planned to expand its services by opening new satellite offices and introduce new services such as dental care, mental health, and palliative care [46]. The organization provides services to all residents in the country regardless of age, including both Qataris and expatriates. The service, which were established in 2009, now has more than 2000 patients (around 2000 adults and more than 300 children); 70% of these are Qataris and 30% non-Qataris. Patients who are under home care services have hypertension, diabetes, cerebrovascular accidents, cerebral palsy, genetic disorders, and chronic respiratory failure, and a few are on mechanical ventilators. During the COVID-19 pandemic, the Qatar Primary Health Care Corporation (PHCC) delivered care and screening for COVID-19 for elderly patients at home [47]. In addition, the pharmacy department of PHCC provided a medication home delivery service as a response to the pandemic. This was to ensure patients received their medications and their refilled prescriptions without any disruption. The service served more than 10,000 patients within the first quarter period of 2020 [48]. PHCC has planned to provide home care since 2013 [49].

Additionally, the Qatar Foundation for Elderly Care provides home care services (e.g., rehabilitation, physiotherapy, nutrition) to the elderly for their convenience, saving time and effort [50]. In addition to the home care services provided by the public sector, several private agencies provide these services (e.g., Home Care Center, QHMC).

Australia

The home care sector is a rapidly growing industry [51]. According to Jackson and Hambleton [52], it is a central element of the national health reforms. In a survey, around 53% of patients say that "they would probably or definitely use pharmacies for in-home services" [53, 54]. Patients have a high level of trust and would be willing to pay for the service. Community pharmacists are appointed to provide medicine use reviews in the patient's home, not in the pharmacy. A monetary incentive is provided for this service [55]. In 2018, the community pharmacy in the healthcare homes trial program was established [56]. The project aimed to improve access to pharmacy services for patients with chronic and complex conditions. Pharmacists are expected to provide medication management, which includes medicines reconciliation, medication reviews, medication adherence service, dose administration aid, blood glucose monitoring, blood pressure monitoring, and development of an asthma management plan.

Canada

It is reported that in 2011, around 1.4 million Canadians received home care, an increase of 55% from 2008 [8]. However, in 2012, many of the people who requiring home care assistance for the management of chronic illness, aging, or disability still did not receive any home care [57]. According to Papastergiou et al. [58], community pharmacists are in a strategic position to provide home care pharmacy services and improve health outcomes. The authors stressed that pharmacist-directed home medication reviews could expand the scope of pharmacy services, maximize healthcare cost savings, and minimize inappropriate use of medications. Houle and MacKeigan [59] indicated that pharmacists do home visits for individuals with complex medication regimens or have problems with medication nonadherence. Furthermore, according to the authors, counseling patients about medication adherence and carrying out medication reviews and reconciliation were the most common services provided.

Lessons learned: Take-home messages

The cases highlighted in this chapter indicate that there are important outcome measures of home healthcare services that should be focused on: quality, efficiency (e.g., cost-saving), cost-effectiveness, convenience, clinical outcomes (e.g., improving adherence, reducing hospital readmissions; improving patient safety), humanistic outcomes (e.g., quality of life, satisfaction, engagement), etc.

The pharmacist can use various study designs (e.g., cross-sectional study, experimental design, quasiexperimental design) and develop different or use existing tools to evaluate the services, e.g., using a questionnaire to assess satisfaction, peer's perspective, or quality; economic analysis method to measure the cost-effectiveness of services and savings; and quality of life tools to measure the impact of the intervention on patients' quality of life. A summary of these studies and methodologies used is provided in Table 1.

Community pharmacists, being some of the most reachable healthcare professionals among the community, have great potential to provide in-home healthcare services. They usually know the people in the community, just as the people in that location are familiar with the pharmacists. This characteristic feature of community pharmacies provides a platform for a more proactive contribution in this setting. The dilemma is in ensuring that the cost, choice, and sustainability continuum is navigated to ensure better patient outcomes while providing value for the providers/payers [60].

Table 1 Summary of home care services, methodologies used, and outcomes.

Study details and authors	Country	Methodology employed to conduct the study	Services provided	Outcomes/aspects studied
Bruning and Selder [26]	United States	Exploratory	Medication reconciliation	Medication errors; medication discrepancies
Corsi et al. [33]	United States	Prospective with intervention	Comprehensive medication review (medication therapy management)	Medication-related problems; cost savings
Department of Health, Australian Government [56]	Australia	Prospective with intervention	Medication management services; medication reconciliation; dose administration aid; blood glucose monitoring; blood pressure monitoring; asthma management plan	Rational use of medications; maximize continuity of care; medication adherence
Flanagan and Barns [20]	Multiple countries	Review	Clinical pharmacy services	Competency of provider; type of patients served; safety of provider; technology used; collaboration of providers; home visits; pharmacist autonomy
Fuji and Abbott [27]	United States	Prospective with intervention	Medication reconciliation	Medication discrepancies
Houle and MacKeigan [59]	Canada	Cross-sectional study	NA	Services provided; remuneration; barriers; facilitators
Jennifer et al. [21]	United States	Retrospective, observational study	Medication review	Medication discrepancies
Kalista et al. [32]	United States	Prospective with intervention	Medication reconciliation; medication teaching	Medication adherence; 30-day heart failure-related hospital readmissions

Reference	Country	Study design	Service	Focus
Kalyango et al. [36]	Uganda	Cross-sectional study	NA	Medication management practices; factors associated with the practices
Mahan et al. [30]	United States	Prospective with intervention and interviews	Pharmacist–patient interactions and consultations	Medication-related problems; medication nonadherence
Malaysian Pharmaceutical Division [43]	Malaysia	NA	Medication reconciliation and review	Optimal and quality use of medications
Meredith et al. [24]	United States	Cross-sectional study	NA	Medication errors
Miner et al. [39]	United States	Qualitative secondary analysis	NA	Medication literacy; perceptions
Myrka et al. [22]	United States	Prospective with intervention	Medication reconciliation	Medication-related problems; reduction in hospital readmissions
UK NHS [13]	United States	NA	Medication delivery	Decreasing long waiting periods; not to carry heavy bulky medicines home; avoid traveling to hospital every month; cost-effective for the NHS
O'Neal et al. [34]	United States	NA	Collaborative care	Medication-related problems
Palesy et al. [51]	Australia	Integrative review	NA	Understanding care recipients and their needs, funding, and regulation; care worker skills, tasks, demographics, employment conditions, and training needs
Papastergiou et al. [58]	Canada	Prospective with intervention	Home medication review and education	Medication adherence; medication storage and disposal; medication-related problems
Poole [60]	United Kingdom	Opinion	Clinical services	Flexible home care model; personalized care; convenient
Rawal [55]	Australia	Opinion	Medicines use reviews	Medication-related problems
Reidt et al. [11]	United States	NA	Collaborative care	Medication-related problems

Continued

Table 1 Summary of home care services, methodologies used, and outcomes.—cont'd

Study details and authors	Country	Methodology employed to conduct the study	Services provided	Outcomes/aspects studied
Reidt et al. [23]	United States	Retrospective study	Home healthcare model	Clinical impact; medication-related problems
Saxena [53]	Australia	Cross-sectional study	NA	Patient's opinion regarding home care services by pharmacist
Schain et al. [31]	United States	Case study	Interprofessional collaborative practice	Risk reduction; improvement of outcomes
Shearer [40]	United States	Review	NA	Evidence-based practices
Smego Jr et al. [37]	Pakistan	Cross-sectional study	Home healthcare	Preparation and distribution of medications
Triller et al. [29]	United States	Cross-sectional study	Clinical pharmacy service model; pharmacy referral service	Medication-related problems
Triller et al. [12]	United States	Retrospective evaluation	Drug information; comprehensive pharmacotherapy assessments	Drug-related problems; optimal therapy
Turcotte [57]	Canada	Survey	Caregiving and home care receiving	Home care needs
Ware et al. [28]	United States	Qualitative study	Complex care program	Basic needs and necessary medical supplies to care for their complex care program at home
Withey and Breault [35]	United States	Cross-sectional study	Medication therapy review; collaboration with other providers	Risk factors associated with falls; potential medication issues

There is also a need to boost research on home healthcare services [61]. Pharmacists need to explore a sustainable reimbursement model, the use of information communication technology services (e.g., telemedicine/ telehealth/telemonitoring), type of services during disasters, the best way to collaborate effectively with other healthcare personnel and deliver the service; they also need to be familiar with medical devices that will benefit patients.

Conclusions

In summary, studies have indicated that there are opportunities for pharmacists to serve patients in their homes. There is established evidence to show that pharmacists' intervention with and without collaborative care produces positive patient health outcomes. The demand for this type of service is increasing worldwide. However, robust research and evidence are needed to generate advance home healthcare pharmacy services.

References

[1] Wiedenmayer K, et al. Developing pharmacy practice. A focus on patient care. WHO in Collaboration with FIP (International Pharmaceutical Federation). WHO/PSM/ PAR/2006.5 https://www.fip.org/files/fip/publications/DevelopingPharmacyPractice/DevelopingPharmacyPracticeEN.pdf; 2006. [Accessed 10 March 2020].

[2] FIP (International Pharmaceutical Federation). Good pharmacy practice. Joint FIP/ WHO guidelines on GPP: standards for quality of pharmacy services, https://www.fip. org/file/1476. [Accessed 22 March 2020].

[3] Bond C. Pharmacy practice research: evidence and impact. In: Babar ZUD, editor. Pharmacy practice research methods. Switzerland: Springer; 2015. p. 1–24.

[4] Law Insider. Definition of health care services, https://www.lawinsider.com/dictionary/health-care-services. [Accessed 22 June 2020].

[5] WHO. Health services, https://www.who.int/topics/health_services/en/. [Accessed 10 March 2020].

[6] Spehar AM, Campbell RR, Cherrie C, et al. Seamless care: safe patient transitions from hospital to home. In: Henriksen K, Battles JB, Marks ES, et al., editors. Advances in patient safety: from research to implementation (volume 1: research findings). Rockville, MD: Agency for Healthcare Research and Quality (US); 2005 February.

[7] MedlinePlus. Home care services, https://medlineplus.gov/homecareservices.html. [Accessed 2 May 2020].

[8] Anon. Portraits of home care in Canada. Mississauga, ON: Canadian Home Care Association; 2013.

[9] OECD. Classification of health care functions (ICHA-HC), https://www.oecd-ilibrary.org/docserver/9789264270985-7-en.pdf?expires=1594551480&id=id&accname=guest&checksum=52768CD77937C3C64CE99E1472F00E41; 2017. [Accessed 8 May 2020].

[10] John Hopkins. Types of home health care services, https://www.hopkinsmedicine.org/health/caregiving/types-of-home-health-care-services. [Accessed 10 March 2020].

[11] Reidt S, Morgan J, Larson T, Blade MA. The role of a pharmacist on the home care team: a collaborative model between a college of pharmacy and a visiting nurse agency. Home Healthc Nurse 2013;31(2):80–9. https://doi.org/10.1097/NHH.0b013e-3182778f5f. [Accessed 2 March 2020].

[12] Triller DM, Hamilton RA, Briceland LL, Waite NM, Audette CM, Furman CA. Home care pharmacy: extending clinical pharmacy services beyond infusion therapy. Am J Health Syst Pharm 2000;57(14). https://www.medscape.com/viewarticle/406898. [Accessed 5 June 2020].

[13] NHS. Pharmacy homecare, https://www.uclh.nhs.uk/OurServices/ServiceA-Z/CSS/PMM/Pages/Pharmacyhomecare.aspx. [Accessed 21 June 2020].

[14] ASHP. ASHP guidelines on the pharmacist's role in home care. Am J Health Syst Pharm 2000;57(13):1252–7. https://doi.org/10.1093/ajhp/57.13.1252. [Accessed 20 June 2020].

[15] Mayo Clinic. Healthy lifestyle. Healthy aging, https://www.mayoclinic.org/healthy-lifestyle/healthy-aging/in-depth/home-care-services/art-20044609?p=1. [Accessed 2 May 2020].

[16] Dolovich L, Tsuyuki RT. Pharmacy practice research produces findings that inform how pharmacists contribute to optimal drug therapy outcomes for Canadians. Can Pharm J (Ott) 2016;149(5):261–3. https://doi.org/10.1177/1715163516663693. https://www.ncbi.nlm.nih.gov/pmc/articles/PMC5032937/. [Accessed 20 April 2020].

[17] Markets and Markets. Home healthcare market, https://www.marketsandmarkets.com/Market-Reports/home-health-care-market-133.html. [Accessed 10 June 2020].

[18] Grand View Research. Home healthcare market size, share & trends analysis report by equipment (therapeutic, diagnostic), by services (skilled home healthcare services, unskilled home healthcare services), by region, and segment forecasts, https://www.grandviewresearch.com/industry-analysis/home-healthcare-industry;   2020–2027. [Accessed 20 June 2020].

[19] Market Research Future. Home healthcare market trends, https://www.medgadget.com/2019/09/home-healthcare-market-trends-2019-global-size-share-growth-analysis-by-top-leading-players-business-opportunity-and-challenges.html;   2019.   [Accessed 10 June 2020].

[20] Flanagan PS, Barns A. Current perspectives on pharmacist home visits: do we keep reinventing the wheel? Integr Pharm Res Pract 2018;7:141–59. https://doi.org/10.2147/IPRP.S148266. [Accessed 10 April 2020].

[21] Jennifer H, Erin N, Amy M, et al. Medication discrepancies and associated risk factors identified in home health patients. Home Healthc Now 2015;33(9):493–9.

[22] Myrka A, Butterfield S, Goss JB, et al. A systems-based medication reconciliation process: with implications for home healthcare. Home Healthc Nurse 2011;29(10):624–35. https://doi.org/10.1097/NHH.0b013e31823454e5. [Accessed 2 April 2020].

[23] Reidt SL, Larson TA, Hadsall RS, Uden DL, Blade MA, Branstad R. Integrating a pharmacist into a home healthcare agency care model: impact on hospitalizations and emergency visits. Home Healthc Nurse 2014;32(3):146–52. https://doi.org/10.1097/NHH.0000000000000024. [Accessed 20 June 2020].

[24] Meredith S, Feldman PH, Frey D, et al. Possible medication errors in home healthcare patients. J Am Geriatr Soc 2001;49:719–24. https://doi.org/10.1046/j.1532-5415.2001.49147.x. [Accessed 22 July 2020].

[25] O'connor MA, Pike A, Ambrefe MM, Greenberg EL. Reducing readmissions through a targeted geriatric pharmacy program. Home Healthc Now 2016;34(2):112–3. https://doi.org/10.1097/NHH.0000000000000341. [Accessed 2 May 2020].

[26] Bruning K, Selder F. From hospital to home healthcare: the need for medication reconciliation. Home Healthc Nurse 2011;29(2):81–90. https://doi.org/10.1097/NHH.0b013e3182079893. [Accessed 20 March 2020].

[27] Fuji KT, Abbott AA. Ensuring effective medication reconciliation in home healthcare. Home Healthc Nurse 2014;32(9):516–24. https://doi.org/10.1097/NHH.0000000000000136. [Accessed 10 May 2020].

[28] Ware EJ, Beveridge MS, Rosado AI, Nageswaran S. Practical needs in the home care of Latino children with medical complexity. Home Healthc Now 2020;38(4):202–8. https://doi.org/10.1097/NHH.0000000000000854. [Accessed 28 June 2020].

[29] Triller DM, Clause SL, Briceland LL, Hamilton RA. Resolution of drug-related problems in home care patients through a pharmacy referral service. Am J Health Syst Pharm 2003;60(9):905–10. https://doi.org/10.1093/ajhp/60.9.905. [Accessed 3 June 2020].

[30] Mahan KR, Clark JA, Anderson KD, Koller NJ, Gates BJ. Development of a tool to identify problems related to medication adherence in home healthcare patients. Home Healthc Now 2017;35(5):277–82. https://doi.org/10.1097/NHH.0000000000000539. [Accessed 2 June 2020].

[31] Schain A, Rees C, Medina C, et al. Reducing risks for older adults with an interprofessional community-academic partnership: a case study. Home Healthc Now 2018;36(6):362–8. https://doi.org/10.1097/NHH.0000000000000696. [Accessed 10 June 2020].

[32] Kalista T, Lemay V, Cohen L. Postdischarge community pharmacist–provided home services for patients after hospitalization for heart failure. J Am Pharm Assoc 2015;55(4):438–42. https://doi.org/10.1331/JAPhA.2015.14235. [Accessed 20 April 2020].

[33] Corsi K, Lemay V, Orr KK, Cohen L. Pharmacist medication therapy management in home health care: investigation of a sustainable practice model. J Am Pharm Assoc 2018;58(Suppl. 4):S64–8. https://doi.org/10.1016/j.japh.2018.04.028. [Accessed 10 March 2020].

[34] O'Neal F, Frame TR, Triplett J. Integrating a student pharmacist into the home healthcare setting. Home Healthc Now 2016;34(6):308–15. https://doi.org/10.1097/NHH.0000000000000397. [Accessed 20 April 2020].

[35] Withey MB, Breault A. A home healthcare and school of pharmacy partnership to reduce falls. Home Healthc Nurse 2013;31(6):295–302. https://doi.org/10.1097/NHH.0b013e318294787c. [Accessed 3 June 2020].

[36] Kalyango JN, Hall M, Karamagi C. Home medication management practices and associated factors among patients with selected chronic diseases in a community pharmacy in Uganda. BMC Health Serv Res 2012;12:323. https://doi.org/10.1186/1472-6963-12-323. [Accessed 10 April 2020].

[37] Smego Jr RA, Khan MA, Khowaja K, Rafique R, Datoo FA. A university-sponsored home health nursing program in Karachi, Pakistan. Home Healthc Nurse 2005;23(11):710–6. https://doi.org/10.1097/00004045-200511000-00007. [Accessed 7 June 2020].

[38] Royal Pharmaceutical Society. Professional standards for homecare services in England, https://www.rpharms.com/; 2014. [Accessed 20 June 2020].

[39] Miner S, McDonald MV, Squires A. Medication literacy and Somali older adults receiving home care. Home Healthc Now 2018;36(5):295–303. https://doi.org/10.1097/NHH.0000000000000673. [Accessed 1 April 2020].

[40] Shearer J. Improving oral medication management in home health agencies. Home Healthc Nurse 2009;27(3):184–92. https://doi.org/10.1097/01.NHH.0000347685.74820.09. [Accessed 10 June 2020].

[41] MAMPU. Domiciliary care services (at home), https://www.malaysia.gov.my/portal/content/27619; 2019. [Accessed 20 June 2020].

[42] Pak J. Malaysia's mobile clinics provide home care for elderly. BBC News 2013. https://www.bbc.com/news/business-24516288. [Accessed 20 June 2020].

[43] Malaysian Pharmaceutical Services. Home care pharmacy services protocol. 2nd ed; 2019. https://www.pharmacy.gov.my/v2/en/documents/home-care-pharmacy-services-protocol-2nd-edition-2019.html. [Accessed 20 June 2020].

[44] Malaysian Pharmaceutical Services. Home care pharmacy services protocol. 1st ed; 2011. https://www.pharmacy.gov.my/v2/sites/default/files/document-upload/home-care-pharmacy-services-protocol-2nd-edition-2019.pdf. [Accessed 20 June 2020].

[45] Rumailah Hospital. Home health care services, https://www.hamad.qa/EN/Hospitals-and-services/Rumailah-Hospital/Hospital-Services/Clinical%20Departments/Occupational-Therapy/Pages/Home-Health-Care-Services.aspx. [Accessed 20 June 2020].

[46] The Peninsula. Home healthcare service to open new satellite offices across the country, https://www.thepeninsulaqatar.com/article/16/01/2019/Home-Healthcare-Service-to-open-new-satellite-offices-across-the-country; January 2019. [Accessed 20 June 2020].

[47] The Peninsula. PHCC delivering COVID-19 screening for elderly at home through home healthcare services, https://thepeninsulaqatar.com/article/10/06/2020/PHCC-delivering-COVID-19-screening-for-elderly-at-home-through-home-healthcare-services; June 2020. [Accessed 20 June 2020].

[48] Gulf Times. PHCC launches home delivery of medicines, https://www.gulf-times.com/story/659996/PHCC-launches-home-delivery-of-medicines; April 2020. [Accessed 20 June 2020].

[49] Gulf Times. Home care for all in Qatar by 2014: PHCC, https://www.gulf-times.com/story/358841/Home-care-for-all-in-Qatar-by-2014-PHCC; July 2013. [Accessed 20 June 2020].

[50] Hukoomi. Home care for the elderly, https://portal.www.gov.qa/wps/portal/services/inviduallandingpages/medical%20services/homecarefortheelderly/!ut/p/a0/04_Sj9CPykssy0xPLMnMz0vMAfGjzOIt_S2cDS0sDNz9fVyNDTyDHT2d_HzdDA1CjPULsh0VAZGTuVA!/. [Accessed 20 June 2020].

[51] Palesy D, Jakimowicz S, Saunders C, Lewis J. Home care in Australia: an integrative review. Home Health Care Serv Q 2018;37(2):113–39. https://doi.org/10.1080/0162 1424.2018.1438952. [Accessed 23 June 2020].

[52] Jackson CL, Hambleton SJ. Australia's health care homes: laying the right foundations. Med J Aust 2017;206(9):380–1. https://doi.org/10.5694/mja16.01470. [Accessed 9 May 2020].

[53] Saxena H. Patients want in-home pharmacy care. Pharmacy News 2018. https://www.ausdoc.com.au/news/patients-want-home-pharmacy-care. [Accessed 18 July 2020].

[54] The Pharmacy Guild of Australia. In-home care, https://www.guild.org.au/about-us/community-pharmacy-2025/framework/in-home-care. [Accessed 22 June 2020].

[55] Rawal P. Pharmacy practice in Australia. Pharm J 2008. https://www.pharmaceutical-journal.com/news-and-analysis/features/pharmacy-practice-in-australia/10033046.article?firstPass=false. [Accessed 24 June 2020].

[56] Department of Health, Australian Government. Community pharmacy in health care homes trial program. Australia https://www1.health.gov.au/internet/main/publishing.nsf/Content/health-care-homes-cp/$File/Community-Pharmacy-in-Health-Care-Homes-Trial-Program-factsheet-Dec-2018.pdf; 2018. [Accessed 5 July 2020].

[57] Turcotte M. Insights on Canadian Society. Ottawa (ON): Statistics Canada; 2014. Sep, Canadians with unmet home care needs. [cited 18 March 2017]. Cat no. 75-006-X. Available from: www.statcan.gc.ca/pub/75-006-x/2014001/article/14042-eng.pdf; 2014. [Accessed 25 June 2020].

[58] Papastergiou J, Zervas J, Li W, Rajan A. Home medication reviews by community pharmacists: reaching out to homebound patients. Can Pharm J (Ott) 2013;146(3):139–42. https://doi.org/10.1177/1715163513487830. [Accessed 24 June 2020].

[59] Houle S, MacKeigan L. Home care pharmacy practice in Canada: a cross-sectional survey of services provided, remuneration, barriers, and facilitators. Can J Hosp Pharm 2017;70(4):294–300. https://doi.org/10.4212/cjhp.v70i4.1680. [Accessed 4 May 2020].

[60] Poole R. The role of local pharmacy in the future of homecare. Pharm J 2018;300(7912).

[61] Krass I. Ways to boost pharmacy practice research. Pharm J 2015;295(7883). https://doi.org/10.1211/PJ.2015.20200088. [Accessed 22 June 2020].

CHAPTER 4

Community pharmacy-based medication therapy management clinic in Saudi Arabia

Basmah Albabtain[a,b], Ejaz Cheema[b], Ghada Bawazeer[c], and Muhammad Abdul Hadi[b]
[a]Department of Pharmaceutical Practice, College of Pharmacy, Princess Nourah Bint Abdulrahman University, Riyadh, Saudi Arabia
[b]School of Pharmacy, Institute of Clinical Sciences, University of Birmingham, Birmingham, United Kingdom
[c]Clinical Pharmacy Department, College of Pharmacy, King Saud University, Riyadh, Saudi Arabia

Saudi Vision 2030 and the National Transformation Program 2020

The Kingdom of Saudi Arabia (KSA) occupies most of the Arabian Peninsula, bordering the Red Sea and the Gulf of Aqaba in the west and the Persian Gulf in the east [1]. It has a population of 34,218,169 with a growth rate of 2.52% in 2017. The legal system is based on absolute monarchy and on Islamic theocracy [2]. KSA's economy is mainly petroleum-based, the largest oil producer in the Middle East, and has the second-largest oil reserve in the world [1].

On April 25, 2016, the government of KSA launched its ambitious national development plan, known as Vision 2030, which worked as a roadmap for economic growth and national development [3]. It is a bundle of social and economic policies that were planned to free the kingdom from dependence on oil exports and to shape a prosperous and sustainable economic future. Vision 2030 is focused on the country's strength; the country's real wealth is considered to lie in the ambition of its human resources and the potential of the younger generation [4, 5].

Vision 2030 comprises of several domains, strategic objectives, and outcome-oriented indicators that require commitment from all public and private sectors. The vision has been designed to accelerate a wide range of reforms aimed at reinforcing and diversifying the economic base, modernizing the health sector, and putting the country's young and growing population on track for maintainable growth and development over the coming decades [4]. The National Transformation Program (NTP) is one

Pharmacy Practice Research Case Studies
https://doi.org/10.1016/B978-0-12-819378-5.00004-0

61

of the programs that has been developed to ensure the rapid completion of projects and initiatives and secure sustainability through periodic review of implementation levels [3].

Saudi healthcare system and health sector transformation

In 1950, the Ministry of Health (MOH) was launched and marked the beginning of the development of a modern healthcare ecosystem in KSA [6]. There has been a substantial improvement in the availability of health resources in the last two decades. A total of 494 hospitals provide 75,225 beds, which is around 22.5 beds per 10,000 population [6, 7].

The healthcare system in KSA is predominantly governmental, offering its services to all citizens [8]. The MOH is the primary provider and financer of health care services in KSA and comprises 60% of the total health services [9]. Although there are some private hospitals and primary healthcare centers, the private sector's role is nominal by comparison to the government sector, making KSA the largest spender on healthcare across the Middle East and North Africa with an allocated government budget of more than $39 billion to "health and social development" in 2018 [5, 10]. The healthcare system provides health services at three levels: primary, secondary, and tertiary [9].

It has been noted that despite healthcare system achievements, significant progress has yet to be achieved for Vision 2030 and its strategic plan [9]. The NTP has 37 strategic objectives mapped into eight themes. The first theme is "transform healthcare," which is divided into three strategic objectives, 34 key performance indicators, and 70 initiatives. To execute this transformation, the MOH has created a dedicated transformation unit, known as the Vision Realization Office (VRO) [5].

In 2017, the Saudi MOH identified some challenges in the current health system to provide better healthcare services. First, the population of the kingdom continues to grow and age. Second, the country has experienced a continued increase in the rates of noncommunicable diseases compared to the regional and international rates. Third, there are significant gaps in the quality of services provided to patients. Much of this is due to a lack of consistent protocols and pathways for treatment, as well as incomplete measurement of patient processes and outcomes. Finally, the system is resource- and staff-centric rather than patient- or person-centric in its orientation. It is also institution-centric rather than population-centric. Eventually, all these challenges will lead to an increase in the overall demand for more frequent, advanced, and expensive treatments, resulting in increased burden on the healthcare system [11].

To overcome these challenges, VRO recommends shifting the Saudi government's role from its traditional one of providing healthcare services to one that focuses on regulating and monitoring them. Therefore, it seeks to increase the private sector contribution by encouraging investments, both local and international. Subsequently, the implementation of a new paradigm of care will improve access to health services and the overall performance of the health system while curbing the growth in health expenditures [5]. In addition, this will ensure fair distribution of medical projects to all parts of the kingdom, following unified and well-known criteria, including hospitals and health and specialized centers [12, 13].

One of the healthcare sector transformation strategies for pharmaceutical care is to change the pharmacy practice model in KSA. Under the new model, most pharmaceutical care services will switch from inpatient to ambulatory and community care. Eventually, most pharmaceutical care services will be provided through community pharmacies (CPs). In this regard, the CP sector has benefited from ongoing initiatives and programs [13]. These initiatives aim to introduce a new approach to healthcare that focuses on prevention and goes beyond merely disease treatment; instead, it will integrate the role of the individual, society, and institutions with the role of health service providers to ensure access to healthcare under best practices [5].

Moreover, the new model will create new extended roles for community pharmacists' contributions to pharmaceutical care beyond accurate dispensing of medication and the provision of basic counseling. The pharmacist's role will become more patient-oriented, resulting in more services being provided by CPs in the future. Extending community pharmacists' roles could lead to many patient-related benefits, including improvement in the quality of care, the optimization of drug therapy [14], a decrease in general practitioner (GP) workload, and a reduction in long-term healthcare costs [15, 16]. In addition, it might ease some pressure from governmental hospitals and healthcare centers in light of the reformation of the Saudi healthcare system [14].

Community pharmacy practice

The pharmacy practice in Saudi Arabia (including community pharmacy) is governed by several authorities, namely, the Ministry of Health (MOH), the Saudi Food and Drug Authority (SFDA), and the Saudi Commission of Health Specialties (SCFHS). The MOH is the body that regulates and dictates the practice of health care professions in general, including pharmacy, as well as developing the laws and regulations that govern pharmaceutical products and institutions. The SFDA governs everything related to medications including medications classification, registration, distribution, and pharmacovigilance. SCFHS oversee licensing, registration, and classification of all health providers in the country [17]. Until recently, the practice of community pharmacists has focused almost exclusively on dispensing, with many restrictions on direct patient care activities with almost no supervision on enforcing medication counseling responsibilities in community pharmacies [18]. Recent changes in the MOH regulations for pharmaceutical products and institutions issued in 1440/2019 released the many restrictions and specifically emphasized pharmaceutical care services that can be practiced in community settings [19]. These new services included vaccination services, assessment and measurement of vital signs, education and patient counseling, medical devices education, medication therapy management and chronic disease management services, acute care services, pharmaceutical consultations, and compounding.

Current services in community pharmacy
Dispensing and medication counseling services
The predominant activity of community pharmacy is dispensing [17, 20]. This aspect of pharmacy is crucial. Historically, dispensing was neglected for a long time and it suffered accumulative negative practices, due to lack of pharmacy leadership, insufficient enforcement of laws related to dispensing without a prescription for almost all medication classes except for controlled substances [21–23], in addition to profit-oriented mindset of community pharmacy owners, whom by law can be of a nonpharmacy background [24]. Moreover, medication education and counseling provided in the community setting are mostly described as deficient and suboptimal [18, 25–29]. Several studies were published to address multiple aspects of the current practice related to safe dispensing of medications [30–33], customers' and patients' satisfaction with the pharmacist role [34–36], as well as pharmacists' and pharmacy students' perception of their role. Despite the methodological issues of these studies, they highlight the need for more improvement in the practice [37, 38] as well as in research [39, 40]. With that being said, the current changes in the healthcare system in Saudi Arabia including the update in regulations and the adamant enforcement to enact MOH laws related to dispensing, in addition to the increase in chain pharmacies along with automation and technology advancement, have significantly reduced such practices and set community pharmacy on the track

toward safe and responsible practice [41]. It is especially important to note here that the quality of education of pharmacists is a crucial component to improve this essential role [42–44], and especially that the setting currently employs mainly expatriates with varied educational backgrounds. The lack of Saudi graduates seeking community pharmacy as a career option is due to unattractive salary, scope of practice, hours of operation, stigma of being a salesperson, and most importantly, the insecurity that many Saudi graduates feel about working in the private sector [45, 46]. Under Vision 2030, nationalization of these jobs will provide an attractive career path for Saudi graduates [47, 48]. In this digital era, the dispensing function of pharmacy has evolved to introduce automation in dispensing and pharmacy warehouses. Loyalty programs, "drive thru pharmacies," online pharmacies, and ATM pharmacy products are available to bring the basic pharmacy services closer to satisfy customers' needs [49]. Table 1 provides a summary of key studies evaluating various community pharmacy services in Saudi Arabia.

Vaccination services

Saudi community pharmacists are allowed to deliver nine types of vaccinations to the public: hepatitis vaccine, shingles vaccine, human papillomavirus vaccine, tetanus vaccine, meningococcal vaccine, hemophilic influenza vaccine, pneumococcal vaccine, influenza vaccinations (including but not limited to H1N1 vaccine), and a combined diphtheria, tetanus toxoids, and pertussis vaccine. The regulations require pharmacists to be certified through a pharmacy-based immunization delivery course. Vaccination are limited to adults (≥ 18 years), and by availability of administration protocol to handle any ADRs, education of the public about the vaccinations, documentation and record keeping, infection control policies, and the availability of a private space to administer the vaccines [52]. In 2018, Balkhi et al. [51] demonstrated that pharmacists in the community are willing to expand their role and offer vaccination services, provided that regulations allow it. Currently, few pharmacies (mainly large chain corporations) are providing such services, which require additional human resources and structure remodeling to satisfy the regulations and considerations regarding the cost [50].

Health education clinics

The Vision 2030 plan made a number of changes in the delivery of health care including a purposeful new pharmacy model that encourages the integration of the private sector in providing all ambulatory care services [13]. Community pharmacies are taking steps to engage in providing direct

Table 1 Summary of pharmacist involvement in different community pharmacy services in Saudi Arabia.

Author (year published)	Year(s) study conducted and location	Study design (number and type of participants)	Type of community pharmacy services evaluation (aim)	Duration/ follow-up	Outcome measures	Summary of results
Al Aloola et al. (2020) [50]	2019, Riyadh	Qualitative in-depth, semistructured interviews (20 Saudi community members who visited Saudi community pharmacies)	Explore the need for immunization services in Saudi community pharmacies from a Saudi community perspective.	20 interviews; each interview took around 20–30 min	Community needs for the service Community expectations from the service Community concerns, attitudes, and beliefs about the service	Participants expressed their need for such services and acceptance of immunization performed by community pharmacists, with the expectation that it would improve their immunization uptake and community health in general. However, some participants expressed concerns about community pharmacists' current level of ability and skill in providing immunization, the lack of a private area for conducting the service, the lack of female community pharmacists, and the cost of the immunization service. Some participants advocated for supervision of such services by the Ministry of Health (MOH) and Saudization of community pharmacy staff.
Khojah (2019) [26]	2018, Madinah	A survey study with simulated clients, i.e., mystery shoppers (88 community pharmacists)	Investigate the level of provision of customer education regarding the effects of sedating antihistamines on driving skills by private community pharmacies.	7 days	Degree and nature of patient counseling provided regarding the effects of sedating antihistamines on driving skills	Only 23 pharmacies offered spontaneous counseling. Although 73.9% of pharmacists (65 of 88), spontaneously or upon request, mentioned sedation as a side effect, only one pharmacist warned the client against driving after taking the medication, and three other pharmacists warned against dealing with hazardous machinery.

Alfadl et al. (2018) [27]	2017, Qassim	Observing the counseling services performed by the community pharmacists (235 sessions observed in 11 community pharmacies)	Evaluate the counseling skills and counseling content delivered by community pharmacists.	2 months	(1) Counseling skills (2) Counseling content (3) Counseling duration	In general, community pharmacists' counseling skills were inadequate. Patient's identity was not routinely checked. The average counseling duration was less than 1 min (51.5 ± 15.8s).
Balkhi et al. (2018) [51]	2016, Riyadh	Cross-sectional paper-based survey (139 community pharmacists)	Assess the readiness and willingness of the community pharmacists to provide an immunization service and to identify the barriers involved in implementing such service in Saudi Arabia.	3 months	Readiness and willingness of the community pharmacists to provide an immunization service. The barriers involved in implementing such a service	76 (55%) expressed their willingness to administer vaccines and establish an immunization service. Among the participants that had shown willingness, many explained their reasons in accepting this role, including their accessibility in the community (56/57, 98.3%) and the possibility of expansion in the rate of immunization coverage in certain age groups, such as the elderly (47/51, 92.2%). The remaining 63 (45%) respondents who were not willing and ready to provide immunization services mainly agreed that a lack of training (46/61, 75.4%) and concerns in maintaining patient safety (31/46, 67.4%) were considered as barriers to deliver immunization services. Most importantly, continuous professional education and training workshops on immunization and pharmacist interest were the main drivers of immunization service implementation.

Continued

Table 1 Summary of pharmacist involvement in different community pharmacy services in Saudi Arabia—cont'd

Author (year published)	Year(s) study conducted and location	Study design (number and type of participants)	Type of community pharmacy services evaluation (aim)	Duration/ follow-up	Outcome measures	Summary of results
Alshammari et al. (2017) [23]	2014–15, six major regions in Saudi Arabia (Riyadh, Jeddah, Madinah, Hail, Qassim, and Sharqiah)	Cross-sectional study (150 community pharmacists)	Assess the compliance of community pharmacies with the regulations that prohibit the dispensing of prescription-only medications in the absence of a physician prescription in Saudi Arabia.	3 months	The prevalence of noncompliance among community pharmacies (compliance rate was calculated per region per drug)	On average, 63% approved dispensing of prescription-only drugs across six regions in Saudi Arabia and the 37% rejected dispensing, representing a significant noncompliance rate regarding the selected list of medications in this study. The frequency of dispensing per medication across six major regions in Saudi Arabia is as follows: isosorbide dinitrate (86%), enoxaparin (82%), nitroglycerin (74%), propranolol (73%), verapamil (70%), warfarin (65%), methyldopa (64%), ciprofloxacin (57%), and codeine (4%).

Study						Findings
Kashour et al. (2016) [28]	Not clear, Riyadh and Jeddah	Cross-sectional observational design with simulated client study (600 community pharmacists)	Determine the prevalence of non-OTC medication sale without prescription by community pharmacists to simulated patients presenting with cardiac symptoms in Saudi Arabia and to evaluate the quality of assessment and counseling provided to these patients.	Not clear	Prevalence of non-OTC medication sale without prescription Assessment and counseling provided by pharmacists	379 (63.2%) sold various prescription medications to simulated patients without prescription. Assessment and counseling provided by pharmacists was inadequate. Almost a quarter of pharmacists did not ask simulated patients any questions; 52% asked one or two questions; and only 24% asked three or more questions. Only 28 pharmacists (4.7%) inquired about drug allergies; 48.5% instructed simulated patients on the dosage and frequency of the sold medications; 21.6% provided instruction on treatment duration; and 19.4% gave instructions on dose, frequency, and duration of treatment. Compared to AHF, ACS simulated patients were more likely to be asked about other symptoms and comorbidities (59.7% vs. 48.7%, $P = .007$ and 46.3% vs. 37.3%, $P = .005$, respectively) and were more likely to be advised to go to hospital (70.3% vs. 56.3%, $P < .001$).

Continued

Table 1 Summary of pharmacist involvement in different community pharmacy services in Saudi Arabia—cont'd

Author (year published)	Year(s) study conducted and location	Study design (number and type of participants)	Type of community pharmacy services evaluation (aim)	Duration/ follow-up	Outcome measures	Summary of results
Al-Tannir et al. (2016) [36]	2014, Riyadh	Cross-sectional survey (500 Saudi adults approached at pharmacists and public places)	Assess the satisfaction level of Saudi adults with the pharmaceutical services provided at the community pharmacies.	1 month	Satisfaction level	Around 41% were satisfied with Saudi pharmacy services. Out of these, 57% attributed their satisfaction to pharmacist counseling on current medication, 96% to appropriate dosage regimen explanation, and 73% to appropriate time spent in counseling ($P < .001$). When asked about reasons for dissatisfaction, 82% of the unsatisfied group stated that pharmacists fail to ask about comorbid diseases and 78% reported unavailability of dedicated pharmacist for patient counseling ($P < .001$).

| Alaqeel et al. (2015) [18] | 2012, Riyadh | Cross-sectional survey with simulated patients (SPs) visits (161 simulated visits and 350 community pharmacists participate in the questionnaire) | Investigate the counseling practices of community pharmacists in Saudi Arabia when dispensing OTC and POM without a prescription. | 2 months | Counseling rate Types of questions asked Information provided during the counseling process | Out of the 161 visits, a medicine was dispensed in 150 visits. When SPs requested medications, pharmacists asked questions during 15 visits (10.0%), provided information during seven visits (4.6%), and both asked questions and provided information, i.e., provided counseling, during four visits (2.6%). When the SPs started to be inquisitive and demanded information, pharmacists asked SPs questions during 71 visits (47.3%), provided information during 150 visits (100%), and both asked questions and provided information, i.e., provided counseling, during 65 visits (43.3%). Information regarding dose was the most common type of information provided in 146 visits (97.3%). After the SPs started to be inquisitive and probed for information, only 10% were counseled on precautions. In the cross-sectional survey, 400 pharmacists were approached and 350 agreed to participate in the questionnaire (87% response rate). Of the respondents, 223 (63.7%) reported that they usually or always tell the patient about the purpose of medicines or the diagnosis, 302 (86.2%) reported that they usually or always give patient information on how to use or apply the medicine; 299 (85.3%) said they were satisfied with their counseling practices. |

Continued

Table 1 Summary of pharmacist involvement in different community pharmacy services in Saudi Arabia—cont'd

Author (year published)	Year(s) study conducted and location	Study design (number and type of participants)	Type of community pharmacy services evaluation (aim)	Duration/ follow-up	Outcome measures	Summary of results
Khan (2013) [31]	2012, Alahsa	Cross-sectional study (50 community pharmacists)	Analyze the community pharmacists' current knowledge and perceived barriers to ADR reporting systems.	6 weeks	The knowledge about ADRs Barriers to ADR reporting systems	In terms of knowledge about ADRs, very few (four, 8.0%) pharmacists were unable to differentiate between the right and wrong definition of ADRs. 42 pharmacists (84.0%) mentioned that patients often report adverse events. However, 45 (90.0%) were not aware of the ADR reporting system in Saudi Arabia. A deficient professional environment was the main barrier to the ADR reporting process. In addition, unavailability of the reporting forms and poor understanding of the reporting process were common barriers to the reporting process.

patient care through fulfilling a number of goals of the national transformation plan for a "healthy society." Beyond the traditional patient education about medications, some pharmacies are now offering services such as specialized education for diabetes, personalized weight management programs to reduce obesity and maintain a healthier lifestyle, vital sign measurement, adherence programs, and specialty pharmacy education geared toward the elderly population [53]. It is important to mention that large chain pharmacies currently have the capacity to add these additional services (mostly for free); however, implementing such services, should occur under the supervision of the MOH and Saudi Patient Safety Centre.

Medication therapy management and chronic disease management services

Medication therapy management (MTM) services that focus on chronic diseases education and management are currently provided in the ambulatory care setting in many large university and governmental hospitals [54–56]. Services include anticoagulation clinics, diabetes management clinics, HIV management, transplant, and oncology medication management, to name a few. "Caring for our health" is one of the main objectives of Vision 2030, which focuses on transforming and raising the standards of healthcare more specifically at the primary care front. The strategic plan advocates a "new care model" that focuses in providing efficient, effective, accessible, and responsive care that empowers people and their families to take control of their health and enables them to be well-informed to make decisions concerning their health [57]. Private sectors (including community pharmacy) are called in to participate in health development. This call for community participation at all levels, combined with the updated regulations that broaden the scope of practice for pharmacists, will generate opportunities to extend MTM services to community pharmacies [58].

Medication compounding

Currently, prescription compounding exists in specified pharmacies that serve mainly dermatology clinics. Some other pharmacies provide limited compounding services based on the 503A guideline, but with extremely limited scope.

Current initiatives

The Ministry of Health initiated program Wasfaty may be the most significant digital transformation in healthcare delivery and prescription dispensing under Vision 2030 [59]. Wasfaty "My Prescription" is a platform for e-prescription services, launched through collaboration with National Unified Procurement Company for Medical Supplies (NUPCO), that connects MOH hospitals and primary care centers (governmental hospitals will follow in the future) with community pharmacies all over the country [13]. It allows all MOH beneficiaries to receive their medications from the nearest registered community pharmacy in their neighborhood. In addition, it is expected that Wasfaty will link to the Unified Patient Record project (still underway) and this will bring opportunities for pharmacists to provide safe and effective comprehensive medication services with access to a patient's medical record, which is currently one of the barriers in providing valuable pharmaceutical care services.

Other initiatives are underway either at the level of individual medical or pharmaceutical entities to introduce new services such as home healthcare and parenteral and infusion therapies, as market needs are currently expanding.

Future development

Several studies showed that community pharmacists believe that pharmaceutical care responsibilities are an essential aspect of the practice [24, 35, 50, 60, 61], and with the recent changes in regulation, more data about how these activities are conducted and their impact on patients and healthcare system will solidify the value of Saudi pharmacists in the community, similar to their colleagues in the hospital setting.

Community pharmacy-based medication therapy management (MTM) service in Saudi Arabia

Globally, the role of community pharmacists has been extended beyond their traditional role of dispensing of medicines to more profound involvement in direct patient care [62, 63]. Unfortunately, as described earlier, the practice of community pharmacy in KSA has not evolved much, with only limited patient-centered services available for patients and the general public [29]. To manage effectively the growing burden of chronic and noncommunicable diseases and an aging population, community pharmacies need to be integrated properly within the healthcare system [64]. Extending community pharmacists' roles could result in many patient-related benefits, including improvement in the quality of care, the optimization of drug therapy [14], decrease in general practitioner (GP) workload, and potential reduction in long-term healthcare costs [15, 16]. In addition, it will ease some pressure from governmental hospitals and healthcare centers in light of the reformation of the Saudi healthcare system [14].

In order to enhance the role of community pharmacies, the Kingdom's Ministry of Health encouraged initiatives and agreements to reform the CP, along with updating the regulations to allow the provision of pharmaceutical care from CP. The community pharmacy-based medication therapy management (MTM) service is one such initiative and is jointly designed by the College of Pharmacy at King Saud University, the Innova Saudi Health Care Company, and the Ministry of Health. This section presents an outline of proposed research to evaluate the effectiveness of the MTM service. The evaluation is based on the UK Medical Research Council's development-evaluation-implementation framework for complex interventions [65]. It is anticipated that the findings of this study will pave the way to introduce MTM and other advanced patient care services in CP and effectively integrate the pharmacist's role as a primary care provider.

MTM service and the MRC's development-evaluation-implementation framework

The MRC's development-evaluation-implementation framework for complex interventions consists of four interlinked but not sequential stages including: development—which includes reviewing literature to identify best quality evidence base, identifying and/or developing appropriate theory, and modeling processes and outcomes; feasibility/piloting—which includes testing procedures/interventions, recruitment and retention rates, and estimating sample size; evaluation—which includes assessing effectiveness and cost-effectiveness and understanding the change process; and implementation—which includes dissemination of findings, monitoring, and long-term follow-up. All these stages feed into each other.

For the development of the MTM service, a comprehensive systematic review and metaanalysis has been conducted to evaluate the effectiveness of the community pharmacy-based MTM service (results are yet to be published). The systematic review not only provided the evidence base for the service development but also guided the design of mixed-methods study. A number of meetings were conducted with stakeholders, field experts, and community pharmacy owners prior to the development of the service. During the meetings, a range of issues with regard to delivery and applicability of service were discussed. The MTM model has been based on the American Pharmacists Association and the National Association of Chain

Drug Stores Foundation framework for implementing effective MTM services in a community pharmacy setting (original framework developed in 2005 and updated in 2008) [66]. The MTM service model in pharmacy practice includes the following five core elements [66]:

- Medication therapy review (MTR)—a systematic process of collecting patient-specific information, assessing medication therapies to identify medication-related problems, developing a prioritized list of medication-related problems, and creating a plan to resolve them.
- Personal medication record (PMR)—a comprehensive record of the patient's medications (prescription and nonprescription medications, herbal products, and other dietary supplements).
- Medication-related action plan (MAP)—a patient-centric document containing a list of actions for the patient to use in tracking progress for self-management.
- Intervention and/or referral—the pharmacist provides consultative services and intervenes to address medication-related problems; when necessary, the pharmacist refers the patient to a physician or other healthcare professional.
- Documentation and follow-up—MTM services are documented in a consistent manner, and a follow-up MTM visit is scheduled based on the patient's medication-related needs, or the patient is transitioned from one care setting to another.

MTM feasibility/piloting using mixed-methods design

A mixed-methods methodology using an embedded design has been developed to evaluate the feasibility of the pharmacist-led MTM program. An embedded design consists of two components: a pilot RCT and semistructured interviews. The data will be collected sequentially and independently. The main question (What is the effect of pharmacist-led medication therapy management program on patients' outcomes?) requires a quantitative approach and it is therefore the principal method, while the qualitative method will be used to explore patients' experience and views on the service (What is patients' experience and views with the pharmacist-led medication therapy management program?) and has a supportive role. The quantitative component will address the effectiveness of the program and the qualitative component will explore issues around patient experience and view, helping to understand and explain why and how the intervention works and how the service can be improved. The use of mixed methods will allow the generation of multiple data sets and perspectives, thus providing a broader understanding than using either a qualitative or quantitative approach alone [67].

Rationale for using mixed-methods approach

As the name suggests, mixed-methods methodology refers to a meaningful integration of the statistical trends of quantitative with stories and personal experiences of qualitative research methodologies to answer a research question within a single study. The goal for researchers using mixed methods is to draw from the strengths and diminish the weaknesses of the quantitative and qualitative research approaches. This collective strength provides a fairer understanding of the research problem than either form of data alone. The rationale to use a mixed-methods approach is the different research questions and illustrations. The primary reason is its ability to answer different research questions requiring different methodologies. Broadly, there are two components to the inquiry: one focuses on the evaluation of "effectiveness" of the MTM service requiring a quantitative approach, and the other looks at exploring patients' experiences and views about the service, requiring a qualitative approach. For illustration reasons—which is one of the most useful applications of a mixed-methods approach, particularly in health services evaluation studies, because a "quantitative only" study can only generate numbers, P values, and effect sizes, which may not be enough for a holistic service evaluation—integrating "numeric" with "words" in the present study makes it possible to answer the study objectives comprehensively.

The embedded design was chosen because it was best suited to answer the different research questions, which required a different method within the single study, taking into consideration that one method is dominant and the other plays a supportive role and answers a different research question. The embedded design enabled choosing a quantitative method to answer the "effectiveness question" and a qualitative method to "explore patients' experience and view with the service" (Fig. 1).

Phase one: The quantitative phase

The quantitative study consists of a pilot RCT, which aims to determine the feasibility of a community pharmacist-led MTM program in KSA. The primary objective is to determine the impact of a pharmacist intervention on patient clinical outcomes, including change in disease-specific clinical outcomes such as diabetes mellitus (DM), hypertension (HTN), and dyslipidemia (DLD), as well as nondisease specific clinical outcomes, such as number and types of drug-related problems (DRP).

This is a two-arm, open-label, parallel-group, pilot randomized controlled study with a 6-month follow-up. Participants in the active arm will receive pharmacist led MTM intervention and participants in the control group will receive usual care only.

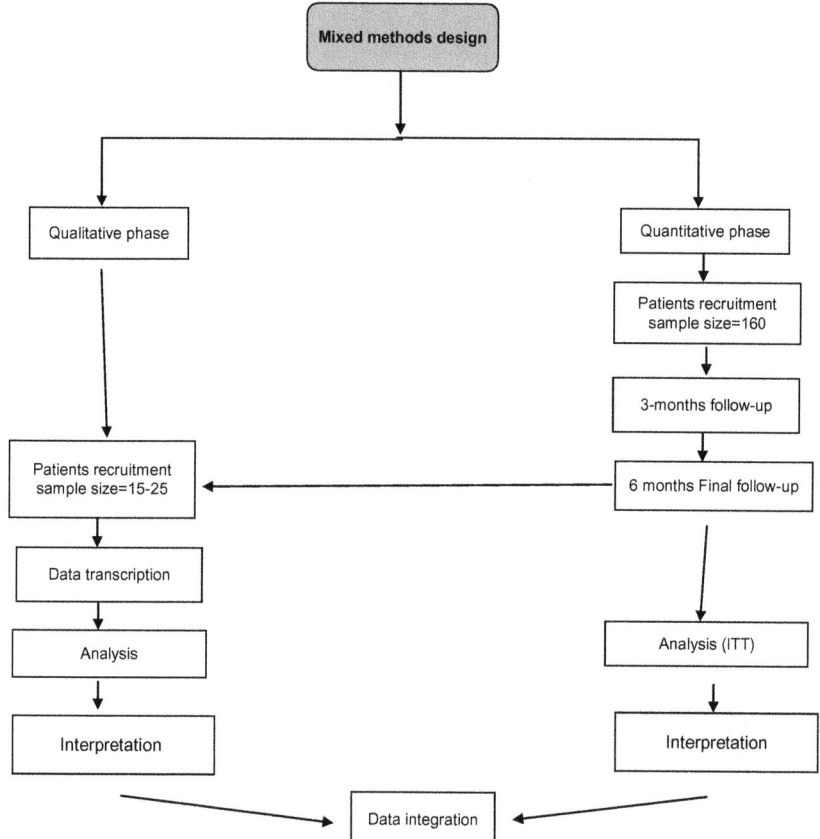

Fig. 1 The research process.

Phase two: The qualitative phase

The qualitative phase will consist of individual face-to-face semistructured interviews with a sample of the patients in the intervention arm to explore their experiences with the service. It is noteworthy that the qualitative interviews will not contribute toward answering the effectiveness question (the primary aim of the study) but it will help us to understand and explain how the intervention might have worked and how the service delivery can further be optimized to improve patient outcomes and experiences.

The need for a qualitative phase in light of the MRC development-implementation-evaluation framework

For the qualitative phase, all interviews will be conducted individually, face-to-face, by the first author in the clinic, using a semistructured approach. It is expected that the interviews will last 20–30 min and will be undertaken within 2 weeks of completion of 6 months follow-up. Participants will be briefed about the purpose of the interview and measures taken to ensure confidentiality will be explained by the first author. The interviews will be audio-taped using two digital audio recorders.

A topic guide will be prepared to ensure uniformity based on the literature review and study objectives. The topic guide will be designed to cover the following areas: expectations from the service; efficacy of the service (did it help? How?); quality of the service; interaction with pharmacist (time given for consultation, engaging patient in discussion and designing of therapeutic plan, listening to and understanding the problem); their opinion of the role of the pharmacist in the MTM program; and overall satisfaction (experience compared to other services in past, aspects of the service which need improvement, etc.) with the service. Discussing these topics through qualitative research can give meaning to numerical results generated through quantitative research. The interviewer (principle researcher) will give a chance for interviewees to express any additional views at the end of the interview.

The use of a qualitative approach will provide a "voice to the patients" and generate more in-depth data on patient perspectives and general experiences with the service. We anticipate that patients' words will enlighten the pharmacists engaged in the MTM program in relation to their needs. Understanding patients' needs and expectations should enable practitioners to improve the care provided. We hope that the findings of this qualitative phase will also help us in understanding the change process and in designing definitive RCT. Developing a strong evidence base underpinned by a robust theoretical framework will help in establishing more patient-centered services within the community pharmacies in the Kingdom.

Conflict of interest

None declared.

References

[1] United Nations Development Programme. Saudi Arabia. Available from: https://www.sa.undp.org/content/saudi_arabia/en/home/countryinfo.html; 2020. (Accessed 16 June 2020).
[2] Nurunnabi M. Transformation from an oil-based economy to a knowledge-based economy in Saudi Arabia: the direction of Saudi Vision 2030. J Knowl Econ 2017;8:536–64.

[3]   Saudi Vision 2030. Available from: http://www.vision2030.gov.sa; 2016. (Accessed 16 June 2020).

[4]   United Nations Interagency Task Force on the Prevention and Control of Noncommunicable Diseases. The investment case for noncommunicable disease prevention and control in the Kingdom of Saudi Arabia: return on investment analysis & institutional and context analysis. Geneva: World Health Organization; 2017. 17.55.

[5]   National Transformation Program 2020. Available from: http://www.vision2030.gov.sa/en/ntp; 2016.

[6]   Al-Hanawi MK, Khan SA, Al-Borie HM. Healthcare human resource development in Saudi Arabia: emerging challenges and opportunities—a critical review. Public Health Rev 2019;40(1).

[7]   Anon. Statistical yearbook. Saudi Ministry of Health; 2018. Available from: https://https://www.moh.gov.sa/en/Ministry/Statistics/book/Documents/book-Statistics.pdf. (Accessed 19 June 2020).

[8]   Bawazir S. Consumer attitudes towards community pharmacy services in Saudi Arabia. Int J Pharm Pract 2004;12:83–9.

[9]   Almalki M, FitzGerald G, Clark M. Health care system in Saudi Arabia: an overview. East Mediterr Health J 2011;17(10):784–93.

[10] Alharbi MF. An analysis of the Saudi health-care system's readiness to change in the context of the Saudi National Health-care Plan in Vision 2030. Int J Health Sci 2018;12(3):83–7.

[11] Anon. Health sector transformation strategy. Saudi Ministry of Health; 2017. Available from: https://www.moh.gov.sa/en/Ministry/vro/Documents/Healthcare-Transformation-Strategy.pdf. (Accessed 17 June 2020).

[12] Aspden P, Wolcott J, Bootman JL, Cronenwett LR, editors. Preventing medication errors. Washington, DC: National Academies Press; 2007.

[13] Alomi YA. New pharmacy model for Vision 2030 in Saudi Arabia. J Pharm Pract Community Med 2017;3(3):194–6.

[14] Smith M, Giuliano MR, Starkowski MP. In Connecticut: improving patient medication management in primary care. Health Aff 2011;30(4):646–54.

[15] Dunlop JA, Shaw JP. Community pharmacists' perspectives on pharmaceutical care implementation in New Zealand. Pharm World Sci 2002;24(6):224–30.

[16] Giberson S, Yoder S, Lee MP. Improving patients and health system outcomes through advanced pharmacy practice. A report to the U.S. Surgeon General. Available from: http://www.accp.com/docs/positions/misc/Improving_Patient_and_Health_System_Outcomes.pdf; 2011. (Accessed 18 June 2020).

[17] Al-Jedai A, Qaisi S, Al-Meman A. Pharmacy practice and the health care system in Saudi Arabia. Can J Hosp Pharm 2016;69(3):231–7.

[18] Alaqeel S, Abanmy NO. Counselling practices in community pharmacies in Riyadh, Saudi Arabia: a cross-sectional study. BMC Health Serv Res 2015;15:557.

[19] Anon. Regulation-of-pharmaceutical-products-and-institutions [document]. Ministry of Health; 2019. Available from: https://www.moh.gov.sa/eServices/Licences/Pages/01.aspx.

[20] Almeman A, Al-jedai A. Pharmacy practice in the Kingdom of Saudi Arabia. In: Fathelrahman AI, Ibrahim MIM, Wertheimer AI, editors. Pharmacy practice in developing countries. Boston: Academic Press; 2016. p. 171–97 [chapter 9].

[21] Al-Mohamadi A, Badr A, Bin Mahfouz L, Samargandi D, Al Ahdal A. Dispensing medications without prescription at Saudi community pharmacy: Extent and perception. Saudi Pharm J 2013;21(1):13–8.

[22] Khan TM. The consequences of nonprescription medication sales in Saudi Arabia's community pharmacies: regulations without implementation. Ther Adv Drug Saf 2014;5(4):173–4.

[23] Alshammari TM, Alhindi SA, Alrashdi AM, Benmerzouga I, Aljofan M. Pharmacy malpractice: the rate and prevalence of dispensing high-risk prescription-only medications at community pharmacies in Saudi Arabia. Saudi Pharm J 2017;25(5):709–14.

[24] Alanazi A, Alfadl A, Hussain A. Pharmaceutical care in the community pharmacies of Saudi Arabia: present status and possibilities for improvement. Saudi J Med Med Sci 2016;4(1):9–14.

[25] Khojah HMJ, Abdalla AME. Do community pharmacies in Saudi Arabia provide medication-related information to nonbuyers? A mysterious shopper survey. Pharmacol Pharm 2019;10(04):169–76.

[26] Khojah HM. Do pharmacists counsel customers about the effects of sedating antihistamines on driving skills? A survey of community pharmacies in Saudi Arabia. J Int Med Res 2019;47(5):2018–25.

[27] Alfadl AA, Alrasheedy AA, Alhassun MS. Evaluation of medication counseling practice at community pharmacies in Qassim region, Saudi Arabia. Saudi Pharm J 2018;26(2):258–62.

[28] Kashour TS, Joury A, Alotaibi AM, Althagafi M, Almufleh AS, Hersi A, et al. Quality of assessment and counselling offered by community pharmacists and medication sale without prescription to patients presenting with acute cardiac symptoms: a simulated client study. Eur J Clin Pharmacol 2016;72(3):321–8.

[29] Al-Hassan MI. A look at community pharmacy practice in Saudi Arabia. Res J Med Sci 2009;3:111–4.

[30] Babelghaith SD, Wajid S, Alrabiah Z, Othiq MAM, Alghadeer S, Alhossan A, et al. Drug-related problems and pharmacist intervention at a general hospital in the Jazan Region, Saudi Arabia. Risk Manag Healthc Policy 2020;13:373–8.

[31] Khan TM. Community pharmacists' knowledge and perceptions about adverse drug reactions and barriers towards their reporting in Eastern region, Alahsa, Saudi Arabia. Ther Adv Drug Saf 2013;4(2):45–51.

[32] Doughan FFA, Alomi YA, Iflaifel MH. Pharmacist's awareness and knowledge of reporting adverse drug reactions in Saudi Arabia. Int J Pharmacol Clin Sci 2019;8(1):60–5.

[33] Faqihi M, Fageehi W. Pharmacist's knowledge, attitude, and practice towards pharmacovigilance and adverse drug reactions reporting process: a cross-sectional survey. Int J Med Dev Ctries 2019;409–14.

[34] AlShayban DM, Naqvi AA, Islam MA, Almaskeen M, Almulla A, Alali M, et al. Patient satisfaction and their willingness to pay for a pharmacist counseling session in hospital and community pharmacies in Saudi healthcare settings. Front Pharmacol 2020;11:138.

[35] Al-Arifi MN. Patients' perception, views and satisfaction with pharmacists' role as health care provider in community pharmacy setting at Riyadh, Saudi Arabia. Saudi Pharm J 2012;20(4):323–30.

[36] Al-Tannir M, Alharbi AI, Alfawaz AS, Zahran RI, AlTannir M. Saudi adults satisfaction with community pharmacy services. SpringerPlus 2016;5(1):774.

[37] Al Juffali L, Al-Aqeel S, Knapp P, Mearns K, Family H, Watson M. Using the human factors framework to understand the origins of medication safety problems in community pharmacy: a qualitative study. Res Soc Adm Pharm 2019;15(5):558–67.

[38] Al-Ghamdi MS. Continuing pharmaceutical education for community pharmacists in the eastern province of Saudi Arabia. J Fam Community Med 2001;8(3):45–52.

[39] Sweileh WM, Zyoud SH, Sawalha AF, Al-Jabi SW. A bibliometric study of community pharmacy-based research activity in middle eastern Arab Countries: 2003–2012. Trop J Pharm Res 2014;13(9):1549.

[40] Sultana K, Al Jeraisy M, Al Ammari M, Patel R, Zaidi STR. Attitude, barriers and facilitators to practice-based research: cross-sectional survey of hospital pharmacists in Saudi Arabia. J Pharm Policy Pract 2016;9(1):4.

[41] Alrasheedy AA, Alsalloum MA, Almuqbil FA, Almuzaini MA, Aba Alkhayl BS, Al-bishri AS, et al. The impact of law enforcement on dispensing antibiotics without prescription: a multi-methods study from Saudi Arabia. Expert Rev Anti-Infect Ther 2020;18(1):87–97.

[42] Al-Ghananeem AM, Malcom DR, Shammas S, Aburjai T. A call to action to transform pharmacy education and practice in the Arab world. Am J Pharm Educ 2018;82(9):7014.

[43] Alhamoudi A, Alnattah A. Pharmacy education in Saudi Arabia: the past, the present, and the future. Curr Pharm Teach Learn 2018;10(1):54–60.

[44] Aljadhey H, Asiri Y, Albogami Y, Spratto G, Alshehri M. Pharmacy education in Saudi Arabia: a vision of the future. Saudi Pharm J 2017;25(1):88–92.

[45] Balkhi B, Alghamdi A, Alhossan A, Alhamami A, Asiri YA. Pharmacy students attitude and perception toward working in community pharmacy in Saudi Arabia. Saudi Pharm J 2020;28(4):397–402.

[46] Al Ghazzawi WF, Abuzaid A, Al-Shareef OA, Al-Sayagh SM. Female pharmacists' career perceptions in Saudi Arabia: a survey at an academic center in Jeddah. Curr Pharm Teach Learn 2017;9(6):1022–30.

[47] AlRuthia Y, Alsenaidy MA, Alrabiah HK, AlMuhaisen A, Alshehri M. The status of licensed pharmacy workforce in Saudi Arabia: a 2030 economic vision perspective. Hum Resour Health 2018;16(1):28.

[48] Alhomoud FK, AlGhalawin L, AlGofari G, AlDjani W, Ameer A, Alhomoud F. Career choices and preferences of Saudi pharmacy undergraduates: a cross sectional study. Saudi Pharm J 2019;27(4):467–74.

[49] Abanmy N. The extent of use of online pharmacies in Saudi Arabia. Saudi Pharm J 2017;25(6):891–9.

[50] Al Aloola N, Alsaif R, Alhabib H, Alhossan A. Community needs and preferences for community pharmacy immunization services. Vaccine 2020;38(32):5009–14.

[51] Balkhi B, Aljadhey H, Mahmoud MA, Alrasheed M, Pont LG, Mekonnen AB, et al. Readiness and willingness to provide immunization services: a survey of community pharmacists in Riyadh, Saudi Arabia. Saf Health 2018;4(1):1.

[52] MOH. Appendix 4: Requirements and procedures for providing pharmaceutical care services in pharmacies. 1st ed. Saudi Arabia: Ministry of Health; 2019.

[53] AlNahdi-Pharmacy. Health educational clinics. Nahdi Medical Company; n.d. Available from: https://nahdi.sa/en/social-sustainability/health-educational-clinics (Accessed 18 October 2020).

[54] Makeen HA. Clinical pharmacists as medication therapy experts in diabetic clinics in Saudi Arabia – not just a perception but a need. Saudi Pharm J 2017;25(6):939–43.

[55] Lubbad NAF, Memone M, AlHazzaa M. Optimizing safe and effective patient care focus on clinical pharmacist services and outcomes at the Medication Therapy Management Clinic: Stroke prevention. In: 18th international conference on neurology and neurological disorders; August 23–24. Paris, France: Allied Academies; 2018.

[56] Dib JG, Abdulmohsin SA. Establishing a pharmaceutical care clinic in a Saudi Arabian health center. Am J Health Syst Pharm 2007;64(1):107–9.

[57] MOH. Health sector transformation strategy. Saudi Arabia: Saudi Ministry of Health; 2017.

[58] Faisal A-O, Mohamed Soliman I, Randa Mansour Abdel-Sattar A, Amsha A, Asma A, Amal A, et al. Privileges of pharmacist in Saudi Arabia: administration and management. PTB Reports 2020;6:1.

[59] Wasfaty, Ministry of Health-Saudi Arabia. Available from: https://wasfaty.sa/about-us/.

[60] Ahmed N, Al-Wahibi N. Knowledge attitude and practice towards pharmaceutical care in community pharmacy in Saudi Arabia. Br J Med Med Res 2016;15(9):1–9.

[61] Almetwazi M, Alhammad A, Alhossan A, Alturki H, Aljawadi M, Asiri Y. Pharmacy students' satisfaction with Introductory Pharmacy Practice Experiences (IPPE) at community pharmacy: the case of Saudi Arabia. Saudi Pharm J 2020;28(1):68–73.

[62] Amien F, Myburgh NG, Butler N. Location of community pharmacies and prevalence of oral conditions in the Western Cape Province. Health SA Gesondheid 2013;18:9–15.

[63] Al-Saleh H, Al-Houtan T, Al-Odaill K, Al-Mutairi B, Al-Muaybid M, Al-Falah T, Ashraf Nazir M. Role of community pharmacists in providing oral health advice in the eastern province of Saudi Arabia. Saudi Dental J 2017;29:123–8.

[64] World Health Organization, Regional Office for the Eastern Mediterranean. Country cooperation strategy for WHO and Saudi Arabia 2012–2016. Regional Office for the Eastern Mediterranean: World Health Organization; 2013. Available from: https://apps. who.int/iris/handle/10665/113227. (Accessed 3 February 2020).

[65] MRC. Developing and evaluating complex interventions. London: Medical Research Council; 2019.

[66] American Pharmacists Association and the National Association of Chain Drug Stores Foundation. Medication therapy management in pharmacy practice: core elements of an MTM service model (version 2.0). J Am Pharm Assoc 2008;48:341–53.

[67] Abdul Hadi M, Phillip AD, Closs SJ, Marczewski K, Briggs M. A mixed-methods evaluation of a nurse-pharmacist–managed pain clinic: design, rationale and limitations. Can Pharm J 2013;146:4.

CHAPTER 5

Pharmacy services and pharmacy practice research in Ukraine

Andriy Zimenkovsky[a], Myroslava Sekh[a], and Zaheer-Ud-Din Babar[b]
aClinical Pharmacy, Pharmacotherapy and Medical Standardization, Danylo Halytsky Lviv National Medical University, Lviv, Ukraine
bCentre for Pharmaceutical Policy and Practice Research, Department of Pharmacy, University of Huddersfield, Huddersfield, United Kingdom

Introduction

Over its years of independence, Ukraine has seen its pharmacy come a long way from almost complete disruption to reaching the appropriate level of drug production and development, product quality control, entrepreneurship, science, and education [1]. Transformation of the content and forms of pharmacy service during the years of independence was carried out in accordance with the changes in political, economic, scientific, technical, and other factors. It is worth noting that throughout this time, there have been more than 15 heads of the Ministry of Health (MOH) of Ukraine. This has hindered the development of the industry, as each minister chose a direction that was not always a continuation of the former one.

As part of the Union of Soviet Socialist Republics, Ukraine produced mainly finished medications, while the synthesis of chemicals and the production of excipients and raw materials were performed predominantly in other republics [1]. At the same time, Ukraine produced more than 800 types of medications and was leading the production of antibacterial medications, vitamins, antipyretics, nonsteroidal antiinflammatory drugs, plant extracts, and medical devices (e.g., sterile bandages, first aid kits) [1, 2]. After the collapse of the Soviet Union, 80% of suppliers remained outside Ukraine. As a result, the production of more than 50 vital medications was stopped. The material–technical basis of production was lagging and outdated [1].

Pharmacy Practice Research Case Studies
https://doi.org/10.1016/B978-0-12-819378-5.00010-6
85

Review of pharmacy services in Ukraine—Historical perspective

First steps in development of pharmacy service in Ukraine, after declaring independence

In the first years of Ukraine's independence, priority measures were taken to bring the pharmaceutical industry out of the crisis. The "Comprehensive Program for the Development of the Medical Industry of Ukraine" for 1992–2003 (1992) [3, 4] was aimed at the reconstruction of enterprises and the development of modern technologies for the manufacture of drugs, primarily the vital ones; Pharmacological and Pharmacopoeial Committees and the State Inspectorate for Quality Control of Drugs were established, which helped to accelerate the development and registration of new domestic medications. The production of 120 medications and prophylactic preparations, which previously were not manufactured in Ukraine, was established and mastered, with 10 of these medications being fundamentally new [1]. Free medication for low-income retirees and children less than 3 years of age was introduced. Children from 3 to 6 years of age were allowed preferential dispensing of medications with a discount of 50% of the cost [5]. However, one of the main problems of that period was the acute shortage of imported medications, which accounted for less than 40% of demand [1]. Nowadays there are more than 11 million welfare beneficiaries in Ukraine [6]. Therefore, there is a need either to review this list with the aim to decrease it, or to seek funds to cover the costs, because there are no resources to provide fully for this population.

Changes in the management structure of the pharmacy service occurred in 1993. At that time, there were 6512 self-supporting pharmacies in the system of the MOH of Ukraine [1] that had extemporaneous drug production, the availability of which, accordingly, required the provision of appropriate pharmaceutical care. A State Committee for the Medical and Microbiological Industry (practically an independent ministry, which oversaw more than 120 pharmaceutical plants, factories and other domestic drug industries) was established, contributing to the further development of pharmacy services.

A characteristic feature of pharmacy payments at that time was the release of drugs on credit, or (rarely) upon delivery. In addition, there was no single structure for the management of drug supply in the regions. There were various forms of state-owned enterprises and associations: state-owned enterprises, corporations, associations, and firms with contractual relations with various pharmacies (state, municipal). In many regions, the organizational and pharmaceutical departments have been significantly re-duced or even eliminated, which has led to a violation of the basic norms of pharmacy service. The rules of storage and release of drugs were violated in pharmacies. In particular, patients could buy prescription drugs with-out a prescription—and that situation persists to this day. There was a state regulation regarding this issue (particularly, order No. 360 of the MOH of Ukraine) [7]; however, regulatory acts (laws, orders) are not implemented, or are not fully implemented. Therefore, only narcotic drugs required a prescription for purchase, while other drugs were easily available without a prescription.

At that time, the issue of intensifying the development of nonstate forms of ownership of pharmacies, pharmaceutical companies and other struc-tures arose. There has been a widespread trend of de facto mergers of state pharmacies with nonstate business structures on the basis of cooperation agreements [1], which resulted in illegal operation of premises, equipment, production facilities, pharmacy staff, government grants, benefits, loans, and repayable funds. In other words, privatization of pharmacies took place. The increase in the share of private pharmacies at that time was beginning to affect pharmaceutical care negatively—instead of operating as healthcare facilities, pharmacies were gradually becoming drugstores.

The turning point in the development of pharmacy service in Ukraine occurred in 1995. At this time, profound changes were observed in the growth of the structure of the range and volume of products produced by pharmaceutical companies [1]. The issue of promotion of medications came to prominence, since it became easier to produce medications than to sell them. Accordingly, the role of marketing activities in the pharmaceutical industry was growing. More attention was paid to the interests and needs of consumers. However, a characteristic feature of that time is the bankruptcy of many pharmaceutical plants and factories, while the rest, which were not unprofitable, became entirely private property. Thus, today there is no state pharmaceutical manufacturer in Ukraine, and accordingly, this situation does not allow the state to regulate fully and adequately both pharmaceuti-cal production and pharmaceutical care or pharmacy service.

The retail network of pharmacies was characterized by a high level of de-velopment of the competitive environment at that time, primarily due to the opening of a large number of densely located pharmacies, pharmacy kiosks, and outlets. Most often they had the same owner. At the same time, represen-tatives of many professions (economists, lawyers, dentists, etc.) took an active part in the pharmaceutical business, as there is no law that would give the right to pharmaceutical activity only to specialists, provisors (the title of pharmacists with higher pharmaceutical education in Ukraine), and pharmacists.

Professional public pharmaceutical associations

In 1998 one of the first professional public associations was established: the Galician Pharmaceutical Association, which is still the largest in western Ukraine. Other public associations were also created in other regions. Pharmaceutical associations aim to regulate the pharmaceutical sector. These nonprofit professional public organizations unite specialists in the pharmaceutical industry, as well as citizens who carry out activities in the field of pharmacy in order to promote its development, carry out research, and protect the common interests of its members in economic, social, and other fields. The main tasks of pharmaceutical associations are to: promote the development of the pharmaceutical industry and improve pharmacy services; ensure the representation and protection of the legitimate rights and interests of their members in cooperation with public authorities and local governments, trade unions; participate in the formation and implementation of economic medicinal policy; and improve the system of training, retraining, and advanced training of pharmaceutical personnel, dissemination of professional knowledge and experience among them, etc. Great hopes were pinned upon the medical and pharmaceutical community organizations, and it was believed that they would play the same important role as in the United States or Europe. However, today they have virtually no influence, either legally or in other respects; the state is currently reluctant to delegate management functions to the professional community.

The logical consequence of the self-regulation of professional community in 2010 was the implementation of the Code of Ethics for Pharmacists in 2010 [8]. It is noteworthy that pharmaceutical associations began to divide into different categories according to the direction and ideology of their members—domestic drug manufacturers, foreign drug manufacturers, pharmacy workers, etc.

The impact of the European integration strategy of Ukraine on pharmacy service development

A new historical stage that affected the development of the pharmacy service and the pharmaceutical industry in general was the strategy of Ukraine's integration into the European Union (EU) (1999). The main directions of pharmacy development of the new period were the creation of appropriate legislation and regulations, harmonization of standardization, regulatory and analytical support, licensing and registration in accordance with EU requirements, ensuring the proper quality of medications, creating a system of information on medications, and more. The problem of accessibility of medications for the population came to the forefront.

In 2002, for the first time in the country, a subcommittee on legislative support for the development of pharmacy and pharmaceutical activities was established under the auspices of the Committee of Healthcare, Maternity and Childhood of the Verkhovna Rada of Ukraine [9]. The main tasks of this subcommittee concerned a wide range of problems of pharmaceutical activity and pharmacy service, starting with the creation of medications, their state registration, production and application in medical practice, etc., and ending with training programs for pharmaceutical staff activities. Although this step was a breakthrough in the development of the pharmaceutical industry, the newly created body unfortunately did not leave a legacy of any significant achievements that would honorably adorn the pages of a history of the domestic pharmacy service.

At the same time, the first private network pharmacies began to appear. However, in Ukraine, in contrast to particularly Germany and Hungary where the law provides that one owner can have only one or two pharmacies, large holdings were created, which may have included several hundred pharmacies. For example, the "Pharmacy Holding," which was founded in 1999 on the basis of municipal pharmacies and is structured both vertically (wholesale/retail) and horizontally (many private pharmacies), covers about 900 outlets, including pharmacies, drugstores, and pharmacy outlets. Some private pharmacy chains are engaged only in retail, while others focus purely on wholesale. Private network pharmacies in Ukraine are, in the authors' opinion, a barrier to Good Pharmacy Practice (GPP), enabling monopolization of drug prices and their range, and slowing down the development of adequate pharmaceutical services. At that time, pharmacies began the process of transforming the "patient" into a "client." Extemporaneous drug production was gradually becoming unprofitable—no one paid attention to the humanistic function in the transition to market relations.

As mentioned above, the vast majority of pharmacies stopped manufacturing extemporaneous dosage forms. Employees with incomplete higher pharmaceutical education (pharmacists) were allowed to work in pharmacies. Pharmaceutical care proper, as a key task of the pharmacist in the pharmacy, began to dissipate. Gradually national drug manufacturers have adopted a system of compliance with the requirements of Good Manufacturing Practice (GMP), and leading national distributors adopted the Good Distribution Practice (GDP). However, many professional associations fiercely opposed the necessity of including in the Licensing Conditions modern international standards that would define the professional requirements for the pharmaceutical worker and the pharmacy itself. Essentially, the professional pharmaceutical community was becoming an active opponent of the introduction of GPP in pharmacies.

At present, the Ukrainian pharmaceutical market is operated mainly through a network of pharmacies, which determine its next dynamics and trends.

Study of the state and the main components of pharmacy service in Ukraine

At the international level of the healthcare system, there is a growing awareness of the importance and the role of the pharmacy as a healthcare institution [10]. Therefore, in the current global trends of development of pharmacy service, there is a significant expansion of the powers of pharmacists in clinical activities (review of prescriptions and rationalization of prescribed medications, improving patient adherence, advice on the use of medical devices, palliative treatment, patient counseling for long-term conditions and weight management [11], chemotherapy and radiopharmacy, providing pharmaceutical care at home, independent and additional prescriptions for chronic patients with certain diseases (diabetes, bronchial asthma, etc.), influenza vaccination, glycemic measurement, etc.) [12–16], increasing their status, and increasing professional independence, autonomy, and responsibility in the process of providing pharmaceutical care [17–19].

In the developed world, this process is well-regulated. There are legislation, protocols, rules, and agreements for the provision of pharmacy services [17]. These are expected to relieve primarily general practitioners and nurses of the burden of the disease, which can be supported by other primary care facilities as well as pharmacies [17]. Pharmacist should be perceived by the population as a reliable source of information and practical advice [20]. This approach obviously contributes to the development of not only commercial but also other functions of the pharmacy as a healthcare institution [21]. However, according to leading researchers, there are significant barriers to changing and perceiving pharmacists' own views on the possibility of involving primary medical care in the team and expanding patient-centered services [17]. The first problem highlighted is the lack of desire to move forward with the model of primary medical care for pharmaceutical workers themselves, who mostly perceive themselves as participants in the retail sale of medications, rather than as providers of primary medical care services [17]. Secondly, there is a lack of incentives and rewards, in particular from the state, for the introduction and expansion of patient-oriented services in the pharmacy [22].

Ukraine is no exception regarding this issue. The pharmacist and the clinical pharmacist became salespeople of medications. Pharmaceutical care in the pharmacy has leveled off, becoming a marketing tool to increase sales and, accordingly, profits, neglecting the humane component and drug safety of the consumer.

The professional functions of pharmacists and clinical pharmacists in Ukraine are limited compared to those of pharmacists and clinical pharmacists abroad. In Ukraine, the content of professional duties of pharmacists is formulated in a number of normative documents (Laws of Ukraine No. 5036-VI and No. 123/96-VR, Order of the Ministry of Health of Ukraine No. 360). In addition, pharmaceutical activity is regulated in the protocols of the provisor (pharmacist) by the order of the Ministry of Health No. 875 dated November 10, 2013 and described in the Code of Ethics of pharmaceutical workers of Ukraine [23]. However, the list of responsibilities is declarative and requires clarification of the responsibility of the pharmacist for the implementation of any functions (specifically) while performing professional activities [23], i.e., pharmaceutical activity is not adequately reflected by law in Ukraine [24].

At the same time, the regulation of pharmacists' activities is an integral part of the concept of the WHO and the International Pharmaceutical Federation (IPF). The Ukrainian pharmaceutical industry is continuing its development focusing on European experience and direction; these standards are an important element in improving the quality of pharmacy service provided to patients in Ukraine. However, as the world experience of pharmacy development shows, the implementation of GPP requirements is a long and continuous process [25]. The prime example is that of New Zealand, where pharmacists were generally interested in taking on a new role, but the pace at which the changes were adopted and implemented was often much slower than expected [17, 26]. To date, Ukraine still does not have enough large-scale research on methods and ways to study and improve the pharmacy services.

Pharmacy practice research in Ukraine

The profession of pharmacist around the world needs a solid foundation, which should also be based on research of pharmaceutical practice, in order to achieve its purpose in society [27, 28]. For example, in 2006, the Canadian Pharmaceutical Practice Research Group identified the study of pharmaceutical practice as a part of scientific research services, which includes research that covers and evaluates various determinants of health, as well as the role of pharmacists and their impact on patients' pharmacotherapy and health outcomes of the population [28]. In particular, the benefits of pharmaceutical interventions in patients with diabetes, hypertension, cardiovascular risk, and dyslipidemia have been repeatedly proven [29–35].

In Ukraine, only a few studies related to pharmaceutical practice have been conducted. One of them is related to the development, testing, and implementation of a program of pharmaceutical care of metabolic syndrome in a pharmacy [36]. The prototypes were the pharmaceutical care programs in pharmacies in Spain (Dader Programme for drug therapy follow-up) [37] and Hungary (Metabolic Syndrome Pharmaceutical Care Programme) [38]. The program consisted of three stages. At the first stage, information leaflets were developed and distributed among the visitors of the pharmacy about the metabolic syndrome, which contained general information about the problem, the main ways of prevention, the importance of a healthy lifestyle, blood pressure, blood glucose, body mass index, and table for noting the corresponding indicators of the patient for their comparison with the norm ($n = 590$). The second stage of the program consisted of identifying and assessing the main and additional risk factors for metabolic syndrome ($n = 465$), as well as the formation of individualized plans for pharmaceutical care of patients in the pharmacy. The third stage was to identify drug-related problems (DRPs) of patients with a doctor-verified diagnosis of "metabolic syndrome," to develop appropriate algorithms for individualized plans for pharmaceutical care of the patient and to form feedback with both the doctor and the patient. Relevant professional documentation was developed, which consisted of: (1) informed consent of the patient to medical/pharmaceutical intervention; (2) forms of assessment of the identified main and additional risk factors; (3) journal of patients who participated in the program of pharmaceutical care of metabolic syndrome; (4) "diary" of a patient with metabolic syndrome (to enter the results of self-monitoring by the patient); (5) forms of evaluation of pharmacotherapy by the patient; (6) the form of DRP assessment by the clinical pharmacist; and (7) the final report of the clinical pharmacist on the program of pharmaceutical care of metabolic syndrome in the pharmacy.

In 6 months, the researchers conducted 465 assessments of risk of developing metabolic syndrome in 162 patients. In 21 patients, risk factors for metabolic syndrome were identified for the first time with the participation of a clinical pharmacist, who referred these patients to a doctor to determine further strategy of treatment.

Challenges in providing pharmacy services in Ukraine

A questionnaire survey was conducted to evaluate challenges related to providing pharmacy services in different regions of Ukraine [39]. It was observed that the main and most important service of the pharmacy is the professional advice of a pharmacist. Most often, visitors ask about the presence of a specific medication (72%–81%); according to the recommendations for the correction of the symptoms of the disease (59%–65%) and the available explanation of the annotation to the drug (54%–57%) [39]. They rarely asked about the interaction with other medications, food, alcohol, and nicotine (36%–43%), and the storage conditions of medicines (30%–43%) [39]. However, this single study cannot be generalized, due to the insufficient number of respondents. The greatest demand of the population is the following services of a doctor in a pharmacy: blood pressure measurement (69%); external inspection (56%); and consultation on the selection of medical devices (45%) and prescription (39%). Patients are less likely to see a doctor for hirudotherapy (9%) and a pregnancy test (9%) [39]. An example of the format of providing simple medical services in a Ukrainian pharmacy by pharmacists is taken from the pharmacy service of Spain, where pharmacists still measure body mass index, weigh individuals, perform glucometry, etc. [37].

The study of the nature of the impact of additional services on the activities of the pharmacy showed that only some types of services contribute to profits. These include medical advice, home delivery of medications, and organization of self-service halls in pharmaceutical markets [39]. Services such as corporate identity, pharmaceutical care, extended operation of the pharmacy, availability of parking, and help desk of the pharmacy contribute to the formation of a permanent circle of pharmacy visitors and the creation of a brand image of the enterprise [40, 41].

Pharmacist's role in the usage of pharmaceutical care principles

Understanding the role of the pharmacist in the aspect of using pharmaceutical care is vital. Professionally provided pharmaceutical care leads to improved clinical outcomes, in particular for patients with cardiovascular pathologies and diabetes mellitus [20]. Therefore, work on the program of the concept of pharmaceutical care opens new prospects in this direction. The pharmacy should become an information and consultation center for doctors and patients [42], and this has been emphasized in Ukraine for the last 10 years. However, at the current time this has still not been implemented in real terms.

The main conceptual principles and characteristics of pharmaceutical care as a component of pharmacy service, as well as factors that affect its quality, were studied in Ukraine (according to the literary data) [42]. The classification of pharmaceutical care depending on the direction, place of sale, assortment groups of drugs, type of medication release was investigated, as a result of which three stages of pharmaceutical care at the level of pharmacist (clinical pharmacist) and pharmacy visitor (patient, his/her relatives, and friends) were identified and characterized: primary stage, support stage, and final stage [42].

Medical and social components of optimizing the quality of medical care/pharmaceutical care in pharmacies and healthcare institutions, using pharmaceutical care as a methodology of professional activity of pharmacists, were studied. As a result, it was established that patient-oriented pharmaceutical care, in accordance with the medical and social needs of society and modern qualification requirements for the professional activities of pharmacists, is important for improving the quality of medical care in Ukraine and forming the policy of rational use of medications [43]. However, the implementation of the given methodology of pharmaceutical care in Ukraine depends on the standardization of identification and resolution of DRPs in accordance with national characteristics and requires legislative regulation to establish the degree of responsibility of pharmacists and clinical pharmacists for its results in pharmaceutical care at all levels of healthcare institutions and pharmacies [43]. It has been shown that a new type of pharmaceutical activity—pharmaceutical care—as an element of social pharmacy reflects the relationship between medications and society, including the relationship among the professional medical and pharmaceutical community, which is associated with individualized pharmacotherapy. The end result of pharmaceutical care should be an improvement in the quality of life of patients both during and after pharmacotherapy, and therefore their satisfaction with the level and volume of pharmaceutical care [43].

An international cross-border study conducted in pharmacies in Lviv (Ukraine) ($n = 139$) and Lublin (Poland) ($n = 129$) examined and compared real pharmaceutical practices in identifying patient needs, and establishing interconnection between this pharmaceutical activity and pharmaceutical care [44]. The design of the study was that the interviewer, in the role of a "disguised visitor," addressed the pharmacist (a total of 150 appeals in each of the cities) with the request to "recommend something for cough," answering the pharmacist's questions according to the modeled clinical situation. Most often, pharmacists from both cities asked about the type of cough (dry or productive) (86.0% and 87.3% in Lviv and Lublin, respectively). Only 12.0% of pharmacists in Lviv and 12.7% in pharmacies in Lublin asked about the duration of the threatening symptom ($p=1$). The question about the patient's age was mentioned in 73.3% (Lviv) and 30.0% (Lublin) cases ($p=1.42$); presence of additional symptoms in 6.7% (Lviv) and 17.3% (Lublin) ($p=0.0077$); and presence of a previous infection or allergy 1.3% (Lviv) and 14.0% (Lublin) ($\chi^2=15.3$, $p=9.39\times10^{-5}$). Recommendations for the use of nonmedication approaches (consumption of plenty of fluids, products rich in vitamin C, use of a warming patch) were provided in 2.0% (Lviv) and 8.7% of cases (Lublin) ($p=0.021$), and correct use of the medication in 99.3% (Lviv) and 91.3% (Lublin) ($p=0.0026$). Regarding the recommended medicines, the pharmacists of Lviv preferred herbal medicines, while the pharmacists of Lublin preferred homeopathic preparations. The average time of pharmaceutical care provided in the presence of a queue in a pharmacy in Lviv was 58.7 ± 44.5 s, and in the absence of the queue it was slightly less, at 49.3 ± 23.5 s. Pharmaceutical care provided in pharmacies of Lublin lasted for an average of 3 min. It was established that the problem of pharmaceutical care of insufficient quality, in particular at the stage of identifying the needs of the patient, is equally characteristic for pharmacies in Lviv and Lublin.

Cooperation between doctors and pharmacists

The principles of teamwork of a doctor, pharmacist, and patient are covered in a number of studies. The aim of this research was to create a model of this type of cooperation, which requires the adoption of the necessary new legal documents and the creation of an extensive type of informational software between clinics and pharmacies [25]. A total of 159 physicians and 199 pharmacists were asked about the feasibility of teamwork in a questionnaire intended to improve the effectiveness and management of patient pharmacotherapy. The results showed that all respondents agreed with the need for cooperation between physicians and pharmacists in the management of patient pharmacotherapy. The pharmacists and physicians agreed on the following statements: "The role of physicians/pharmacists in the management of patient pharmacotherapy is important" (73.0% physicians and 83.4% pharmacists); "Pharmacists and doctors complement each other" (78.5% and 92.5%, respectively); "Cooperation is a necessary component that should be encouraged" (82.8% and 89.5%), "Cooperation will improve patient treatment outcomes" (87.3% and 95.0%); "Cooperation will improve the quality of service" (75.6% and 97.0%); and "Cooperation will improve interdisciplinary relations" (85.9% and 97.0%) [25].

The study confirms that pharmacists tend to seek to develop cooperation with doctors, although they are more inclined to work together and are not very active in the implementation of such cooperation. Almost all respondents agree that the collaboration of doctor and pharmacist will improve the quality of care and treatment of patients, interdisciplinary relationships, and effective management of pharmacotherapy of patients. However, historically, doctors have not generally accepted the medicine-related interventions suggested by the pharmacists. In addition, a low level of communication in the form of doctor-pharmacist and unrealized resources of the pharmacist's pharmaceutical care directed to the doctor were revealed [25]. On the other hand, there were almost no conflicts of interest between clinical pharmacists and physicians in hospitals; however, these conflicts were evident in the pharmacy between pharmacists and clinical pharmacists, provided that clinical pharmacists adhere to the proper ideology of rational pharmacotherapy. Training of pharmacy service in Ukraine includes training in proper communication between specialists involved in medical and pharmaceutical practice [43, 45].

The role of the clinical pharmacist in a pharmacy and inpatient healthcare institution

The number of registered over-the-counter and prescription drugs in Ukraine today is in the ratio of approximately 1:6 [25]. In nonspecialized pharmacies the nomenclature of prescription drugs can reach 70%, and in pharmacies (of any form of ownership) located on the territory of specialized hospitals (cardiology, tuberculosis, oncology, psychiatric, pediatric, etc.), the share is even greater [25]. Therefore, the presence of the position of "clinical pharmacist" in the staff list of a pharmacy engaged in the retail sale of medications is a sign of providing high-quality pharmaceutical service, which should be taken into account in the certification of pharmacies [25, 43, 46].

The results of a survey conducted on 1500 respondents on the realities and prospects of clinical pharmacy in Ukraine showed that 43.7% of health professionals identify the emergence of clinical pharmacy in the domestic healthcare system with the beginning of training of clinical pharmacists, and 69.2% believe that the activity of this specialist is necessary in both hospitals and pharmacies. At the same time, 18.7% are still unfamiliar with the direction of clinical pharmacy. Among the surveyed doctors, this figure was slightly higher (20.6%) than among pharmaceutical workers (13.7%) [47].

Another large-scale anonymous survey among healthcare professionals in Ukraine ($n = 10,737$) revealed inconsistencies in the attitude to the peculiarities of clinical pharmacy compared to a general pharmacy, the relation to the specialists who provide clinical pharmacy services, and the healthcare settings to them. Most respondents considered the activity of clinical pharmacists necessary (74.2%). Clinical pharmacist activity was identified as a priority in pharmacies by 55.3%, in the hospital by 47.7%, and in the hospital pharmacy by 45.0%. Among the activities of the clinical pharmacist in the hospital was the monitoring of safety and efficacy of drugs (69.9%), the provision of pharmaceutical care (50.5%), evaluation of pharmacotherapy (42.1%), and extemporaneous production of drugs (26.8%). More than half of the respondents (54.2%) mentioned the prospects for the development of clinical pharmacy in Ukraine. There were difference of opinion on key issues of clinical pharmacy throughout Ukraine and insufficient support for its prospects [48].

Researchers in Ukraine have also developed conceptual and methodological approaches to potential ways to improve the quality of medical care and pharmaceutical care through the implementation of functional responsibilities of the clinical pharmacist. Particular examples are examination of PT quality, development of models of multidisciplinary pharmaceutical care, application of clinicoeconomic and pharmacoeconomic analysis in clinical practice, etc. [49]. It was proved that the development and control over the implementation of the pharmaceutical component of medical care protocols is directly related to the functional responsibilities of the clinical pharmacists [49].

The importance of the clinical pharmacist is scientifically grounded in the process of quality improvement of pharmacotherapy in type II diabetes by means of pharmacy service based on pharmaceutical care. The algorithm of construction of the individual plan of pharmaceutical care at this pathology is developed. The role of patients' pharmaceutical care and a set of measures are scientifically substantiated; they include patient education in ensuring effective and safe PT, further rehabilitation of patients in the postinfarction period and their adaptation to new living conditions, as well as the theoretical foundations of the concept of education, self-education, and training of patients in the postinfarction period as elements of pharmacy service with multivector pharmaceutical care [49].

Moreover, the main elements of clinical pharmacists' activity in the context of pharmaceutical care in pharmacotherapy of patients with different methodologies were studied. Pharmacy services are included in disease conditions such as bronchial asthma, type II diabetes mellitus [49], chronic cardiovascular diseases [50], community-acquired pneumonia [51, 52], etc. The individual plan of pharmaceutical care, aimed at all participants in the diagnostic and treatment process (doctor, middle medical staff, patient), was improved [52]. It was also proved that the rational use of drugs and positive compliance (adherence) in combination with pharmaceutical care are optimal for achieving the desired clinical effect at minimal cost [49].

Exploring the relationship between DRP identification and individual PC

Another priority in the development of modern pharmacy service in Ukraine is the introduction of detection and evaluation of drug-related problems (DRPs) in the healthcare sector of Ukraine. The first studies substantiate the importance of documenting DRP-related information in the process of pharmaceutical care [53]. The presence of common components of DRPs and pharmaceutical care is established, as well as their close connection with the concept of rational PT, which is reflected in the professional clinical and pharmaceutical activities aimed at assessing and improving the quality of the medicinal process. It is determined that the DRP system is linked to pharmaceutical care. Correctly constructed pharmaceutical care is based on a deep understanding of the nature of DRPs and the process associated with their identification, solution, and (most importantly) prevention [54].

It is suggested that the purpose of DRP-related documentation should be quality control of patient counseling, continuous professional development of pharmacists, and optimization and individualization of effective and safe PT. The researchers separately modeled and proposed a classification system of DRPs for use in pharmacies in Ukraine, which addresses the problems of domestic community pharmacies. This will improve the quality of both pharmaceutical service and pharmacotherapy. The introduction of the DRP system in the domestic pharmaceutical practice will, according to scientists, increase the medical and social function of pharmacists and help restore the status of the pharmacy as a healthcare establishment [55].

Development of computer systems to support clinical decision-making

Ukrainian researchers have identified and developed the structure of a computer system to support clinical decision-making using a software product based on MySQL. The system allows the search to be organized for highly evidenced information at the right time and, consequently, the quality of individualized care and pharmaceutical care for patients is improved. The use of information from the State Formulary of Medications and Instructions for Medical Use also allows a database of drug interactions to be created, which is relevant for use in domestic healthcare institutions [56].

Table 1 provides a summary of different studies related to the pharmacy service and pharmacy practice research in Ukraine, and their reported outcomes.

New directions of development of pharmacy service in Ukraine

In 2016, pharmacy services and the pharmaceutical sector were harmonized to EU standards in Ukraine. This was in response to a request from the Ministry of Health of Ukraine. The National Medication Supply Policy of Ukraine need to be guided by WHO recommendations, and the main goals and strategies should be the availability, quality, and rational use of medicines. This also includes: increasing the level of pharmacy services, the implementation of which will require the establishment of an effective and transparent system of procurement of medications at state expense; improved access to medications and medical devices through effective regulation in accordance with WHO recommendations; and introduction of strategic long-term planning of procurement of vaccines and basic vital medications. The direction of "personnel policy" provided, in particular, the introduction of a clinical pharmacist in each healthcare institution. The creation of a document such as the "Yellow Card," as established in the United Kingdom, was meant to be the result of this cooperation. Unfortunately, some of these changes have not yet been implemented.

Future prospects

Although the list of specialties for the training of future specialists does not include the specialty "Clinical Pharmacy," a course was introduced as "Specialization in Clinical Pharmacy" for fourth-year students at the Faculty of Pharmacy Danylo Halytsky Lviv National Medical University. The aim is

Table 1 Summary of study the pharmacy service and pharmacy practice research in Ukraine.

Authors and studies	Aims and objectives	Type and nature of article	Synthesis of results
Hromovyk et al. (2009) [42]	Determining the main conceptual provisions and characteristics of pharmaceutical care as a component of pharmacy service for the population	Opinion piece	The main conceptual provisions and characteristics of pharmaceutical care as a component of pharmacy service and the factors influencing its quality are determined. Three stages of pharmaceutical care at the level of the pharmacist (clinical pharmacist) and the visitor of a drugstore are isolated and characterized (the patient, his/her relatives, and other close individuals).
Zimenkovsky et al. (2010) [49]	To evaluate the role of clinical pharmacist in improving the quality of medical care and pharmaceutical care in Ukraine	Narrative review	The main conceptual and methodological approaches to potential ways to improve the quality of medical care and pharmaceutical care through the implementation of the functional responsibilities of the clinical pharmacists were identified. The project of the "State program of development of clinical pharmacy in Ukraine" was processed.
Zimenkovsky et al. (2010) [49]	Development of a model of individualized pharmaceutical care of patients with bronchial asthma and type II diabetes	Retrospective study Medical prescriptions for patients with bronchial asthma and type II diabetes ($n = 474$)	For the first time the main components of pharmaceutical care in the pharmacotherapy of bronchial asthma and type II diabetes mellitus were identified, which is focused on the doctor, medical staff, and patient. The algorithm of construction of the individual plan of pharmaceutical care at the given pathologies was processed.

Author	Aim	Type	Findings
Boretska and Zimenkovsky (2011) [55]	Research regarding theoretical bases of DRP, process of their monitoring and documentation in some developed countries of Europe	Narrative review	Ways of DRP monitoring in pharmacies of eight developed European countries were investigated. Based on this, the DRP classification system for use in pharmacies of Ukraine was modeled and proposed.
Boretska et al. (2011) [56]	Creation of a computer system, "interaction of medications," for the possibility of its use in the practice of healthcare professionals	Computer program development	A computer system to support clinical decision-making using a software product based on MySQL was created. The use of the system in the practice of pharmacists, clinical pharmacists and doctors, in order to prevent drug interactions, aims to organize the search for highly evidence-based information at the right time and, consequently, improve the quality of individualized medical and pharmaceutical care of patients.
Zimenkovsky et al. (2011) [53]	Research of international DRP standardization systems and determination of further ways of their implementation in the field of healthcare of Ukraine	Narrative review	The main possible ways of using DRP classifications by the clinical pharmacist in the assessment of the quality of pharmacotherapy and the formation of a plan of pharmaceutical care were established.
Zimenkovsky et al. (2011) [54]	Study of common components of DRP, pharmaceutical care and their relationship	Narrative review	The presence of common components of DRP, pharmaceutical care, and their close connection with the concept of rational pharmacotherapy was established. The own definition of DRP was formed. The need for individualization of pharmacotherapy and pharmaceutical care for each patient to increase compliance with treatment was identified.

Continued

Table 1 Summary of study the pharmacy service and pharmacy practice research in Ukraine—cont'd

Authors and studies	Aims and objectives	Type and nature of article	Synthesis of results
Siatynia et al. (2012) [47]	The study of the current state and prospects of clinical pharmacy in Ukraine	Survey of healthcare professionals in Ukraine ($n = 1500$)	Of the healthcare professionals surveyed, 43.7% identify the appearance of clinical pharmacy in Ukraine with the beginning of training of clinical pharmacists specialists; 69.2% consider clinical pharmacist activity necessary in both inpatient and pharmaceutical healthcare establishments; 18.7% are not familiar with the direction of clinical pharmacy (among the surveyed doctors, the rate is higher (20.6%) than among pharmaceutical workers (13.7%)).
Zayats et al. (2012) [36]	Development, testing and implementation of a program of pharmaceutical care of metabolic syndrome in a pharmacy	Prospective study of patients with metabolic syndrome ($n = 162$)	465 assessments of the risk of developing metabolic syndrome were performed in 162 patients. 461 risks of developing metabolic syndrome were identified. In 21 patients the risk factors for metabolic syndrome were identified for the first time with the participation of a clinical pharmacist.
Zimenkovsky et al. (2017) [44]	Study of the real pharmaceutical practice regarding the identification of patient needs in pharmacies of Ukraine and Poland Establishing the relationship between this pharmaceutical activity and pharmaceutical care	Prospective study of pharmacists in Ukraine ($n = 139$), pharmacists in Poland ($n = 129$)	The most frequently asked questions were about the type of cough: 86.0% (Lviv) and 87.3% (Lublin). 12.0% (Lviv) and 12.7% (Lublin) of pharmacists asked about the duration of the threatening symptom; about the patient's age—73.3% (Lviv) and 30.0% (Lublin) ($p = 1.42$), the presence of additional symptoms—6.7% (Lviv) and 17.3% (Lublin) ($p = 0.0077$), the presence of a previous infection or allergy—1.3% (Lviv) and 14.0% (Lublin) ($x^2 = 15.3, \rho = 9.39 \times 10^{-5}$). Recommendations for proper use of the medication were provided in 99.3% (Lviv) and 91.3% (Lublin) ($p = 0.0026$). The average time of provided pharmaceutical care was 58.7 ± 44.5 s (Lviv), and 3 min (Lublin).

| Auhunas (2019) [25] | Study of the opinion of doctors and pharmacists on the feasibility and readiness of teamwork to improve the effectiveness and management of pharmacotherapy of patients | Survey of doctors in Ukraine ($n = 159$); community pharmacists in Ukraine ($n = 199$) | Respondents agreed on the following statements: "The role of physicians/pharmacists in the management of patient pharmacotherapy is important" (73.0% physicians and 83.4% pharmacists); "Pharmacists and doctors complement each other" (78.5% and 92.5%, respectively); "Cooperation is a necessary component that should be encouraged" (82.8% and 89.5%); "Cooperation will improve patient outcomes" (87.3% and 95.0%); "Cooperation will improve the quality of service" (75.6% and 97.0%); and "Cooperation will improve interdisciplinary relations" (85.9% and 97.0%). |
| Bushuyeva (2019) [39] | Investigation of the state of pharmacy service and the service sector of pharmacies. Determining their socio-economic significance | Survey of community pharmacists in Ukraine ($n = 130$) | 72%–81% of visitors were interested in the availability of a specific medication; 59%–65% sought after recommendations for the correction of disease symptoms; 54%–57% sought after the available explanation of the drug usage annotation; 36%–43% sought after the information about interaction with other drugs, food, alcohol, and nicotine. The most popular services of a doctor (pharmacist) in a pharmacy are: measurement of blood pressure (69%); external inspection (56%); consultation on the selection of medical devices (45%); prescription (39%). |

Continued

Table 1 Summary of study the pharmacy service and pharmacy practice research in Ukraine—cont'd

Authors and studies	Aims and objectives	Type and nature of article	Synthesis of results
Zimenkovsky et al. (2019) [48]	Study of realities and prospects of clinical pharmacy development in Ukraine	Survey of medical professionals of Ukraine ($n = 10{,}737$)	54.2% noted the prospects for the development of clinical pharmacy in Ukraine; 74.2% considered clinical pharmacist activity necessary; 55.3% saw the priority of the activity of clinical pharmacist in pharmacies, 47.7% in hospitals, and 45.0% in hospital pharmacies. Among the activities of clinical pharmacist in hospital are: monitoring the safety and effectiveness of medications (69.9%); provision of pharmaceutical care (50.5%); evaluation of pharmacotherapy (42.1%); and extemporaneous production of medications (26.8%).
Sekh et al. (2019) [52]	To propose an algorithm for creating system messages of pharmaceutical care, in relation to specific nosology, aimed at clinicians	Retrospective study Medical records of patients with community-acquired pneumonia ($n = 540$)	A retrospective assessment of the quality of pharmacotherapy of patients was performed. 8386 DRPs were detected. An algorithm for the development of system messages of pharmaceutical care aimed at clinicians was proposed. In total 276 system messages of pharmaceutical care were formed.

to provide specified specialty at the postgraduate level for the pharmacists. This is the first time that the position of clinical pharmacist at the primary level of healthcare in Ukraine was introduced. Promoting private clinical pharmacy was also suggested for the first time. This is a prototype of the development of private pharmaceutical service in Ukraine in the format of a private office of a clinical pharmacist. This role is intended to act as an independent specialist in rational pharmacotherapy.

In line with European integration, the "State Strategy for Implementation of the Medication Provision Policy for the Period until 2025" was approved in Ukraine (Resolution of the Cabinet of Ministers of Ukraine No. 1022 from December 5, 2018) [57]. This was developed on the basis of WHO recommendations. It envisages harmonization of Ukrainian legislation on healthcare with EU legislation, as well as the development of quality assurance and management system at all stages of medication through further implementation of the provisions of international standards of product and service quality assurance (in particular, GPP). The possibility of the introduction and harmonization of all pharmacies in GPP format in the near future will give a new impetus to the development of pharmacy services in Ukraine.

Summary

In Ukraine, legislative changes are needed to strengthen the pharmaceutical care services further. The weakness in legislation is causing a number of problems in society: on the one hand, the main costs of pharmacotherapy fall on the patient or his/her family (the patients buy the vast majority of drugs at personal expense), while on the other hand, self-medication is becoming extremely common among the population, which is usually irresponsible, especially on the basis of the possibility of receiving all drugs (except narcotics) freely without a prescription. It is almost impossible to monitor the rational use of medications by patients, especially at the stage of outpatient treatment. Since most prescription drugs can be purchased at a pharmacy without a prescription, there is an uncontrolled market for antibacterial agents. The very low salaries of doctors and the existing technologies of market promotion of medicines have also created conditions in which a clinician or pharmacy worker becomes an informal or illegal distributor of the manufacturer's company.

As a result of unsystematic liberalization of the pharmaceutical sector, there is an unfortunate trend of changing public opinion about the role of a pharmacist from a healthcare worker to a person who just sells medicines. This leads to the leveling of its role in the treatment process and society in general. It is considered that a pharmacist is not a person who provides a professional pharmacy service, but someone who only sells medicines.

References

[1] Chernykh V. Pharmaceutical industry during the years of independence of Ukraine. Bull Pharm 2002;3:3–12.

[2] Almakaieva L, Maslova N, Heorhievskyi V. The leader of the national pharmacy is 90 years old. Pharm J 2019;2:3–8.

[3] Resolution of the Cabinet of Ministers of Ukraine on the development of the medical, veterinary and microbiological industry, improving the provision of the population and the needs of livestock sector with medicines, medical and veterinary equipment: validated on October 8th, 1992, № 573. Available at: https://zakon.rada.gov.ua/laws/show/573-92-%D0%BF#Text; 1992. [Date of request 22 June 2020].

[4] Resolution of the Cabinet of Ministers of Ukraine on the approval of the comprehensive program for the development of the medical industry for 1997–2003: validated on December 18th, 1996, № 1538-96-p. Available at: https://kodeksy.com.ua/norm_akt/source-%D0%9A%D0%9C%D0%A3/type-D0%9F%D0%BE%D1%81%D1%82%D0%B0%D0%BD%D0%BE%D0%B2%D0%B0/1538-96-D0%BF-18.12.1996.htm; 1996. [Date of request 22 June 2020].

[5] Resolution of the Cabinet of Ministers of Ukraine on the organization of free and preferential dispensing of medicines on doctors' prescriptions in case of outpatient treatment of certain groups of the population and for certain categories of diseases: validated on August 17th, 1998, № 1303. Available at: https://zakon.rada.gov.ua/laws/show/1303-98-%D0%BF#Text; 1998. [Date of request 22 June 2020].

[6] Order of the Ministry of Social Policy of Ukraine on the approval of the Strategic Action Plan of the Ministry of Social Policy of Ukraine for the 2020 budget year and the two budget following periods (2021 – 2022): validated on February 7th, 2020, №97. Available at: https://www.msp.gov.ua/documents/5641.html; 2020. [Date of request 22 June 2020].

[7] Order of the Ministry of Health Care of Ukraine On the approval of the Rules for prescribing medicines and medical devices, the Procedure for release of medicines and medical devices from pharmacies and their structural units, Instructions on storage, accounting and destruction of prescription forms: validated on July 19th, 2005, № 360. Available at: https://zakon.rada.gov.ua/laws/show/z0782-05#Text; 2005. [Date of request 22 June 2020].

[8] Ethical code of a pharmacist of Ukraine. Kharkiv; 2010. 13 p.

[9] Parliament of Ukraine. Available at: http://itd.rada.gov.ua/mps/info/expage/5568/5.

[10] Babar Z-U-D, Almarsdottir AB. The future of pharmacy practice research. In: Babar ZU, editor. Pharmacy practice research methods. 2nd ed; 2020, ISBN:978-981-15-2992-4. 271 p.

[11] El-Dahiyat F, Curley LE, Babar ZUD. A survey study to measure the practice of patient counselling and other community pharmacy services in Jordan. J Pharm Health Serv Res 2018;10(1):133–9.

[12] Goode JV, Owen J, Page A, Gatewood S. Community-based pharmacy practice innovation and the role of the community-based pharmacist practitioner in the United States. Pharmacy (Basel) 2019;7(3):106.

[13] Yuan C, Ding Y, Zhou K, Huang Y, Xi X. Clinical outcomes of community pharmacy services: a systematic review and meta-analysis. Health Soc Care Community 2019;27:e567–87.

[14] Hurley-Kim K, Goad J, Seed S, Hess KM. Pharmacy-based travel health services in the United States. Pharmacy (Basel) 2018;7(1):5.

[15] Aleksandra M, Trudi A, Jeff H. Community pharmacist-led interventions and their impact on patients' medication adherence and other health outcomes: a systematic review. Int J Pharm Pract 2018;26(5):387–97.

[16] Hazen ACM, de Bont AA, Boelman L, et al. The degree of integration of non-dispensing pharmacists in primary care practice and the impact on health outcomes: a systematic review. Res Soc Adm Pharm 2018;14(3):228–40.

[17] Babar Z-U-D, Scahill S. Medicines access, use and pharmaceutical health system issues: reflections, thoughts and points to consider. In: Babar Z-U-D, editor. Global pharmaceutical policy. Palgrave Macmillan; 2020, ISBN:978-981-15-2723-4.

[18] Buss VH, Shield A, Kosari S, Naunton M. The impact of clinical services provided by community pharmacies on the Australian healthcare system: a review of the literature. J Pharm Policy Pract 2018;11(22). https://doi.org/10.1186/s40545-018-0149-7.

[19] Benson H, Lucas C, Benrimoj SI, Williams KA. The development of a role description and competency map for pharmacists in an interprofessional care setting. Int J Clin Pharmacol 2019;41(2):391–407.

[20] Babar Z, Kousar R, Murtaza G, Azhar S, Khan S, Curley L. Randomized controlled trials covering pharmaceutical care and medicines management: a systematic literature review. Res Soc Adm Pharm 2018;14(6):521–39.

[21] Babar Z-U-D, Edlin R. Economic evaluation of a medicines management model in New Zealand. In: Babar ZU, editor. Economic evaluation of pharmacy services; 2016, ISBN:9780128036594. 248 p.

[22] Scahill SL, Harrison J, Sheridan J. The ABC of New Zealand's ten year vision for pharmacists: awareness, barriers and consultation. Int J Pharm Pract 2009;17(3):135–42.

[23] Pestun IV, Mnushko ZM. Review of current trends in the professional activity of provisors (pharmacists) in Ukraine and abroad. Soc Pharm Health Care 2017;3(1):52–9.

[24] Paramonova OS. The content of professional duties of a medical and pharmaceutical worker within the meaning of Article 140 of the Criminal Code of Ukraine. J Kyiv Univ Law 2011;4:327–31.

[25] Auhunas SV. Comprehensive scientific and theoretical substantiation of the laws of development of the system of medication supply of the population of Ukraine from no pharmaceutical and emergent positions [Ph.D. thesis]. Kyiv: Pl Shupyk National Medical Academy of Postgraduate Education; 2019.

[26] Scahill S, Harrison J, Carswell P, Babar ZU. Organisational culture: an important concept for pharmacy practice research. Pharm World Sci 2009;31(5):517–21. https://doi.org/10.1007/s11096-009-9318-8.

[27] Donovan J, Tsuyuki RT, Al Hamarneh YN, Bajorek B. Barriers to a full scope of pharmacy practice in primary care: a systematic review of pharmacists' access to laboratory testing. Can Pharm J (Ott) 2019;152(5):317–33.

[28] Dolovich L, Tsuyuki RT. Pharmacy practice research produces findings that inform how pharmacists contribute to optimal drug therapy outcomes for Canadians. Can Pharm J 2016;149(5):261–3.

[29] Mansell K, Edmunds K, Guirguis L. Pharmacists' scope of practice: supports for Canadians with diabetes. Can J Diabetes 2017;41(6):558–62.

[30] Wibowo Y, Parsons R, Sunderland B, Hughes J. Evaluation of community pharmacy-based services for type-2 diabetes in an Indonesian setting: pharmacist survey. Int J Clin Pharmacol 2015;37(5):873–82.

[31] Al Hamarneh Y, Charrois T, Lewanczuk R, Tsuyuki RT. Pharmacist intervention for glycemic control in the community (the RxING study). BMJ Open 2013;3, e003154.

[32] Ali M, Schifano F, Robinson P, Phillips G, Doherty L, Melnick P, Dhillon S. Impact of community pharmacy diabetes monitoring and education programme on diabetes management: a randomized controlled study. Diabet Med 2012;29(9):e326–33.

[33] Tsuyuki RT, Al Hamarneh YN, Jones CA, Hemmelgarn BR. The effectiveness of community pharmacist prescribing and care on cardiovascular risk: the multicenter randomized controlled RxEACH trial. J Am Coll Cardiol 2016;67(24):2846–54.

[34] Tsuyuki RT, Houle SK, Charrois TL, et al. Randomized trial of the effect of pharmacist prescribing on improving blood pressure in the community: the Alberta Clinical Trial In Optimizing Hypertension (RxACTION). Circulation 2015;132:93–100.

[35] Aslani P, Rose G, Chen TF, Whitehead PA, Krass I. A community pharmacist delivered adherence support service for dyslipidaemia. Eur J Pub Health 2011;21(5):567–72.

[36] Zayats MM, Zimenkovsky AB. Program of pharmaceutical care of patients with metabolic syndrome in the community pharmacy of Ukraine Clinical Pharmacy. Pharmacother Med Stand 2012;4:167–74.

[37] Martinez-Romero F, FernandezLlimos F, Gastelurrutia MA, Parras M, et al. Programa Dader de Seguimiento del Tratamiento Farmacologico. Resultados de la fase piloto. Ars Pharmaceutic 2001;1:53–65.

[38] Hungarian National Committee of Pharmaceutical Care. Metabolic Syndrome Pharmaceutical Care Programme. [Internet]. Available at: http://www.europharmforum. org/file/12596; 2020. [Cited 18 June 2020].

[39] Bushuyeva I. Marketing research of the state of service of pharmaceutical establishments. [Internet]. Available at: http://sophus.at.ua/publ/2014_05_22_23_ kampodilsk/sekcija_5_2014_05_22_23/marketingovi_doslidzhennja_stanu_servisu_ aptechnikh_ustanov/63-1-0-989; 2014. [Cited 25 June 2020].

[40] Khomyakov GV. Trends in the Ukrainian pharmaceutical market and forecast for the future. Provisor 2007;3:11–3.

[41] Hromovyk BP, Hasyuk HD, Moroz LA, Chukhray NI. Pharmaceutical marketing: textbook; coll. exercises. Lviv: Nautilus; 2000. 320 p.

[42] Hromovyk BP, Propisnova VV, Zupanets IA. Conceptual issues of pharmaceutical care. Clin Pharm Pharmacother Med Stand 2009;1–2:39–42.

[43] Zimenkovsky AB, Boretska OB. Organizational and methodological principles of creation and activity of clinical and pharmacy service in pharmacies of Ukraine. Clin Pharm Pharmacother Med Stand 2011;3–4:21–6.

[44] Zimenkovsky A, Nastyukha Y, Boretska O, Drozd M, Devinyak O. Quality of pharmaceutical care at the stage of patients needs identification under conditions of community pharmacies as a transborder problem. Acta Pol Pharm Drug Res 2017;74(3):1011–9.

[45] Boretska OB, Zimenkovsky AB, Nastyukha YS. Model of activity of a clinical pharmacist in providing pharmaceutical care in a pharmacy. In: Kharkiv National Pharmacy University, Formation of the National Medical Policy under the conditions of introduction of health insurance: questions of education, theory and practice, Proceedings of the II Ukrainian scientific and educational internet conference, Kharkiv, Mart 14, 2012; 2012. Available at: http://medrep.com.ua/dox/55555.pdf.

[46] Ponomarenko NS, Kokhanov IV, Auhunas SV. Research of interaction of the doctor and pharmaceutical workers in management of pharmacotherapy of out-patient policlinic patients in Ukraine. Prescription 2017;2:128–45.

[47] Siatynia VY, Nastyukha YS, Zimenkovsky AB. The current state and prospects of clinical pharmacy in Ukraine according to health care professionals. Clin Pharm Pharmacother Med Stand 2012;1–2:90–4.

[48] Zimenkovsky A, Nastyukha Y, Kostyana K, Devinyak O, Zayats M, Koval A, Denysiuk O, Gorodnycha O, Siatynia V. Clinical pharmacy in Ukraine according to the healthcare professionals' assessment. Pharmacia 2019;66(4):193–200.

[49] Zimenkovsky AB, Lopatynska OI, Grem OY, Bokshan EV, et al. The role and place of the clinical pharmacist in improving the quality of medical care of the population of Ukraine. Clin Pharm Pharmacother Med Stand 2010;1–2:24–34.

[50] Solomenchuk TM, Zaruma LE, Skybchyk VA, Grem OY. Prevention and treatment of cardiovascular diseases at the family doctor's office: the role of clinical pharmacist and pharmaceutical care. Clin Pharm Pharmacother Med Stand 2008;1:39–43.

[51] Sekh M, Zimenkovsky A. Community-acquired pneumonia: quality of pharmacotherapy and expense of irrationality. Pharmacia 2018;65(4):25–37.

[52] Sekh M. Clinical and pharmaceutical substantiation of a quality improvement model for the pharmacotherapy of community-acquired pneumonia [Abstract of Ph.D. dissertation]. Lviv: Danylo Halytsky Lviv National Medical University; 2019. 24 p.

[53] Zimenkovsky AB, Ryvak TB, Khanyk NL. Drug-related problems (DRP) in pharmacotherapy and methodology for their evaluation and standardization. Clin Pharm Pharmacother Med Stand 2011;1–2:16–23.

[54] Zimenkovsky AB, Ryvak TB, Khanyk NL. The concept of DRP as part of the philosophy of rational pharmacotherapy, integrated with the system of pharmaceutical care. Clin Pharm Pharmacother Med Stand 2011;1-2:23–31.

[55] Boretska OB, Zimenkovsky AB. Development of a model of the classification system of drug-related problems (DRP) for use in a domestic pharmacy. Clin Pharm Pharmacother Med Stand 2011;1–2:131–6.

[56] Boretska OB, Zimenkovsky AB, Horilyk DV. Computer system for clinical decision support based on software product based on MySQL for detection and prevention of drug interactions in health care establishments of Ukraine. Clin Pharm Pharmacother Med Stand 2011;3-4:179–84.

[57] Resolution of the Cabinet of Ministers of Ukraine on State Strategy for Implementation of the Medication Provision Policy for the period until 2025: validated on December 5, 2018, № 1022. Available at: https://zakon.rada.gov.ua/; 2018.

CHAPTER 6

Understanding pharmacy staff attitudes and experience relating to suicide

Hayley C. Gorton[a], Claire O'Reilly[b], Hayley J. Berry[c], David Gardner[d], and Andrea Murphy[e]
[a]School of Applied Sciences, University of Huddersfield, Huddersfield, United Kingdom
[b]Faculty of Medicine and Health, University of Sydney, Sydney, NSW, Australia
[c]Centre for Pharmacy Postgraduate Education (CPPE), University of Manchester, Manchester, United Kingdom
[d]Department of Psychiatry and College of Pharmacy, Dalhousie University, Halifax, NS, Canada
[e]College of Pharmacy, School of Nursing, Department of Psychiatry, Dalhousie University, Halifax, NS, Canada

An international focus on suicide prevention

The prevention of suicide is an international priority. The World Health Organization (WHO) set a target of a 10% reduction in suicide, compared to the 5 preceding years, by the year 2020 [1]. Previously recorded estimates are of 800,000 suicides annually, although this is almost certain to be an underestimate due to deviations in reporting among countries [1]. Some of this is scientific or technical, relating to reporting systems; and some relates to beliefs about suicide and perceived stigma. The Global Burden of Disease (GBD) study showed an increased number of suicides but reduced standardized mortality rate worldwide between 1990 and 2020 [2]. Suicide was the most common cause of age-standardized years of life lost and inversely associated with sociodemographic index. Rates varied between countries, with particular countries skewing regional data. The highest recorded rate was in Lesotho (39.0/100,000 deaths, 95%CI 25.5–55.7) and lowest in Lebanon (2.4/100,000 deaths, 95%CI 1.6–3.5). Notwithstanding the personal tragedy, with an estimated 135 people affected by each suicide [3], the societal implications are vast. Given that bereavement by suicide is itself a risk factor for suicide [4], one can see the ripple effect of every single death.

The WHO reflected the different levels of maturity of suicide prevention plans across the world in their guidance [1]. For countries with more developed plans, there was a call to consider the responsibilities and activities of a multitude of stakeholders and support training for healthcare professionals. We believe that pharmacists can have an important role to play

Pharmacy Practice Research Case Studies
https://doi.org/10.1016/B978-0-12-819378-5.00006-4

in suicide prevention activity owing to their relationships with people and as gatekeepers of medication [5, 6]. This chapter will explore pharmacists and their teams as potential contributors to suicide prevention activities, suicide prevention frameworks, and overall research agenda. A case study from the United Kingdom will supplement a review of suicide prevention in pharmacy practice internationally. The experience gained by the authors through the fellowship that linked them (detailed in Ref. [5]) will be intertwined throughout.

Potential role of pharmacy teams in suicide prevention

The involvement of pharmacists in suicide prevention was first mentioned in the literature almost 50 years ago [7]. In this paper, Gibson and Lott implored pharmacists to "assume a viable and active role in drug suicide prevention," by virtue of their role as public health practitioners. With the exception of two opinion pieces in the intervening 40 years [8, 9], this role was not discussed in the literature again until 2012 and the majority of papers have been published in the last 3 years. Opinion pieces continue to dominate the literature in this area, with very few experimental or observational studies [6]. Our representation (Gorton) in a newly-formed special interest group on "suicide prevention in primary care" under the auspices of the International Association for Suicide Prevention [10] brings this important field of research and practice to the fore.

The contribution of pharmacists to suicide prevention has begun to be explored in some high-income countries. The majority of the work is from Canada [11–17], Australia [11, 13, 14, 18], the United States [19–23], and the United Kingdom [5, 24]. Almost all studies focus on pharmacists caring for patients in a primary care context. There was also a study from Japan focusing on pharmacists with a special interest in psychiatry [25]. A summary of research methods are provided in Table 1, for studies that have been published since the Murphy et al. [6] review.

Experience of suicide in pharmacy practice and beyond

Some studies have mapped the experience of suicide prevention among pharmacists, and occasionally their teams. The reported level of experience varied among studies. In one survey of community pharmacists and their support staff in North Carolina, United States, 22% of the 501 respondents were aware of a patient's suicide [19]. In another survey in the same population but restricted to community pharmacists, 58% knew

Table 1 Summary of studies published since Murphy et al.'s scoping review [6]. Includes studies that focus on attitudes or experience, not exclusively training.

Author	Objectives	Design	Sample	Country	Summary of results
Carpenter et al. [19]	Assess the experience that pharmacy staff have in suicide prevention, and understand training preferences. Validate the Pharmacy Suicide Interaction Scale (PSIS) measure.	Survey	Community pharmacy staff ($n = 501$) working in North Carolina	United States	22.4% knew of a patient who had died by suicide. 8.8% had training in suicide prevention. 89.6% expressed desire for training. PSIS had construct validity.
Cates et al. [20]	Measure pharmacists' attitudes to suicide against the Attitudes to Suicide Prevention scale (ASP). Establish knowledge of suicide.	Survey	Pharmacists attending a continuing professional education program at a single school of pharmacy ($n = 227$)	United States	25% were aware of a patient suicide. 4%–8% felt that they had the required skills and knowledge to help suicidal patients. The mean ASP score was 32.3 ± 5.5.
Gillette et al. [21]	Measure pharmacists' attitudes to suicide against the Attitudes Toward Suicide (ATTS) scale. Establish nature of interactions with people who were suicidal; and barriers to this.	Survey	Community pharmacists working in North Carolina ($n = 225$)	United States	The median ATTS score was 70 (IQR 7). Reporting few barriers (OR 0.70, 99.5%CI 0.51–0.98) and high preparedness to help someone (OR 6.63, 99.5%CI 1.74–25.23) were associated with likelihood of suicidal ideation assessment.

Continued

Table 1 Summary of studies published since Murphy et al.'s scoping review [6]. Includes studies that focus on attitudes or experience, not exclusively training—cont'd

Author	Objectives	Design	Sample	Country	Summary of results
Gorton [5]	Compare and contrast the role of community pharmacy teams in suicide prevention across nations. Produce recommendations for implementation in the United Kingdom.	Opinion piece	Observational travel Fellowship	United States, Canada, and United Kingdom	Pockets of research and activity in suicide prevention exist. More research is needed to understand this role fully and to produce evidence-informed training.
Gorton et al. [24].	Understand the current and potential role of community pharmacy teams in suicide prevention.	Qualitative interviews	Interviews with community pharmacy staff in the north-west of England ($n = 25$)	England	There are examples of pharmacy teams supporting people with suicidal behavior. There was a distinct absence of formal training but a desire for this training, alongside facilitated referral pathways. Participants felt that this could enhance their role.
Kassir et al. [18].	Present an argument for involvement of pharmacists in suicide prevention through summary of key literature.	Narrative review	Narrative review (not systematic)	Australia	Supports the need for careful enhanced role of pharmacists in suicide prevention, if supported by sound training and ongoing research.
Murphy et al. [11]	Understand the experiences of community pharmacists in helping people at risk of suicide.	Survey-thematic analysis of open-ended questions	Community pharmacists in Canada ($n = 235$) and Australia ($n = 161$)	Canada and Australia	The identified themes were: stigma, accessibility for confiding, emotional toll, and referral/triage. Pharmacists were deemed to have an enhanced role, but training and support needs were identified.

Murphy et al. [12]	Establish attitudes to suicide using the Attitudes Toward Suicide Scale (ATTS) and understand implications for both suicide and medical assistance in dying.	Survey-preliminary analysis	Community pharmacists in Canada ($n=235$) and Australia ($n=161$)	Canada and Australia	Interactions between pharmacists and people with thoughts or plans of suicide or medically assisted dying are likely to be underestimated. Permissiveness toward suicide was not influenced by personal experience.
Murphy et al. [13]	Determine community pharmacists' stigma related to suicide.	Survey	Community pharmacists in Canada ($n=235$) and Australia ($n=161$)	Canada and Australia	Low levels of stigma were detected, through low agreement with stigmatizing terms. Personal/familial experience with mental health problems was associated with lower agreement ($P<.05$) with terms including irresponsible and cowardly. Australian pharmacists tended to agree with stigmatizing terms more than their Canadian counterparts.
Murphy et al. [14]	Determine the experience with people at risk of suicide of community pharmacists.	Survey	Community pharmacists in Canada ($n=235$) and Australia ($n=161$)	Canada and Australia	85% of pharmacists had interacted with someone about suicide. Community pharmacists in Australia were more likely to have had mental health crisis training and felt more prepared than their Canadian counterparts did.

someone who had died by suicide and 76% knew someone, in either their professional or personal life, who had made a suicide attempt. Of the pharmacists attending a continuing education program in Alabama, United States, one-quarter knew a patient who had died by suicide, and 20% had been affected by suicide of a close family member [20]. Eight-five percent of respondents to a survey of community pharmacists in Australia and Canada could recall one or more interactions with a patient they believed was at risk of suicide [14]. Thirty-nine percent disclosed that a close friend or family member had attempted or died by suicide [13]. Due to the heterogeneity in study populations and definitions of both suicidal behavior (ranging from death to suicidal thoughts) and being affected (personally, professional, or both), we cannot meaningfully combine these estimates. Nevertheless, it is evident that community pharmacy staff and their teams are affected by suicide in their practice, through personal and professional connections that influence their care, thus supporting the argument that they have a role to play in this agenda. This corroborates with evidence from other healthcare professionals, which highlights the complexity of factors that direct a healthcare professional's interactions with patients about suicide [26].

Studies that obtained qualitative data [19, 24, 11] can provide further insight into the nature of these experiences. Common to studies in the United Kingdom [24], and Canada and Australia [11], the pharmacy staff viewed their accessibility and relationships with patients as central to the conversations they had and as a facilitator to suicide prevention activity. Often, pharmacists and their staff expressed uncertainty about how to respond, or admitted to evasiveness through not directly asking about suicide [19, 24, 11]. As a common theme, referral and triage was as a key role identified by all. In the United Kingdom, it was identified that the implementation of clear and facilitated referral pathways was an essential component of any enhanced role of pharmacy teams in suicide prevention [24]. The use of displays regarding mental health, and specifically suicide, was deemed to facilitate conversations [24, 11].

Attitudes to suicide and suicide prevention

Much of the published work has ascertained attitudes to suicide prevention. The largest body of this work was conducted by coauthors Gardner, Murphy, and O'Reilly—a survey of community pharmacists' experience of suicide in Canada and Australia [11–14]. These papers described a study of 161 and 235 community pharmacists practicing in Australia and Canada, respectively. Experiences, attitudes, and stigma of community pharmacists relating to suicide were explored.

Questions regarding attitude were modeled on the Attitudes Toward Suicide (ATTS) scale [27]. From a subset of these questions that related to permissiveness, it was found that having personal experience (self, family, or friend) of mental illness did not influence one's attitude to suicide [12]. This was a different perspective to that offered in our study of community pharmacy staff in the United Kingdom, where personal experience was cited as a motivation for involvement in suicide prevention [24].

We cannot draw a direct comparison due to the methodological differences but it should be noted that in the latter [24], this view was often from pharmacy support staff. Such team members might cite use of their personal experience in the absence of professional training. In the former [12], all participants were pharmacists, who will likely have been influenced by professional training, experience, and responsibility, rather than consciously using their personal experience. In a survey of community pharmacists in North Carolina, United States, those who knew someone who had died by suicide were more likely to endorse suicide prevention, represented by lower ATTS score, than those who did not [21]. Similarly, those who were aware of a patient who had died by suicide scored higher on a bespoke Pharmacy Suicide Interaction Scale, which indicated greater behavioral indicators of suicide, compared to those who were not aware of such a patient [19]. Conversely, in the study of pharmacists in Japan with an interest in psychiatry, pharmacists who reported experience of suicidal thoughts themselves were more permissive about suicide than those who did not [25]. The opposite was true for participation in education about suicide prevention, which was associated with a preventative outlook.

Suicide prevention training

Across published studies, the proportion of participating pharmacists who had previously completed some education and training in suicide prevention varied. The majority of participants in these studies had not previously competed any training in suicide prevention. The percentage who had been trained ranged from 4% (of 227) in Alabama, United States [20] to 9% (of 501) in North Carolina, United States [19], 12% (of 235) in Canada [13], and 29% (of 161) in Australia. The highest reported proportion was in the Japanese study, in which 36% of 327 pharmacists had undertaken training [25]. This study included those with a specific interest in psychiatry; thus, estimates may not generalizable to the wider population of pharmacists in Japan. The differences in estimates among international studies could be the result of a host of factors. Importantly, the scope of practice and extent of the activities expected of community pharmacists in those countries may significantly influence pharmacy teams' abilities to actively engage in roles and participate in suicide prevention frameworks. Alternatively, the range of estimates could be attributed to variations in study populations, sample size, and methods. These nuances aside, there is overwhelming international consensus that evidence-informed suicide prevention gatekeeper training would be valuable for pharmacists [5, 19, 20, 24, 11, 14, 25]. Some studies went as far to recommend that suicide prevention training be extended to pharmacy support staff, not just for the pharmacist [24, 14].

Features that were recommened to be encompassed in such training programs included: education regarding the minimization of stigma [13], guidance on facilitating referral pathways [24], altering attitudes of permissiveness [25], mitigating barriers, and improving efficacy as well as increasing knowledge [21]. Indeed Gillette et al. [21] identified lack of training as the major barrier to pharmacists assessing someone for suicidal ideation. For some, the desire for enhanced training was prompted explicitly or implicitly by uncertainty relating to their previous interactions with people about suicide [19, 24, 11]. Responding to crises might also be incorporated via mental health first aid training. This is being increasingly adopted by pharmacists and pharmacy schools in Australia [28].

Carpenter et al. [22] reviewed the range of suicide prevention training programs specific to pharmacists and/or pharmacy students in the United States. Some commonalities were identified, but programs were generally disparate. The authors identified a mandatory suicide prevention training requirement for pharmacists in Washington State in 2018 [22]. This was introduced into legislation, which covered various healthcare professional groups. Anecdotal conversations with pharmacists to whom this training is applicable, during the implementation period, were suggestive of perceived importance but highlighted lack of urgency versus competing demands [5].

In Scotland, essential training on suicide prevention has been introduced for pharmacists employed by the National Health Service (NHS) [29]; however, community pharmacists are not part of this program. In England, the requirement for such training has now been included as part of a quality-based payment scheme [30].

The impact of training is difficult to objectively measure and it is likely impossible to determine any causative influence on suicide rate reduction.

Rather, evaluation is restricted to subjective measures, as recalled by the participants [5]. Often, this is based on self-reported confidence and self-reported likelihood to intervene. Attempts to mirror practice have been made through simulated patients [28]. However, this practice also focuses on communication skills and confidence, rather than direct impact on suicide. Gatekeeper training has been linked with suicide rate reduction in other settings (e.g., military) whereas community-based interventions are somewhat limited in their evidence [31]. These concepts must be borne in mind when considering the utility of available suicide prevention training programs for pharmacy teams.

Suicide prevention in other sectors of pharmacy

To our knowledge, the published literature has almost exclusively focused on community pharmacy and within that, pharmacists, with some studies extended to the wider pharmacy teams. Pharmacists work in a multitude of settings in which suicide prevention could be part of their role. This wider role has not yet been formally scoped, and we continue to emphasize the need for this, as we did as a consequence of the fellowship that brought many of the authors together [5].

Public views of pharmacy could be inconsistent across countries and settings; therefore, understanding of this is fundamental to contextualizing the potential role of pharmacy teams in suicide prevention. In the United Kingdom, the increasing provision of pharmacists in independent, patient-facing roles amplifies this need. Additionally, such pharmacists might streamline the referral systems that have been called for [24] and begin to bridge the communication gaps between settings that have been identified as problematic. As pharmacists work in settings including family doctors' surgeries, prisons, urgent care, and emergency departments, the need for understanding the approach to suicide prevention in these roles is increasing.

Medicines and suicide prevention

It is plausible that pharmacists and their teams could contribute to two aspects of suicide prevention activity; firstly, supporting people who may be contemplating or planning suicide. Many of the described studies above focused on the experiences and interactions of pharmacy teams with patients from a holistic standpoint. This is perhaps reflective of more modern and patient-focused roles in pharmacy, where communication and consultation often play a central role. The second potential role relates to restricting or monitoring access to medicines, which may be used in suicide, or self-harm.

In the original call to action in 1972, the potential role of pharmacists was attributed specifically to "drug suicides" [7], referring to intentional overdose. Consideration of the role of medicines in intentional poisoning is a vital and modifiable risk factor for suicide. In Europe, poisoning by medication is one of the most common methods of suicide [1]. As restriction of access to means is the most effective method of suicide prevention, management of medication access could be a useful preventative tactic.

The involvement of medicines in suicide prevention was specifically mentioned in some, but not all studies. In the UK study, participants gave limited credence to the involvement of medicines in suicide [24]. Medicines access was mentioned by pharmacists in Australia and Canada, but discussion of suicide plans related to medicines featured less prominently in conversation than discussion regarding patients' thoughts of suicide (i.e., the more holistic approach) [14]. It is notable, however, that there have been examples cited of patients wanting to access certain medicines or large quantities of medicines with the explicit intention of dying [19, 11]. Pharmacists have been explicitly identified as a gatekeeper of medicines for suicide prevention [11].

In a small Canadian survey ($n = 86$) relating to medicine overdose, misuse, and diversion, the role of pharmacists in the education of patients about their medicines was endorsed [16]. Restricted supply of medication (e.g., to 1 week) was also considered useful, with suggestions that access to electronic patient records could support this. In the United Kingdom, pharmacists have less flexibility in the issue of repeat prescriptions than may be feasible in other countries. Supplies usually require endorsement by the prescriber, and quantities are defined by the prescriber. In Australia, pharmacists can supply medicines in periodic installments based on an agreement with a prescriber or carer, under the Staged Supply Program [32], while in Canada, the scope of practice of pharmacists differs among provinces and territories, with some allowing for independent prescribing and most allowing for adaptations of prescriptions written by the original prescriber [33]. In a study conducted by coauthors, there were examples where quantities were restricted, but the pharmacist had not been informed that this was as a protective mechanism for suicide [24]. Improved communication between prescribers and pharmacists could join the holistic and medication supply aspects for maximum potential.

Differences in the perspectives that have been ascertained internationally could be, in part, a reflection on medication access over-the-counter and problematic medicines in those regions. Anecdotally, the focus on such medicines is in relation to misuse or addiction, rather than use in intentional poisoning [5]. There is, however, increasing interest regarding the implications of over-the-counter medications in poisoning [34, 35]. Furthermore, studies provide evidence at a regional, state, or provincial level, and thus may not fully depict national practice. There is an opportunity to learn among national and international colleagues to consider medicines access and suicide prevention. The recent key therapeutic topic from the National Institute for Health and Research (NICE) on medicines optimization and suicide [36] could be a useful starting point.

UK case study
UK landscape in suicide prevention

Healthcare in all UK nations falls under the auspices of the NHS, where healthcare is free at point of care. In recent years, there has been considerable policy and political momentum to enhance suicide prevention activity in the United Kingdom [37–39]. Activities are led at a devolved and then regional level, with England, Wales, Scotland, and Northern Ireland having distinct plans. This enables local intelligence to be incorporated into suicide prevention activities. In 2019, a cross-government suicide prevention work plan was introduced [39]. This is overseen by a dedicated governmental suicide prevention minister. The plan incorporates a range of organizations, including those related to health, public health, education, transport, justice, and social care. This exemplifies the multifaceted nature of suicide prevention and the need for a coordinated effort between agencies, speaking to the "suicide is everyone's business" mantra [40].

Experiences of UK pharmacy teams in suicide prevention

In the past 2 years, the potential contribution of pharmacy teams to the suicide prevention agenda in the United Kingdom has piqued some interest [36, 41]. In 2018, collaborative suicide and self-harm competency frameworks were published [41]. These were wide-ranging to cover various public-facing professions. Pharmacists were mentioned, but it remains unclear which parts of the framework pertain to pharmacists and their teams in different settings.

To date, Gorton and colleagues have conducted two studies in the United Kingdom to explore attitudes and experiences of pharmacy teams in suicide prevention activities. The first is the aforementioned qualitative study [24]. In this study, community pharmacy teams often gave examples where they had interacted with patients about suicide. Pharmacy teams described their two-way relationships with patients and the accessible pharmacy environment as facilitators for this. With training, which no participants had previously had, they felt that this role could be enhanced if they could access facilitated referral pathways. We now present a case study in which we will describe one part of an anonymous, online survey that explored attitudes to and experience of suicide, as perceived by pharmacy teams.

Pharmacy staff and suicide prevention: A case study in the UK context

Aim

The aims of this study were to: (i) measure attitudes and preparedness of pharmacy staff in relation to suicide prevention; (ii) identify any variation in attitudes and confidence in relation to demographic factors such as role and sector; and (iii) explore the experiences as described by staff.

Method

The survey was available at the start of an optional "on-the-sofa" style interview video on suicide awareness that was produced and hosted by the Centre for Pharmacy Postgraduate Education (CPPE) [42]. All registered pharmacists and pharmacy technicians in England access much of their training via CPPE. Some programs are additionally open to other members of the pharmacy team. Anyone working in any role in any sector of pharmacy in England was eligible to access the video and associated survey. They were invited to do so through communications via professional networks, social media, and direct communications from CPPE. Pharmacy professionals and staff could access the awareness-raising video without participating in the survey. Ethical approval was granted by the University of Huddersfield School of Applied Sciences School Research, Ethics, and Integrity Committee (SAS-REIC-19-0309-1).

The survey was provided on a third-party platform so that the participants' identities could not be linked to the CPPE online learning platform, which hosted the video. The survey included questions on demographics, personal experience with mental health problems and suicide, previous training, attitudes, and experiences. The Attitudes Toward Suicide Prevention Scale [43] is a 14-item scale that was used to measure participants' attitudes to suicide prevention. It has been used by others for this purpose in the United States [20]. Preparedness was measured by adapting questions that have been used elsewhere to measure pharmacy students' confidence in suicide prevention [23]. Both scales are Likert scales, and aggregate scores were obtained through sum of the components of each set.

Attitude statements were measured on a scale from 1 = strongly disagree/ none to 5 = strongly agree/all, with a possible range of aggregated score of 14–70. The lower the score, the more positive the attitude to suicide prevention.

Preparedness statements were rated from 1 = not at all prepared to 5 = fully prepared. The possible range of aggregated scores was 5–20, with higher scores indicating a greater level of preparedness.

Open-ended questions were included to enable participants to describe interactions relating to suicide in their practice.

Analysis

Data were analyzed using IBM SPSS version 26. Descriptive statistics were used to report demographic data and answers to questions relating to personal experience. Summary statistics of central tendency were used to describe aggregates, which were also inspected graphically. Comparative analyses were used to compare aggregates between subgroups, with Mann–Whitney U tests used to compare distributions. A thematic analysis was planned for qualitative comments. Due to a limited return of comments, we have drawn out specific comments to illustrate our quantitative findings.

Results

Eighty people completed the questionnaire, of whom 83% were female (Table 2). Participants spanned usual working ages, with 51% aged between 35 and 54. There was representation from a variety of sectors, with some participants working in multiple sectors. Sixty-one percent practiced in community pharmacy, 14% practiced in hospital pharmacy, and 9% of respondents worked in specialist mental health services. Most participants were pharmacists (60%) or pharmacy technicians (29%), with the remainder representing a variety of roles including dispensing/counter assistants, pre-registration pharmacists/technicians, and drivers. In the United Kingdom, pharmacy technicians are registered with the pharmacy regulator (General Pharmaceutical Council); other support staff are not registered. A quarter of participants declared having a current or previous personal mental health diagnosis, and 40% reported having a close relationship with someone who had died by or attempted suicide. Just 13% of participants reported having undertaken suicide prevention training.

Table 2 Demographics of survey participants.

Demographic	Frequency n (%) N=80
Female	66 (83%)
Age	
<25	7 (9%)
25–34	16 (20%)
35–44	22 (27%)
45–54	19 (24%)
55–64	14 (18%)
>64	2 (2%)
Sector of pharmacy practice[a]	
Community	49 (61%)
Hospital	11 (14%)
Specialist mental health	7 (9%)
General practice (family doctors' surgeries)	6 (8%)
Care home	1 (1%)
Academia	11 (14%)
Industry	2 (3%)
Other	5 (6%)
Professional role	
Pharmacist	48 (60%)
Pharmacy technician	23 (29%)
Preregistration pharmacist	5 (6%)
Preregistration pharmacy technician	1 (1%)
Dispensing assistant	2 (3%)
Pharmacy student	1 (1%)
Personal experience	
Experienced own mental health problems	20 (25%)
Someone close has attempted or died by suicide	32 (40%)
Previous suicide prevention training	10 (13%)
Estimate of number of interactions with patients about suicide	
0 or did not answer	20 (25%)
1–2	31 (38%)
3–5	19 (24%)
6–10	2 (3%)
>10	8 (10%)

[a]Does not sum to 100% due to participants working in multiple sectors.

When asked to estimate the number of times that they had interacted with patients who were contemplating or planning suicide, the most common estimation was once or twice (38%). Few participants (9%) reported asking someone about suicide; the majority were told by the patient (46%) or someone else (14%). Other ways that participant had identified patients included communication on discharge from hospital and noticing new scars that were suggestive of self-harm.

The median aggregate score relating to attitude (scale: 14–70) was 33.0 (IQR 26.0–36.8), thus representing an uncertainty among participants. A median aggregate preparedness score of 10.0 (IQR 7.0–12.0) indicated partial preparedness to respond to suicide (Fig. 1). Responses to individual statements are shown in Table 3.

In sensitivity analyses, some comparisons were made between subgroups. However, these should be interpreted with caution due to limited power to detect differences at these levels and to control for covariates. The comparison of community pharmacy staff versus hospital pharmacy staff attitudes toward suicide prevention ($P = .02$) and preparedness suggested variance in the former but not the latter ($P = .752$). The attitude aggregate was higher for community pharmacy staff versus hospital staff, suggestive of more negative attitudes to suicide prevention. When pharmacists were compared to nonpharmacist participants, no statistically significant differences in attitude or preparedness scores were observed. The nonpharmacist group was a heterogeneous group varying in role, level, and length of experience.

When exploring attitudes, participants were invited to provide free-text comments. They used these fields to emphasize they had not done any suicide prevention training before. The following particularly striking comment was made by one pharmacist:

"I have been that suicidal patient. I wish my pharmacist had asked me how I was doing."

Interpretation

The proportion of participants who worked in specialist mental health services was low. This suggests that pharmacy staff working in other settings have identified a need for suicide awareness, given that they took part in the survey by virtue of interest in watching the video relating to this. This is supported by our earlier extensive discussion of training needs. In previous work [24], no participants had received any formal training in suicide prevention, but there was an overwhelming call for this to be provided. The expectations of pharmacists regarding the benefits of participating in suicide prevention training have not been measured.

Table 3 Median (IQR) responses to agreement with individual statements and aggregate score. Not all respondents answered each statement, so not all rows equal $n = 80$.

Statement	Median score (IQR)
Attitude statement	1 = strongly disagree, 5 = strongly agree
I resent being asked to do more about suicide.	1.0 (1.0–2.0)
Suicide prevention is not my responsibility.	1.0 (1.0–2.0)
Making more funds available to the appropriate health services would make no difference to the suicide rate.	1.0 (1.0–3.0)
Working with suicidal patients is rewarding.[a]	2.0 (2.0–3.0)
If people are serious about suicide, they don't tell anyone.	3.0 (2.0–4.0
I feel defensive when people offer advice about suicide prevention.	2.0 (1.0–3.0)
It is easy for people not involved in clinical practice to make judgments about suicide prevention.	4.0 (3.0–4.0)
If a person survives a suicide attempt, then it was a ploy for attention.	2.0 (1.0–2.0)
People have the right to take their own lives.	3.0 (2.0–4.0)
Since unemployment and poverty are the main causes of suicide, there is little that an individual can do to prevent it.	2.0 (1.0–2.0)
I don't feel comfortable assessing someone for suicide risk.	3.0 (2.0–4.0)
Suicide prevention measures are a drain on resources, which would be more useful elsewhere.	1.0 (1.0–2.0)
There is no way of knowing who is going to die by suicide.	3.0 (2.0–4.0)
What proportion of suicides do you consider preventable?[a]	2.0 (1.0–2.0)
Attitude aggregate	33.00 (26.0–36.8)
Preparedness statement	1 = not at all prepared, 5 = fully prepared
How prepared are you to identify the signs of suicide?	2.0 (1.0–2.0)
How prepared are you to respond appropriately to people who have plans or thought of suicide?	2.0 (1.0–2.0)
How prepared are you to reassure people who talk about plans or thoughts of suicide?	2.0 (1.0–2.0)
How prepared are you to decide whether intervention from another healthcare professional is necessary for someone who has plans or thoughts of suicide?	2.0 (2.0–3.0)
Preparedness aggregate	10.0 (7.0–12.0)

[a]Numbering was inversed on calculation of aggregate score.

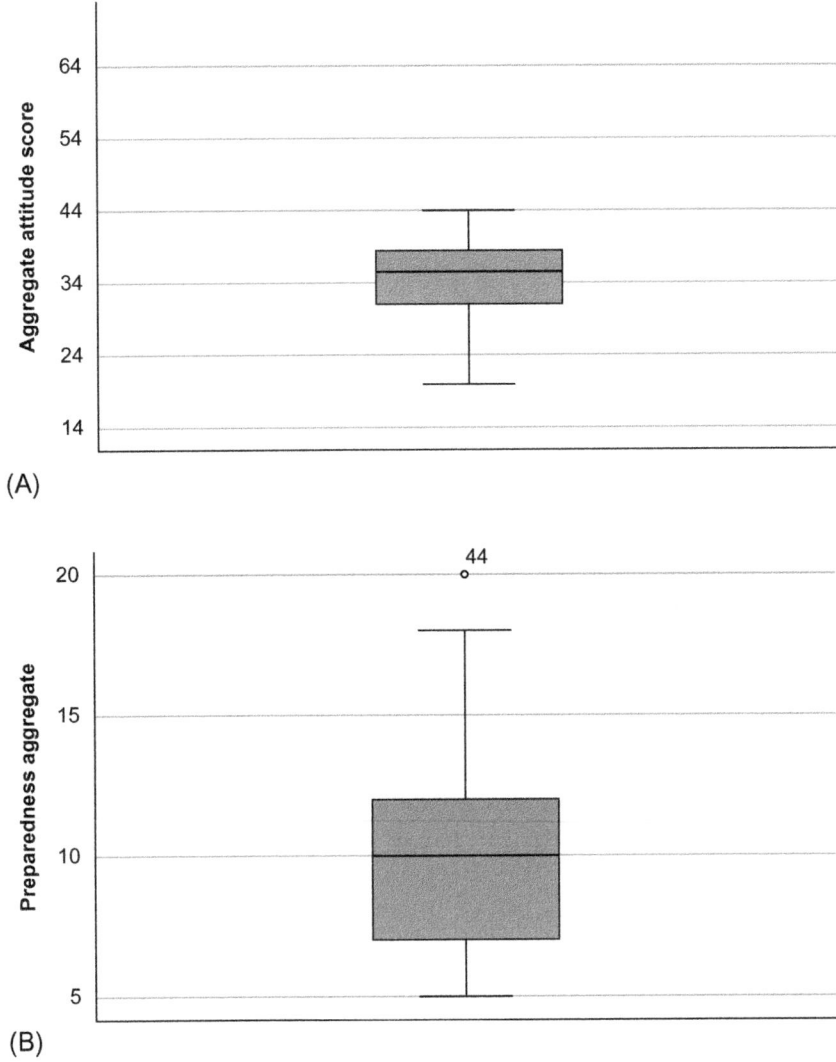

Fig. 1 (A) Aggregate attitude score-viable range: 14–70. (B) Aggregate preparedness score-viable range: 5–20.

Our results also suggest that participants had an uncertain attitude toward suicide overall. In questions relating to personal experience of mental health and suicide, 10%–12% of participants stated "rather not say." It is plausible that participants did not want to disclose this information for fear of stigma, despite the survey being anonymous. There was a comment in the survey that advocated for the need to reduce stigma relating to suicide. In the qualitative interview study, participants often cited concerns regarding stigma, yet inadvertently used stigmatizing language themselves [24]. The perception of stigma might affect one's practice. In the Australian and Canadian survey [13], pharmacists who had experience of someone close to them having a mental health problem were less likely to use stigmatizing descriptors, such as "pathetic" ($P = .008$), "irresponsible" ($P = .01$), or "stupid" ($P = .007$), than those who did not. Pharmacists did not generally endorse the use of stigmatizing terms, but Australian pharmacists were more likely than Canadian pharmacists to describe someone who dies by suicide as "cowardly" ($P = .02$), "disconnected" ($P = .02$), or "irresponsible" ($P = .02$).

Pharmacy staff gave a sense of partial preparedness for suicide prevention activities, as indicated by the aggregated preparedness scores. In the qualitative interview studies, participants were not directly asked to rate level of preparedness, but did indirectly discuss this in relation to training needs. Many discussed this in the context of having helped someone who was suicidal, where they felt prepared enough to try, but not to be certain they had acted in the most appropriate way [24].

Participants reported being told about suicide far more frequently than asking the patient. Similarly, Murphy et al. [14] reported that 66% of interactions to do with suicide were initiated by the patient. This indicates a reactive rather than proactive practice pattern. This was evident in our previous qualitative work, where participants often gave examples of patients making disclosures rather than proactively asking them [24].

Conclusion and recommendations

In the literature, we are beginning to see exploration of the contribution that pharmacy teams do, or might, make to suicide prevention agendas, albeit in a few developed countries. The potential extent of this role must be considered within the complex and expanding role of pharmacists and their teams. The existing evidence may not be generalizable to less developed countries and other sectors of pharmacy; both of which pose important lines of enquiry. We advocate for continued and shared development in this area to understand better the interlinked role of medicines and pharmacy in suicide prevention.

References

[1] World Health Organization. Preventing suicide: a global imperative, https://www.who. int/mental_health/suicide-prevention/world_report_2014/en/; 2014. [Accessed 26 June 2020].

[2] Naghavi M. Global, regional, and national burden of suicide mortality 1990 to 2016: systematic analysis for the Global Burden of Disease Study 2016. BMJ 2019;364:l94.

[3] Cerel J, Brown MM, Maple M, Singleton M, Van De Venne J, Moore M, Flaherty C. How many people are exposed to suicide? Not six. Suicide Life Threat Behav 2019;49:529–34.

[4] Pitman AL, Osborn DP, Rantell K, King MB. Bereavement by suicide as a risk factor for suicide attempt: a cross-sectional national UK-wide study of 3432 young bereaved adults. BMJ Open 2016;6.

[5] Gorton H. What could UK community pharmacy teams learn from the United States and Canada about their role in suicide prevention? Clin Pharm 2019;11.

[6] Murphy A, Hillier K, Ataya R, Thabet P, Whelan A, O'Reilly C, Gardner D. A scoping review of community pharmacists and patients at risk of suicide. Can Pharm J (Ott) 2017;150:366–79.

[7] Gibson MR, Lott RS. Suicide and the role of the pharmacist. J Am Pharm Assoc 1972;12:457–61. passim.

[8] Brushwood DB. Pharmacist liability for suicide by drug overdose. Am J Hosp Pharm 1983;40:439–43.

[9] Kozma CM. Do we need a more aggressive approach to suicide prevention? Manag Care Interface 2004;17:37–8.

[10] International Association for Suicide Prevention. Suicide prevention in primary care, https://www.iasp.info/suicide_prevention_in_primary_care.php; 2020. [Accessed 26 June 2020].

[11] Murphy A, Ataya R, Himmleman D, O'Reilly C, Rosen A, Salvador-Carulla L, et al. Community pharmacists' experiences and people at risk of suicide in Canada & Australia: a thematic analysis. Soc Psychiatry Psychiatr Epidemiol 2018;53:1173–84. https://doi.org/10.1007/ss00127-018-1553-7.

[12] Murphy AL, O'Reilly C, Martin-Misener R, Ataya R, Gardner D. Community pharmacists' attitudes on suicide: a preliminary analysis with implications for medical assistance in dying. Can Pharm J 2018;151:17–23.

[13] Murphy AL, O'Reilly CL, Ataya R, Doucette SP, Martin-Misener R, Rosen A, Gardner DM. A survey of Canadian and Australian pharmacists' stigma of suicide. SAGE Open Med 2019;7. 2050312118820344.

[14] Murphy AL, O'Reilly CL, Ataya R, Doucette SP, Burge FI, Salvador-Carulla L, Chen TF, Himmelman D, Kutcher S, Martin-Misener R, Rosen A, Gardner DM. Survey of Australian and Canadian community pharmacists' experiences with patients at risk of suicide. Psychiatr Serv 2020;71:293–6.

[15] Hamilton AAC. Detecting and dealing with suicidal patients in the pharmacy. Can Pharm J 2012;145:172–3.

[16] Leong C, Alessi-Severini S, Sareen J, Enns MW, Bolton J. Community pharmacists' perspectives on dispensing medications with the potential for misuse, diversion and intentional overdose: results of province-wide survey of community pharmacists in Canada. Subst Use Misuse 2016;51.

[17] Murphy AL, Gardner DM, Chen TF, O'Reilly C, Kutcher SP. Community pharmacists and the assessment and management of suicide risk. Can Pharm J 2015;148:171–5.

[18] Kassir H, Eaton H, Ferguson M, Procter NG. Role of the pharmacist in suicide prevention: primely positioned to intervene. J Pharm Pract Res 2019;49:567–9.

[19] Carpenter DM, Lavigne JE, Colmenares EW, Falbo K, Mosley SL. Community pharmacy staff interactions with patients who have risk factors or warning signs of suicide. Res Social Adm Pharm 2020;16:349–59.

[20] Cates M, Cochran-Hodges J, Woolley T. Pharmacists' attitudes, interest, and perceived skills regarding suicide prevention. Ment Health Clin 2019;9:30–5.

[21] Gillette C, Mospan CM, Benfield M. North Carolina community pharmacists' attitudes about suicide and willingness to conduct suicidal ideation assessment: a cross-sectional survey study. Res Social Adm Pharm 2020;16:727–31.

[22] Carpenter D, Lavigne J, Roberts C, Zacher J, Colmenares E. A review of suicide prevention programs and training policies for pharmacists. J Am Pharm Assoc 2018;58:522–9.

[23] Painter N, Kuo G, Collins S, Palomino Y, Lee K. Pharmacist training in suicide prevention. J Am Pharm Assoc 2018;58:199–204.

[24] Gorton HC, Littlewood D, Lotfallah C, Spreadbury M, Wong KL, Gooding P, Ashcroft DM. Current and potential contributions of community pharmacy teams to self-harm and suicide prevention: a qualitative interview study. PLoS ONE 2019;14.

[25] Kodaka AM, Inagaki M, Yamada M. Factors associated with attitudes toward suicide: among Japanese pharmacists participating in the board certified psychiatric pharmacy specialist seminar. Crisis 2013;34:420–7.

[26] Boukouvalas E, El-Den S, Murphy A, Salvador-Carulla L, O'Reilly C. Exploring health care professionals' knowledge of, attitudes towards and confidence in caring for people at risk of suicide: a systematic review. Arch Suicide Res 2020;24(S1):S1–S33.

[27] Renberg E, Jacobsson L. Development of a Questionnaire on Attitudes Towards Suicide (ATTS) and its application in a Swedish population. Suicide Life Threat Behav 2011;33:52–64.

[28] El-Den S, Chen TF, Moles RJ, O'Reilly C. Assessing mental health first aid skills using simulated patients. Am J Pharm Educ 2018;82:185–93.

[29] Scottish Government. Edinburgh: Scottish Government, https://www.gov.scot/publications/scotlands-suicide-prevention-action-plan-life-matters/; 2018. [Accessed 26 June 2020].

[30] NHS Business Service Authority. Drug Tariff [Internet], 2020. Available at: https://www.nhsbsa.nhs.uk/pharmacies-gp-practices-and-appliance-contractors/drug-tariff [Accessed 16 September 2020].

[31] Kutcher S. Suicide risk management. London: BMJ Best Practice; 2018.

[32] Pharmaceutical Society of Australia. Guidelines for pharmacists providing staged supply services, https://www.ppaonline.com.au/wp-content/uploads/2019/01/PSA-Staged-Supply-Guidelines.pdf; 2019. [Accessed 10 July 2020].

[33] Canadian Pharmacists' Association. Pharmacists' scope of practice in Canada, https://www.pharmacists.ca/pharmacy-in-canada/scope-of-practice-canada/; 2020. [Accessed 10 July 2020].

[34] Cairns R, Brown JA, Buckley NA. Adolescent self-harm: over-the-counter medicines fly under the radar. Aust Prescr 2019;42:151.

[35] Cairns R, Brown JA, Wylie CE, Dawson AH, Isbister GK, Buckley NA. Paracetamol poisoning-related hospital admissions and deaths in Australia, 2004–2017. Med J Aust 2019;211:218–23.

[36] National Institute for Health and Care Excellence. Suicide prevention: optimising medicines and reducing access to medicines as a means of suicide [KTT24], https://www.nice.org.uk/advice/ktt24; 2019. [Accessed 26 June 2020].

[37] HM Government. Preventing suicide in England. A cross-government outcome strategy to save lives, https://assets.publishing.service.gov.uk/government/uploads/system/uploads/attachment_data/file/430720/Preventing-Suicide-.pdf; 2012. [Accessed 26 June 2020].

[38] HM Government. Preventing suicide in England: third progress report on the cross-government outcomes strategy to save lives, https://assets.publishing.service.gov. uk/government/uploads/system/uploads/attachment_data/file/582117/Suicide_ report_2016_A.pdf; 2017. [Accessed 26 June 2020].

[39] HM Government. Cross-government suicide prevention workplan, https://assets. publishing.service.gov.uk/government/uploads/system/uploads/attachment_data/ file/772210/national-suicide-prevention-strategy-workplan.pdf; 2019. [Accessed 26 June 2020].

[40] National Scottish Suicide Prevention Leadership Group. Making suicide prevention everyone's business, https://www.gov.scot/publications/national-suicide-pre-vention-leadership-group-annual-report-2019-making-suicide-prevention-every-ones-business/pages/3/; 2019. [Accessed 26 June 2020].

[41] Health Education England. Self-harm and suicide prevention competence framework: adults and older adults, https://www.ucl.ac.uk/clinical-psychology/competency-maps/ self-harm/adult-self-harm-map.html; 2018. [Accessed 26 June 2020].

[42] Centre for Postgraduate Pharmacy Education. Suicide awareness, https://www.cppe. ac.uk/programmes/l/suicide-e-01/; 2019. [Accessed 26 June 2020].

[43] Herron J, Ticehurst H, Appleby L, Perry A, Cordingley L. Attitudes toward suicide prevention in front-line health staff. Suicide Life Threat Behav 2001;31:342–7.

CHAPTER 7

Making Time, Making History, Transforming Lives: Community pharmacy service development and evaluation for people living with learning disabilities

Sue Jones[a], Saira Khan[a], Hadar Zaman[a], Ruth Buchan[b], and Kevin Flint[a]
[a]School of Pharmacy and Medical Sciences, University of Bradford, Bradford, United Kingdom
[b]Community Pharmacy West Yorkshire, Leeds, United Kingdom

Introduction

The *Making Time* service was launched by multiagency health and social care providers in the United Kingdom (UK) involving National Health Service (NHS) Leeds North Clinical Commissioning Group and Community Pharmacy West Yorkshire in partnership with Leeds City Council Adult Social Care Learning Disability Services and Leeds and York Partnership NHS Foundation Trust. The main aim and objective of this service was:

> to try and make sure that People Living With Learning Disabilities (PLWLD) got the best service in respect of health and lifestyle and support from their local community pharmacy. It was about making sure that pharmacy services could offer the kind of person centred service that PLWLD really needed to stay safe and well.

Inspiration for the service came from listening to the concerns of people who were using the Leeds Disability Care Services.

Making Time was about building upon the services that PLWLD already received and enhancing these by being more proactive using a "year of care" approach. This service allowed PLWLD to look at their health and lifestyle-related goals with their community pharmacist to make them realistic and achievable. The *Making Time* service also enabled PLWLD to create time with pharmacy staff to discuss medication and how this could be optimized to improve health and lifestyle outcomes. *Making Time* allowed PLWLD to receive accessible and reasonably adjusted community pharmacy services that were person-centered, supporting a healthy and safe lifestyle.

Pharmacy Practice Research Case Studies
https://doi.org/10.1016/B978-0-12-819378-5.00003-9

Background

Overview of learning disability in UK healthcare context

In the United Kingdom, it is estimated that 1.5 million people have a learning disability (LD) which is 2% of the population [1, 2]; however, only a quarter of these individuals are on the LD register with their local General Practitioner (GP) [2]. Hatton et al. [3] in their report estimated 1,087,100 individuals with LD, of whom 252,446 people were officially identified on LD registers. This meant only one in four PLWLD were registered and known [3].

PLWLD are at an increased risk of health inequalities resulting in early mortality. Compared to the general population, PLWLD died much younger (13–20 years younger for men with LD and 20–26 years younger for women with LD) [4, 5]. Furthermore, they are at an increased risk of a range of other health issues compared to the general population [6].

In 2016, the NHS project *Health and Care of People with LD 2014–15*, developed in collaboration with Public Health England (PHE), found that obesity was twice as common in people aged 18–35 with LD and one in two eligible females with LD received breast cancer screening, compared with females without LD, more than two of three of whom received such screening [7].

Moreover, a report from the Disability Rights Commission suggested that the levels of ill-health for this group were significantly higher than the figures imply. Both the localized demographics and variations in the place where persons live created considerable challenges at the local level in providing the appropriate forms of support, as this evaluation made obvious in Leeds [4].

In 2014, *A Confidential Inquiry into Premature Deaths of People with LD* by Heslop et al. reviewed the deaths of 247 PLWLD over a 2-year period, as well as 58 comparator cases of adults without LD. Findings were that 28% ($n = 69$) of PLWLD died from avoidable causes compared to 9% ($n = 5$) in a comparison population of people without LD. Nearly a quarter (22% $n = 54$) died under 50 years; median age at death was 64 years. For males and females, the median ages at death were 65 and 63, respectively, with the general population median ages being 78 and 83, respectively [8].

Research has also demonstrated that 20%–40% of PLWLD were prescribed antipsychotics, which was double that of the general population. In many instances, antipsychotics, which were the most prescribed medications for PLWLD, were prescribed for their sedative effects rather than for specific antipsychotic effects [9, 10]. A study in primary care by Sheehan et al. [10] found around 70% of antipsychotics were given to PLWLD in the absence of a record of several mental illnesses. This finding was comparable to other studies that found most antipsychotics prescribed to PLWLD were given to manage behavioral problems rather than mental illness [10, 11].

Making Time in worlds of practice

For a patient who does not have an LD, the common language is English, and community pharmacists are taught to empathize and work with the patient at their level of understanding to optimize their healthcare, medication, and well-being. This was previously possible because the common thread for the patient–pharmacist interaction was the English language and an expectation of understanding from both parties; this created the possibility of a meaningful dialogue, understood by both parties. For PLWLD, the common thread of their method of communication was more complex and nuanced than that of the standard patient.

The dominant assumption in the literature on health was that somehow scientific measurement, aligned with appropriate medication and other guided measurable physical and dietary regimes, provided the basis for measured evaluations of the health of a person [12]. Consequently, in remaining with this dominant medical model, as uncovered from the literature, a wide range of vital cultures reproduced in the lives of persons were simply merged by the very same institutions of state—institutions that, ironically, in their rhetoric continue to express concerns about how to listen to and to support persons labeled with LD. As revealed, these include not least medicine, research, education, law, and the national evaluation of the health of persons. Putting these all together revealed a complex, multifaceted range of cultures in play with each other in everyday clinical practice.

Making Time identified many cultures at play in the care of people. Fig. 1 represents six identified in the process of this evaluation.

National and health cultures represent places where often the door may be closed to innovation, and are seen to be objective and capture what might be missing, as described earlier. Innovation and transformation can be seen from the service and communication cultures. At the central point are the individuals and groups of individuals associated with these cultures in their everyday lives (person and population cultures). By exploring these in more detail, a model of practice may be developed to support PLWLD.

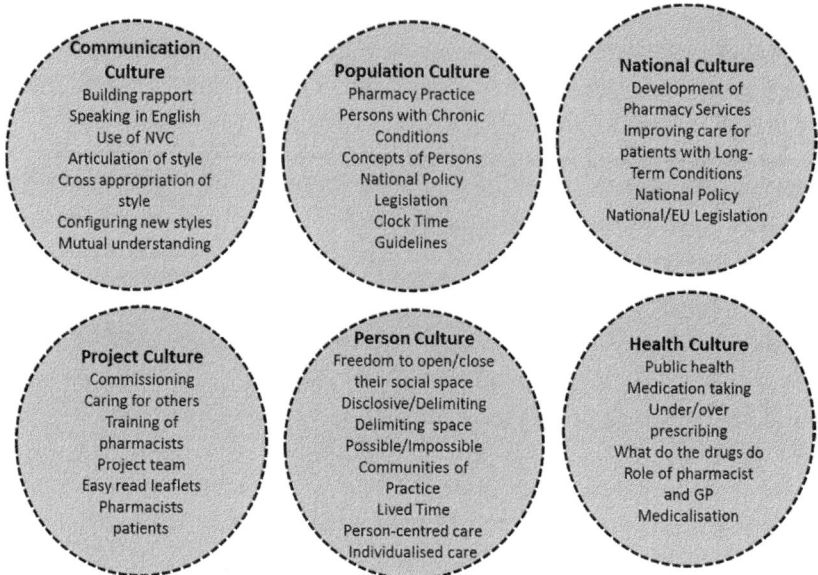

Fig. 1 *Making Time* in worlds of practice; cultures at play.

Development of the Making Time service

Methodologically, the service was designed following feedback from PLWLD, guardians, carers, healthcare professionals (HCPs), and other stakeholders such as policy makers who identified a need. Pharmacy teams were encouraged to participate in the research and each pharmacy team involved was invited to training events run by service users and Community Pharmacy West Yorkshire (CPWY). They were trained to provide tailored support for PLWLD to help them to achieve their goals and, more importantly, deliver person-centered care in a way that was accessible and easy to understand using the resources provided. These included easy-to-read literature to support PLWLD in understanding how their pharmacy team could support them with their health and medicines. A novel aspect of *Making Time* was that the service was remunerated and based on a "year of care" approach, rather than a one-off consultation service, which was the most common format for many pharmacy services such as Medicine Use Reviews (MUR) and flu vaccinations.

At the initial assessment stage, the patient's medicines were discussed together with lifestyle, health, and well-being. This was followed by a series of monthly consultations, over a year, to support and encourage PLWLD to set and achieve self-determined goals and have discussions about their medicines, or issues important to them relating to their health and lifestyle. The types of support provided by pharmacies included prevention of ill-health, self-care, medicines optimization, and management of long-term conditions.

Methods used to evaluate the Making Time service

A challenge of clinical practice in pharmacy, medicine, and other aligned disciplines is that of working with and involving persons with chronic health conditions. There is a natural human tendency to reduce the body of a single person to a group of persons or populations, as described in the introduction. Healthcare is fraught with developing guidelines that are for a disease, e.g., National Institute for Health and Care Excellence (NICE) guidelines, which do not really focus on the individual person, but consider the disease. This is a challenge as HCPs seek to metricize and generalize, and quantitative research focuses on a population, not individuals. Hence, this research was exploratory to develop theories and ideas about this service that could be tested subsequently on a larger scale. The evaluation focused on both the person and the collective body of persons, and they were each located in their various communities of practices: community pharmacies, their home, their office.

Given the nuances of the service, methodologically the evaluation was a mixed methods service evaluation with a broadly ethnographic philosophy. Ethnography gave a systematic way of understanding the practices, behaviors, and perceptions of all participants involved in *Making Time*. It allowed collection and analysis of the qualitative data required for the evaluation to occur in their everyday setting: the community pharmacy or their place of residence [13–15]. The research remained descriptive, cross-sectional, and retrospective, and focused on the effectiveness and feasibility of the service. This was from the perspectives of the extent to which the service achieved its intended outcomes, and processes and problems encountered, respectively.

Methods of data collection

The various options for this evaluation included self-completed questionnaires, participant observations, focus groups, and reflective diaries. Whatever the method, it needed to reflect the ethnographical dimension to this work and so be close to the participant natural setting: their home or their pharmacy.

Semistructured interviews

The format used for the method of data collection of this evaluation was broadly a semistructured interview. These were seen to be most appropriate as participant views were more likely to be expressed in a "semistructured" design compared to a standard interview or questionnaire [16, 17]. They created social space for participants to express themselves in their own terms in response to a series of open-ended prompting questions. Topic guides were developed to capture perspectives of participant community pharmacists and stakeholders [16]. These were audio recorded, anonymized, given pseudonyms, and transcribed verbatim for subsequent data analysis.

In approaching this evaluation, what remained less well explored or elaborated was the ways of "listening to" PLWLD. While talking to stakeholders and community pharmacists, the common language was English and the level of communication and cues between the researcher and participant was common and known. For PLWLD, the practice of listening to them was not a matter of grasping and placing what was said within the same context as the community pharmacists and stakeholders; the evaluation needed another perspective of maximizing communication between the researcher and the PLWLD. To do this, the "off the shelf" semistructured interviews were not sufficient and interactions with persons with LD required the researcher to open space for them as persons, in which their unique community-based context could be seen (disclosed/disclosive space).

Therefore, in listening to persons in a clinical setting it was vital to remain mindful of the requirement to create disclosive space for the other person, together with the recognition that each person lived within the interplay of both what was possible for that person and what was impossible. It was in the space opened by the interplay of possible/impossible that persons gave expression to their own particularities, idiosyncrasies, and desires, and in this space, persons had the freedom to live their lives as persons. Clearly, too, the outline approach, involving listening to others—which respected and opened space for them as unique persons involved in the interplay of the possible and impossible—also had implications for the methodological approach used in this study. It also affected how the analysis of the practices of persons with LD in their interactions with community pharmacists and other support staff was undertaken.

Sample size and sampling

The sample was "purposive," which is common in qualitative studies [15]. For the purposes of this evaluation, a range of stakeholders identified by CPWY, all community pharmacists, and patients who had signed up for *Making Time* were approached to participate in the evaluation. On agreeing to participate, a mutually convenient time was arranged for the interviewer to meet with the interviewee at their place of work or residence/day center (PLWLD). Some stakeholders had moved to another part of the United Kingdom and these were contacted and interviewed over the telephone.

Methods of data analysis

Data was collected largely in the form of recordings, which were transcribed, and field notes and memos to self were added to complete the data set. For participant community pharmacists and stakeholders, a framework approach to analysis was adopted, which sought to identify trends and differences between community pharmacist views and develop themes and ideas about the data. Transcripts and recordings were listened to/read repeatedly looking for emergent themes and ideas across the data set. This gave uniqueness to the developed methodological approach with PLWLD as it combined ethnography and illuminative enquiry.

Triangulation

To ensure the quality of qualitative data, it was necessary to triangulate any findings to other elements of the study. Triangulation is a term used in navigation and surveying: people discover their location on a map by taking bearings from landmarks, identifying their location from where these bearing lines intersect. Initially, the forms of triangulation sought to uncover more understandings of the practices of each of the three groups involved in the service (i.e., the project team, the community pharmacists, and the persons). The move toward "thick descriptions" of each person's practices, characteristic of ethnography, were based on many hours of engagement with the findings to produce a clear focus upon the practices of persons—with other theories "bracketed" out of the way.

Four forms of data triangulation were used:
- *Methodological triangulation*: This used the principles of ethnography coupled with reviewing emerging phenomenon about how the participants lived in their world and the nature of their communication.

- *Data triangulation:* This used different sets of data: in working with each of the persons, the interviewer collected data concerned with their use of signs in addition to noting what each was said in the semistructured interviews.
- *Investigator triangulation:* The interviews of the five community pharmacists in the study were conducted by one interviewer, while the interviews of the project team and the PLWLD were conducted by a different interviewer and this was led by another member of the team. The discussions and reflections upon the data following the interviews then gave the basis for generating a complex range of perspectives on the practices involved.
- *Theory triangulation:* By drawing insights from a number of theories around the phenomenon, about how participants lived in their world and the nature of their communication, this opened up a language for the understandings of practice involving persons who have limited use, and in two cases, no use, of formal English.

Results and discussion

The greatest impact for the research team in this evaluation was from the engaging and thought-provoking conversations that were had about the *Making Time* service. In order to give justice to the findings, this section presents results and discusses some of them, leading to a more integrated and reflective account. Integration of findings from different participants' perspectives provides a more holistic approach to reading of the findings of this analytical illuminative evaluation.

The service was piloted in 24 pharmacies in Leeds (United Kingdom) and almost 100 patients were registered on the service, aged between 35 and 85. Only half of the pilot sites ($N=12$) managed to register patients and 31 patients had a *Making Time* initial assessment with an average consultation time of 20 minutes. Of these, three were smokers, 13 were overweight or obese, and 18 described themselves as moderately inactive or inactive. From the perspective of medication, 87% ($N=26$) were taking regular medicines, of which 88% ($N=23$) used monitored dosage systems (MDS) and 61% ($N=19$) had more than four regular medicines. When goal-setting, 24 patients had an average of two goals set and these related to the following areas (see Fig. 2).

Making Time: Caring for persons

A major success of the service revealed in this evaluation was in creating space for a small number of persons with LD in ways that encouraged them to make significant and sustained transformations in their lifestyles

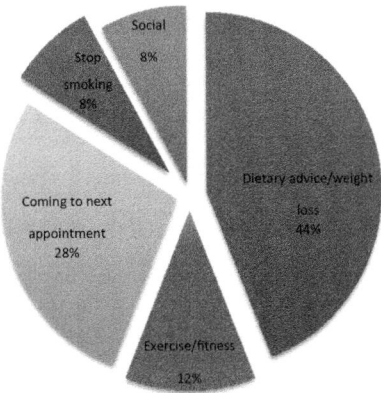

Fig. 2 Types of goals set for PLWLD.

and radical transformations in their everyday worlds of practice. The service began to provide a focus upon the success of HCPs in caring for persons. The provisional evidence from three community pharmacists involved in the service indicated some of the challenges involved in supporting and caring for persons labeled with LD. One of the Community Pharmacists (A) noted how the services they provided at his pharmacy were "very successful for one lady." In response to the question of the extent to which the service helped to create this success, he reported:

I would have helped this lady if she'd have asked us in the first place, but the Making Time service gave us the opportunity to ask:
  "What do you want to do," or:
  "What can we help you with."
  So, (presenting her with this service) just got that conversation going a bit quicker: that was brilliant and we also helped get her back into exercise. She did start exercising and managed to lose weight, but then stopped and we helped her get back into swimming and doing some activity.
  The first thing we did was to help her stop smoking. She went down from forty cigarettes per week and has completely given up now. I mean, it took about six months or so. But, she was a very unique individual in that she'd already managed to lose loads of weight.
  We also did an MUR with her and sorted some of her medication so actually ended up stopping some of her Parkinson's med's which has stopped her restlessness. I think she was a little bit overprescribed on Parkinson's medication so she is a lot less restless now. Consequently, that particular lady really benefited from the Making Time service.

This success, of course, in turn challenged many patterns of data presented in the literature, as described in the introduction, where there were guidelines and documents around generic issues but none with a focus on the challenges of working and communicating with PLWLD. As noted earlier in this report, Community Pharmacist A's actions in caring for "this lady" demonstrated that it is quite possible, given the appropriate clinical support, as Richard (stakeholder) indicated in conversation, "to create the space and the time" for persons with LD to transform pivotal aspects of their own lives, with each person transforming their own world of everyday practice.

Another Community Pharmacist (B), who was working as part of a team in a community pharmacy with PLWLD, also commented on the considerable success of this service and how they had been able to "get over twenty patients signed up" for the service. This was a major success for the service reflecting both their team-based approach to the care given to persons with LD and the juxtaposition of a local care home.

PLWLD who signed up at Community Pharmacist B's pharmacy were based in a local home, which supported independent living for this heterogeneous group. They each attended, with support from their carers, and Community Pharmacist B spoke about the challenge of getting this group to attend the pharmacy in the first place. Ordinarily, he explained, the pharmacy supplied persons at the home with a "tray of medications" and this gave them little motivation to attend. Consequently, one of the goals set for these PLWLD at the community pharmacy had been "to come for an appointment." In Community Pharmacist B's mind, for most of this group, "that was quite a big achievement for them."

Other goals Community Pharmacist B's pharmacy set for particular patients included weight loss, smoking cessation, and socializing. He recognized that the goals had to be negotiated and tailored for each person. "Probably about seven stayed working with us," said Community Pharmacist B. "They just liked to come in and have a chat—it was something good for them." By consideration of the world of practice of persons in this situation, this evaluation could begin an understanding of the importance for persons of being with others in a place where they each feel safe. Community Pharmacist B recalled that being with others in the pharmacy and chatting "made a difference to their confidence and (helped) them to feel comfortable with the pharmacy staff coming into the pharmacy."

Community Pharmacist B's pharmacy, then, had become a safe place for this heterogeneous group of persons with LD. He observed that "it made a massive difference to them" in terms of their expressed confidence, and while not medication related, it was health (mental) related.

Making Time: Contributions to public health and education

The community pharmacists who provided the service were very positive about the pivotal role of *Making Time* in promoting public (health) education. Pharmacist C indicated that it "fits perfectly with our role (as community pharmacist) in promoting public health." They elaborated:

> Many goals for our clients in Making Time were very simple. For example, there was one client who was drinking a large bottle of coke every day. And pharmacists could explain to her some of the risks and dangers to her health: rotting her teeth; her weight; the caffeine levels. Following that conversation, she drank much less coke. She received a massive health benefit.

Equally, Pharmacist D was very clear on why the service had been successful in promoting public health with PLWLD. Pharmacist D spoke of "the pharmacist (being) able to talk them round and have a more detailed conversation about some of the issues involving public health." Unconsciously, here Pharmacist D gave voice to the community pharmacists' emerging educational and pedagogical aspects of public health. Everyone involved in the service agreed that public education constituted a powerful and important dimension of the *Making Time* service.

One of the stakeholders (F) could place in context the contribution of the service to public education:

> We've seen, over the years, pharmacists making tremendous advances and contributions in supporting healthy lifestyles and healthy living through harm reduction protocols, supporting people to lose weight, doing walking clubs, getting people active ... We've seen pockets of these. The more we do in systemising these in the work of pharmacists, the better we do for local populations. You know, seeing pharmacies as the hubs for health and wellbeing, using the estate, the resources and the skills we already have. You know, pharmacists with a five-year Masters' degree trained in nearly every high street in the country is just a phenomenal asset we need to do more with.

All community pharmacist participants agreed that community pharmacists/pharmacies had a significant potential role in promoting public health. What remained was a question for further research of just how effectively the different pedagogies of public health are used to engage PLWLD and more generally with other persons.

Pharmacist E (a community pharmacist) wished for community pharmacists to be able to take a bigger role in public health. However, while he recognized the importance of gaining extra time with clients in the service, more generally he acknowledged that in "spending more time in being people facing, I need more Accuracy Checking Technicians (ACTs)."

Certainly, as one of the individuals who worked closely with the pharmacies involved in the service and who took a lead in developing the easy-to-read leaflets, one of the stakeholders (G) was in no doubt that the *Making Time* service had made community pharmacies "more accessible" to the public and "raised awareness that pharmacies are more useful than maybe they have been perceived before."

Similarly, as far as stakeholder G (a significant contributor to the development of the easy-to-read leaflets) was concerned, talking about community pharmacy with groups with LD had never happened before. Nor, it would appear, had there been any consideration given, before this publication, to the pedagogies that best promote public health for PLWLD. Stakeholder G reflected:

> Now we've been to the lead people and we've talked to them about what you might want to use your pharmacy for. What you might get out of it. We know that a number of people have gone. And they have seen their pharmacy in a different way. So, we certainly have had some kind of impact in terms of people's understanding of what a pharmacy might be able to do.

Pharmacists were keen to discuss their role in public health and all of them felt that services such as *Making Time* represented the future direction of community pharmacists' role in providing services to patients and moving away from a dispensary-based role.

> It's a brilliant service (MURs) but there is too much focus on 400 as a target … Although they don't make it out to be a business target that's ultimately how it comes across that you need to do 400 or you're not performing. (Community Pharmacist B)

Community pharmacists were positive about this, though many still spent most of their time in the dispensary. Stress, time constraints, and the current funding model based on quantity rather than quality, were also mentioned by the community pharmacists in this study [18]. This reiterates the need for transformation in the pharmacy profession to ensure consistency as well as change by community pharmacists themselves to be more service-orientated.

In summary, all the professionals involved in this service remain entirely driven by a powerful moral force that directed each of them in their own particular ways to move toward improving the care given to PLWLD.

Challenges faced by pharmacists in delivering Making Time
Communication/consultation skills

One key theme that emerged from interviews with pharmacists was around the challenges they faced in delivering the service in terms of communication skills. Despite communication/consultation skills training being provided before the service was launched, all pharmacists commented that more support (training) should have been provided for pharmacists to help them improve their communication skills when providing any pharmacy services to PLWLD:

> *… how do you identify individual patients with learning disabilities, it could be a difficult conversation to start in the pharmacy. If you already know the patient then that would help but often with mild learning disabilities it could be difficult. Some of the patients had communication difficulties so although I was communicating with the patients, the carers had to provide a lot of support too in the consultation. Often the carers did need to rephrase what I was saying. (Pharmacist E)*
>
> *The one thing we did find difficult was triggering off the conversation in the first place. I spoke to the carers initially to try and have the conversation beforehand to try and find out if there were any burning issues. (Pharmacist A)*

Providing safe and effective care is a key professional standard set by the General Pharmaceutical Council, the regulator of Pharmacists/Pharmacy Technicians in the United Kingdom, which includes the need to "communicate effectively." The standard states that pharmacy professionals must "adapt their communication to meet the needs of the person they are communicating with." Effective communication is therefore at the heart of education and training, and pharmacy professionals must be accountable for meeting these standards [19].

In 2016, an Australian study explored the level of understanding of PLWLD in relation to their asthma medication to inform the design and provision of future education support to manage their asthma. The research found that pharmacists' communication skills were a barrier for PLWLD. The study described strategies with which pharmacists can improve their communication and consultation skills when managing or advising PLWLD and/or their caregivers. Suggestions ranged from active listening to determine understanding of concepts about health beliefs of the PLWLD, exercising care with language, and working with the person's known routines to maximize adherence with medications [20]. This evaluation reaffirms the findings of this study, whereby communication/consultation skills still seem to be an area for improvement for pharmacy professionals, who thus need upskilling. This could be due to lack of training specifically aimed at consulting/communicating with PLWLD.

Recruitment into Making Time

Recruitment and identifying suitable individuals that would benefit from participating in this service was identified as another key challenge pharmacists experienced. All the community pharmacies involved in this service had recruited PLWLD using various means such as opportunistic recruitment and links with local care homes and carers. Although carers were initially good at bringing PLWLD to pharmacies, some of the feedback regarding carers suggested that they were reluctant to return for consultations due to time constraints, which resulted in follow-up appointments being missed:

> *We really struggled ... I thought it would be easier than it is especially because they've already had carers in with them. It's quite unusual to put that much effort in and not get that conversion rate so I think it is quite a difficult set of patients to work with unfortunately or to convert. (Pharmacist A)*
> *There was a decent drop out rate. Mainly when we started to do the initial assessment some just couldn't communicate and it was difficult ... I think communication was challenging for some patients. I think finding goals for some of the patients were difficult. (Pharmacist D)*

The majority of PLWLD came in with an employed carer; however, other PLWLD who accessed the service had either family members support them or were independent to care for themselves. This suggests that most pharmacies were recruiting patients in supported housing. Pharmacists who were successful at recruiting patients often had links with a local care home that supported PLWLD. Pharmacists mentioned that they faced difficulties recruiting PLWLD who were not being cared for in a formal care setting. One of the Pharmacists (C) stated:

> *If I could do this service again I would put more effort into approaching homes where I know there are patients with learning disabilities. In general I am just wondering whether carers were made aware of the service and more could have been done on that front to encourage them to visit the pharmacy.*

Pharmacy teams, including pharmacy assistants, were involved in recruiting PLWLD for the *Making Time* service. Recruitment and retention into community pharmacy services has historically been an issue. There is paucity of research undertaken into the service received by PLWLD in community pharmacies. Research has shown that this may be because service users are often unknown as having LD [3]. However, difficulty communicating was a barrier in recruitment and this has been an issue with other pharmacy services. One further study looked at the views of pharmacy assistants recruiting patients into a smoking cessation service in London and found that the pharmacy assistants felt they lacked the interpersonal skills to engage with smokers effectively to recruit into the service. This study concluded that regular communication skills training to provide person-centered care for the wider pharmacy team is vital in improving recruitment and retention into pharmacy services [21].

A qualitative study on the implementation of community pharmacy services in Australia found that poor recruitment into pharmacy services was due to several factors including lack of stakeholder involvement, lack of pharmacy team involvement, poor leadership of local healthcare/pharmacy leaders, and low levels of awareness of pharmacy services in the general population [22]. One of the key strengths of *Making Time* was the multiagency approach taken to identify and engage with PLWLD and their carers to raise awareness of this service. Despite significant investment in relationship building with these agencies, uptake of the service was low. The reasons behind uptake and drop-out rate need to be explored further in order to provide bespoke pharmacy services to PLWLD in the future.

Making Time: A model for understanding of PLWLD

The conversations with patients uncovered interesting findings for the service and in order to make sense of what happened, each patient who was interviewed formed a case and from extended reviewing of the data from these conversations, a proposed model was developed to help to understand the meaning of these conversations. The view at this stage was to understand better how to support building effective relationships with PLWLD and their community pharmacists. For PLWLD in this study, their understanding and expression of their world, which was sought deliberately by this service, was by bringing their communication practices into the research consciousness this evaluation could seek to understand their world of practice.

This service enabled PLWLD to engage and interact more closely with their community pharmacist, and to improve their health as a result. This pilot service may support the development of a more sophisticated understanding of how the whole concept of creating time and space through a funded service could be developed for future services. All PLWLD had their own unique ways of giving expression (equipment), each in their own languages, to what mattered for them in their own terms. For many, this amounted to using an unpredictable mixture of formal and informal signs, sounds and silences, incomplete sentences, and various words that had significance for each of them.

The logics of practice that follow in this section were developed by researchers with competence in language. Such logics gave a useful starting point for developing a systematic analytical framing in which listening to persons remained possible. But, in listening to the person, in practice, there was a need to keep in the foreground the requirement that such listening to the other involved learning afresh, in each case, aspects of the others' languages.

Models of practice

It would have been easy in opening discussion upon the qualitative results from this service to remain focused upon individuals with LD. However, as suggested earlier, the many layers of national cultures along with the layers of localized cultures grown around this *Making Time* service all set out to represent persons in their community settings.

These arose from consideration of the dominant style of organization used in working with individuals/people with LD. The dominant style of organization that emerged from the literature, in terms of cultural layers mirrored the localized cultures grown around the *Making Time* service. In that way, various questions emerging from consideration of the style of organization in turn gifted us with a series of questions that could be employed in critical examination of the findings from the qualitative study.

Clearly, in moving to discuss the results from the qualitative study, there was a desire to look forward at the style of organization that could be further explored in working with persons in their various communities of practice. Fortunately, despite the very limited outcomes from the patients themselves, each of the patients' practices, along with each of the community pharmacists' practices, involved in the service, have suggested a provisional model concerning persons' making-lived-time for themselves.

Discussion of Making Time: Transformation of practice

Through extensive revisiting of the findings, the transformation of clinical and communication practice can be reflected upon by considering the PLWLD and community pharmacists' existing and transformational styles of practice (see Fig. 3).

Making Time required both PLWLD and their community pharmacists to build successful relationships to communicate between each other, at an understandable and translational level, to enhance care. Fig. 3 tries to capture some of the elements of transition.

In moving to discuss the findings, it was vital to look back at the style of organization (national and local) originally envisaged for the *Making Time* service, and, in radical contrast, looking forward at the style of organization

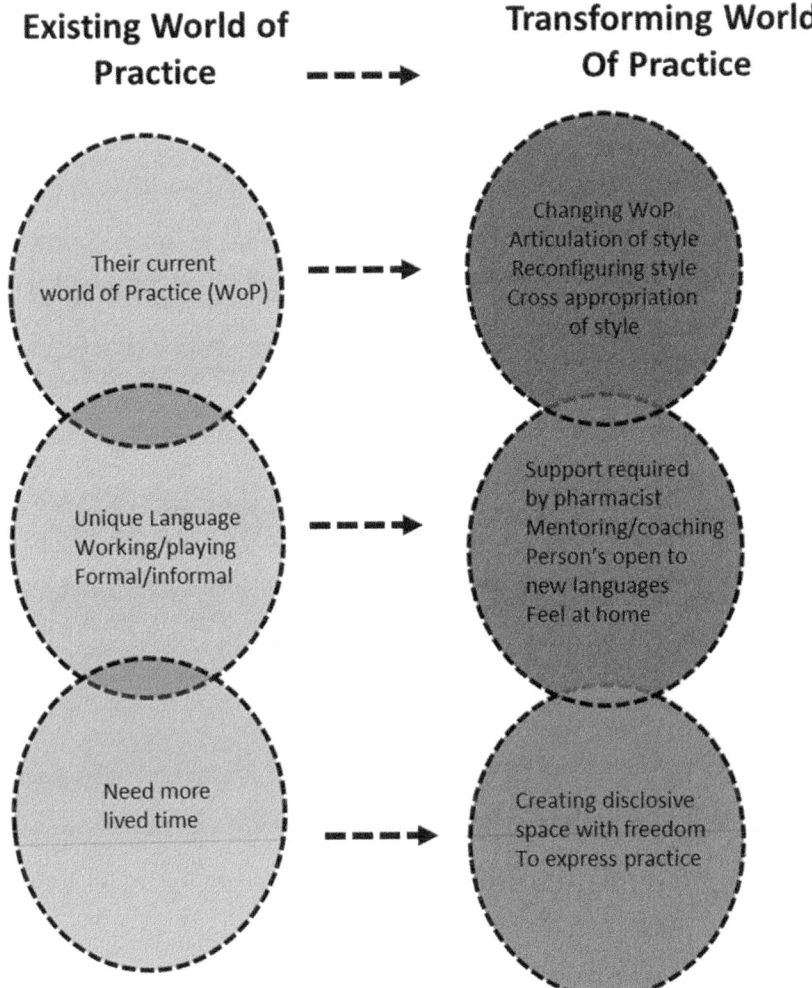

Fig. 3 A suggested model for the transformation seen by PLWLD when working with their community pharmacist.

required to support persons in their making-lived-time in their various communities of practices—persons who endure the daily experience of living with the label of "learning disabled." The aim of looking forward, therefore, was to uncover from the qualitative data the basis for understanding more concerning just what is required in order to open space for persons— space in which they each have the possibility of becoming empowered in their own personhood to work on maintaining and improving the quality of their own health.

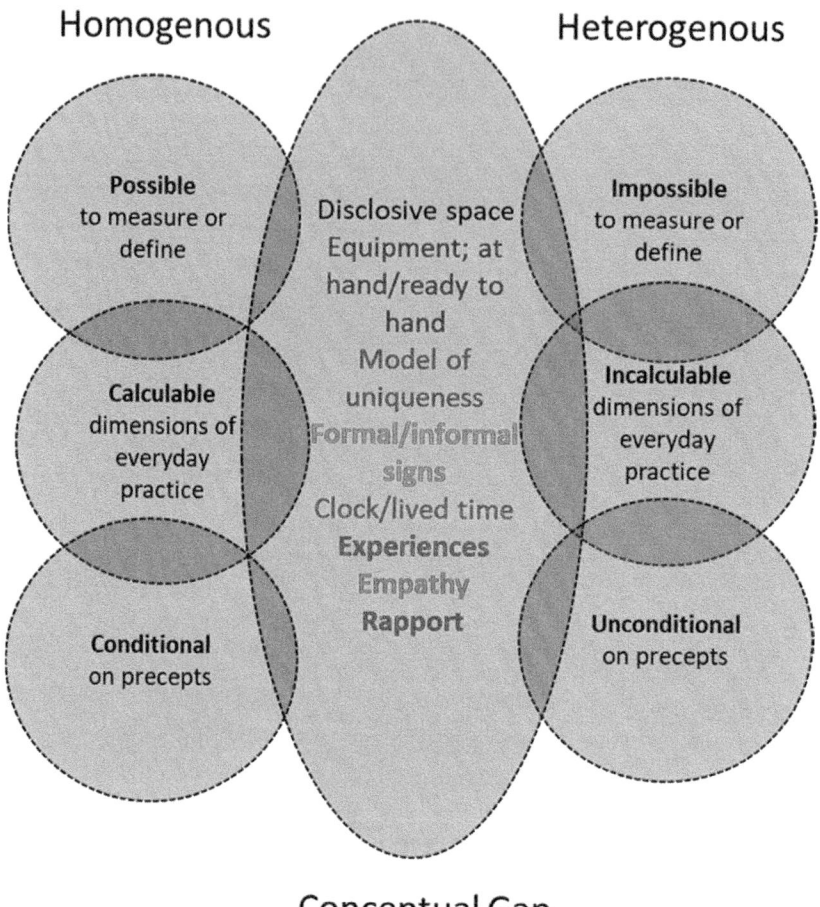

Conceptual Gap

Fig. 4 Patient care in pharmacy; dimensions at play.

Having reflected and reanalyzed the findings of this evaluation, Fig. 4 was developed as a visual illustration to reflect the findings. Having explored areas where the service was very successful, together with limitations of the research, opened a conceptual gap for working with patients living with long-term conditions. On the left-hand side is a representation of the current medical model where things are objective and factual. As has been seen from this evaluation, PLWLD require much more engaged, person-centered, tailored approaches, as represented on the right-hand side—subjective factors. In the middle are some of the concepts, theories, and ideas emerging from this evaluation that deserve further investigation to really engage in true person-centered care.

By attempting to uncover the basis for modeling a person's health in ways that extended beyond the scope of measurement and of medications, there was curiosity to uncover whether such a model was possible and what it might mean in terms of extending understandings of health, healthcare, and person-person interactions. In the longer term, the aim of these discussions was to open space for new understandings of health that complement and may be used in parallel with more standard medically based therapies. In moving toward that point, there is a desire to open the basis for further research, which may be used in helping persons, each in their own style of language, to understand more about themselves and their own health in their own terms.

Conclusion

This study began with the aim of investigating the work of community pharmacy professionals in healthcare in *Making Time* for persons. In working with PLWLD, from this evaluation, several provisional conclusions with wider ramifications for the approach to care given by professionals to patients suffering from a range of chronic conditions can be posited.

The *Making Time* service and its evaluation opened up a new disclosive space for some PLWLD, enabling them to revitalize, reenergize, and radically refresh aspects of their own lives in moves to maintain and improve their own health. It provided a complementary model for healthcare, which focused upon not only the existing grammar of medical practice, pharmacy practice, and other aligned healthcare practices, but also complemented this focus with concerns directed toward the languages and worlds of practices of persons. *Making Time* has generated new knowledge and in doing so, opened a new language for the practice of caring for chronically ill patients that provides the basis for further evaluation of a similar service rolled out for a year for other persons living with chronic conditions with the aim of examining ways of further improving the care given by professionals in the health service.

The evaluation has highlighted the importance of mentoring and coaching of healthcare professionals in developing their practice of caring for chronically ill persons. This has also indicated what additional research is required in order to uncover and to characterize how to make further transformations in team work in the community directed toward improving the care given to chronically ill persons.

Acknowledgment

The authorship team would like to express their deep gratitude to Nigel Hughes, who sadly is no longer with us. Nigel was a real powerhouse for this project, and motivated and engaged everyone connected with this service. His passion to provide equitable healthcare services to all people living with learning disabilities was unrivaled.

References

[1] Mencap. What is a learning disability? [online]. Available from: https://www.mencap.org.uk/learning-disability-explained/what-learning-disability; 2017. [Accessed 10 January 2020].

[2] Russell AM, Bryant L, House A. Identifying people with a learning disability: an advanced search for general practice. Br J Gen Pract 2017;67(665):e842–50. https://doi.org/10.3399/bjgp17X693461.

[3] Hatton C, Glover G, Emerson E. LD observatory: people with LD in England 2015: main report. London: Public Health England (PHE); 2016. November.

[4] Disability Rights Commission (DRC). Equal treatment: closing the gap. A formal investigation into physical health inequalities experienced by people with LD and/or mental health problems. [online]. Available from: http://disability; 2006, studies.leeds.ac.uk/files/library/DRC-Health-FI-main.pdf. [Accessed 30 January 2020].

[5] PHE. Pharmacy and people with learning disabilities: making reasonable adjustments to services. [online]. Available from: https://www.ndti.org.uk/uploads/files/Pharmacy_RA_report_final.pdf; 2017. [Accessed 4 January 2020].

[6] Emerson E, Baines S. Health inequalities and people with learning disabilities in the UK. Tizard Learn Disabil Rev 2011;16(1):42–8.

[7] NHS Digital. Health and care of people with LD. [online]. Available from: http://www.content.digital.nhs.uk/catalogue/PUB22607/Health-care-learning-disabilities-2014-15-summary.pdf; 2016. [Accessed 25 February 2020].

[8] Heslop P, Blair PS, Fleming P, Hoghton M, Marriot A, Russ L. The confidential inquiry into premature deaths of people with intellectual disabilities in the UK: a population-based study. Lancet 2014;383(9920):889–95.

[9] Johnny L, Mahan S. Antipsychotic drug side effects for persons with intellectual disability. Res Dev Disabil 2010;31(6):1570–6.

[10] Sheehan R, Hassiotis A, Walters K, Osborn D, Strydom A, Horsfall L. Mental illness, challenging behaviour, and psychotropic drug prescribing in people with intellectual disability: UK population based cohort study. Br Med J 2015;351:h4326. https://doi.org/10.1136/bmj.h4326.

[11] DeKuijper G, Hoekstra P, Visser F, Scholte FA, Penning C, Evenhuis H. Use of antipsychotic drugs in individuals with intellectual disability in the Netherlands: prevalence and reasons for prescription. J Intellect Disabil Res 2010;54:659–67.

[12] Barber S, Thakkar K, Marvin V, Franklin BD, Bell D. Evaluation of my medication passport: a patient-completed aide-memoire designed by patients, for patients, to help towards medicines optimisation. BMJ Open 2014;4(8).

[13] Babar ZU. Pharmacy practice research methods. 2nd ed. Springer; 2020.

[14] Miles M, Huberman M. Qualitative data analysis: an expanded source book. 2nd ed. Sage Publications; 1994. p. 3–180.

[15] Smith F. Conducting your pharmacy practice research project. 2nd ed. London: Pharmaceutical Press; 2010.

[16] Flick U. An introduction to qualitative research. 2nd ed. London: Sage Publications; 2006. p. 16–80.

[17] Muijs D. Doing quantitative research in education with SPSS. 2nd ed. London: SAGE Publications; 2010.

[18] Jacobs S, Hassell K, Johnson S. Managing workplace stress to enhance safer practice in community pharmacy: a scoping study. Pharmacy Research UK; 2013. p. 1–139.

[19] General Pharmaceutical Council. Standards for pharmacy professional. [online]. Available from: https://www.pharmacyregulation.org/sites/default/files/standards_for_pharmacy_professionals_may_2017_0.pdf; 2017. [Accessed 1 July 2020].

[20] Davis SR, Durvasula S, Merhi D, Young PM, Traini D, Bosnic Anticevich SZ. Knowledge that people with intellectual disabilities have of their inhaled asthma medications: messages for pharmacists. Int J Clin Pharm 2016;38(1):135–43.

[21] Sohanpal R, Rivas C, Steed L. Understanding recruitment and retention in the NHS community pharmacy stop smoking service: perceptions of smoking cessation advisers. Br Med J 2016;6. https://doi.org/10.1136/bmjopen-2015-010921.

[22] Moullin J, Sabater-Hernandez D, Benrimog S. Qualitative study on the implementation of professional pharmacy services in Australian community pharmacies using framework analysis. BMC Health Serv Res 2016;16:439.

CHAPTER 8

Pharmacist-led interventions to promote cardiovascular health: A review of studies from Portugal

Filipa Alves da Costa[a,b] **and Ema Paulino**[c,d]

[a]Research Institute for Medicines (iMED.ULisboa), Faculty of Pharmacy, University of Lisbon, Lisbon, Portugal
[b]Centre for Interdisciplinary Research Egas Moniz (CiiEM), University Institute Egas Moniz, Caparica, Portugal
[c]Farmácia Nuno Álvares, Almada, Portugal
[d]Ezfy, Lda., Lisboa, Portugal

Introduction

Cardiovascular disease (CVD) is among the top causes of premature death worldwide. It is classified as a noncommunicable disease (NCD) for which various risk factors contribute in a synergic way to its development. The World Health Organization (WHO) has issued a global approach to NCDs, detailed in the WHO Global Monitoring Framework, where the main domains and their indicators are presented. The framework is divided into three major domains, including morbidity and mortality, risk factors, and national systems response, totaling 25 indicators. This document also sets targets for 2025, summarized into the ambitious global target of reducing premature death due to NCDs by 25% [1]. For its achievement, cross-sectorial work is needed, where all partners in care provision must be aligned, including those living with CVD. Pharmacists may have an enormous contribution to meeting some, if not all, of the nine targets set, working collaboratively and especially focused on their expertise as medicines experts, also taking advantage of their privileged proximity to the community. This role has been highlighted by the International Pharmaceutical Federation (FIP) in a recent report, which compiles best practice and examples of pharmacists' contribution to beating noncommunicable diseases in the community [2].

Pharmacy services and identification of at-risk individuals

Mass screening at the population level is one means for early detection of a disease, within the scope of public health initiatives. Opportunistic screening is another possible approach, described as more cost-effective,

Pharmacy Practice Research Case Studies
https://doi.org/10.1016/B978-0-12-819378-5.00011-8

through which we select particular individuals known to be at higher risk of the disease; and this is often more efficiently put in practice by working in specific settings, which may have the advantage of proximity and easy access to such individuals. Increasingly, community pharmacies are being used worldwide as an ideal place for opportunistic screening and awareness-raising events, through which the identification of signs and symptoms of disease may trigger the need for specific testing and onward referral for further medical evaluation to confirm potential diagnosis and eventual institution of therapy.

Community pharmacies are conveniently located, easily accessible, and serve many individuals, including those who are asymptomatic, making pharmacists ideally positioned to undertake initiatives for the early detection and management of chronic diseases [3, 4].

Portugal is one of the pioneer countries in Europe where various initiatives have been conducted aiming to identify individuals at high-risk of cardiovascular disease in a timely manner. In this section, we provide some examples of meaningful contributions that have been initiated, often within the context of pilot studies, either research-led or promoted through representative organizations, which, obtaining good results, have in the medium and long-term changed practice in a sustainable way. For more than 5 years now, Portuguese pharmacies have been among those offering a wider range of services [5]. Point of care testing is one of the services most widely implemented in European countries, which may support both the early identification of people at risk of cardiovascular disease and their monitoring, once diagnosis is established and therapy instituted [6]. In Portugal, over 90% of community pharmacies regularly provide point-of-care testing to the population and these focus on four major risk factors: blood pressure, cholesterol, body mass index, and glycaemia; arrhythmia is the most recent addition to this list of services that pharmacies may provide, but given the novelty, even though it is not yet spread nationally, we consider it worth the mention.

Blood pressure

Hypertension is the leading risk factor for cardiovascular events globally, contributing to 45% of all deaths [7]. In Portugal, the overall hypertension prevalence in 2015 was 36%, with the highest values observed in males (39.6%) and in individuals aged between 65 and 74 years old (71.3%) [8]. Among hypertensive individuals included in this study, 69.8% were aware of their condition, 69.4% were being pharmacologically treated, and of these,

71.3% were controlled. These numbers show that there are many opportunities to improve early diagnosis as well as treatment effectiveness.

In 2005, the WHO, through the Countrywide Integrated Noncommunicable Disease Intervention (CINDI) initiative, proposed a pharmacy-based hypertension management model aiming to improve hypertension control at the community level [9]. This model consisted of three levels of intervention, including primary prevention, early detection of undiagnosed people, and management of hypertensive treatments instituted for diagnosed people. Fifteen years later, according to the Pharmaceutical Group of the European Union (PGEU), 90% of countries within the region provide blood pressure measurement in community pharmacies, with 37% of these undertaking structured hypertension management services [10].

In Portugal, virtually all pharmacies have blood pressure measurement as a service. However, although three randomized controlled trials focusing on pharmacist-led intervention programs in Portugal have shown them to enhance hypertension control, sustained hypertension management services are still scarce, including structured documentation of provided care [11–13]. A study assessing the effects on clinical outcomes of an outsourced pharmaceutical care service, which documented the follow-up of 379 patients enrolled between 2008 and 2014, demonstrated that 74.6% of the initially uncontrolled patients achieved systolic control over a mean period of follow-up of 9.1 ± 0.63 months per patient. Moreover, both mean systolic and diastolic blood pressure significantly improved from baseline ($P < .001$). The proportion of patients achieving established therapeutic goals increased from 44.8% to 84.3% [14]. More recently, a collaborative care intervention between pharmacies and a primary healthcare center targeting hypertension and hyperlipidemia has been implemented in one region. This service resorts to care protocols as decision algorithms in the pharmacy dispensing software; exchange of information technology-driven between settings and with patients; and interprofessional meetings between pharmacists, physicians, and nurses, commonly known as quality circles [15]. Although results from this collaborative approach are not yet published, there is great expectation that this model can be replicated to other parts of the country.

Cholesterol

Offering point-of-care measurement of cholesterol at community pharmacies has been shown to assist with patient outcomes by providing information on at-risk patients for onward referral [16]. According to PGEU, 73% of EU countries provide cholesterol measurement in pharmacies [10].

Portugal is one of these countries, with pharmacies progressively moving from simply measuring total cholesterol to providing total lipid profile results. The contextualization of these results within the individual global cardiovascular risk at 10 years, using models such as SCORE, has been mostly used for research studies, but is less implemented in daily practice, despite being the recommended method by the Portuguese Health-Directorate [17]. A cross-sectional survey carried out in 60 community pharmacies, involving 1043 individuals, showed 20% of participants were at high 10-year risk of fatal CVD, among which 39.4% were asymptomatic. The most frequent cardiovascular risk factors identified were hypercholesterolemia (63.1%), hypertension (54.8%), obesity (29.0%), diabetes (13.4%), and smoking (10.4%) [18]. In 2010, a national campaign named "Know your heart values" was conducted, with 412 pharmacies reporting the involvement of 12,930 participants, 44.9% of which were considered at high risk of developing a fatal cardiovascular event in the next 10 years [2]. A high proportion of patients (65.4%) identified as having total cholesterol above reference values had no pharmacological therapy instituted, thus requiring onward referral for follow-up evaluation. Similar figures were reported during an awareness campaign held in 2016, where among the 1268 evaluated individuals, 48% had total cholesterol above the reference values [19]. Among the 634 participants aged 40–65 years old, the SCORE value showed a moderate risk for 59.0% of individuals, high risk for 4.0%, and very high risk for 12.4%.

In a study assessing the effects on clinical outcomes of an outsourced pharmaceutical care service designed for diagnosed patients, 85.5% of the 379 participants presented hypercholesterolemia, and 45.7% of these had values outside of therapeutic goals [14]. Due to the pharmacist interventions, from the 148 patients initially uncontrolled for cholesterol, 55 achieved established therapeutic goals after a mean follow-up period of 9.1 ± 0.63 months per patient, translating into an increase in controlled patients from 54.3% to 71.3%.

Body mass index

A global systematic review focusing on pharmaceutical interventions for the management of type 2 diabetes in various countries and including 5761 patients has highlighted the variability of outcomes reported, among which reduction in BMI was demonstrated for 12 out of 14 studies [20]. Even though this review did not include any studies conducted in Portugal, this is a parameter measured in most community pharmacies.

According to the PGEU, in 93% of European countries, pharmacies provide weight measurement services [10]. Portugal is one of these countries, where in addition to weight measurement, there is a specific service to check for BMI and educate people on its meaning. Pharmacists' intervention in the field of obesity and overweight has been for long anchored on school-based interventions through which the pharmacist collaborates with the local community by health education activities directed at schoolchildren.

Much of this work was initiated over 30 years ago with a program called "The pharmacist at school," which consisted of periodic visits by a local pharmacist who would educate children on a specific topic. The topics were agreed annually, and the educational content developed by the sectorial organization National Association of Pharmacies. This led individual pharmacies then to take on this role progressively in a more independent manner through which they established collaborations locally, and agreement of topics and frequency was also reached according to local needs. More recently, in 2012, another nationwide initiative emerged, this time led by the Pharmaceutical Society, entitled "Healthy Generation." This program has different characteristics as there is no direct involvement of pharmacists, but instead there is a group of trained pharmacy students that act as health champions, who together with the mascot "GS" (standing for healthy generation in Portuguese, see Fig. 1), go to all the schools in the country, including faculties, and engage with children, adolescents, and young adults in

Fig. 1 Mascot of the program visiting schools and exercising with children.

educational activities aiming to demonstrate the benefits of healthy eating and engaging in regular physical exercise. The program started modestly in 12 schools, involving 4450 students in the first year, but progressively grew and the most recent data indicate this program throughout the years has contributed to the education of 91,287 students and 4253 teachers, and over 22,000 people, including pharmacists, parents, and members of the public, have had contact with the program. The outreach is indeed impressive, and it has been internationally recognized as an example of good practice in health promotion by the International Pharmaceutical Federation [21].

Glycaemia

The number of people with diabetes worldwide rose from 108 million in 1980 to 422 million in 2014, taking global prevalence among adults, aged over 18, from 4.7% in 1980 to 8.5% in 2014 [22, 23]. According to the WHO, between 2000 and 2016, there was a 5% increase in premature mortality from diabetes. In fact, adults with diabetes have a two- to threefold increased risk of heart attacks and strokes [23]. Portugal has one of highest prevalence rates of diabetes in Europe [24]. The latest data from the National Diabetes Observatory refers to a prevalence of 13.3% in citizens between 20 and 79 years old, with an estimate of undiagnosed diabetes of 5.8% in 2015 [25]. A systematic review and meta-analysis, which assessed community pharmacy-based screening for risk factors for diabetes and cardiovascular disease risk, has shown that pharmacies are feasible sites for screening for diabetes [26].

The PGEU reports 76% of countries in the region providing glucose measurement in community pharmacies, with 43% of countries also reporting to have diabetes management services [10]. In Portugal, a recent comprehensive review of pharmacy-based diabetes interventions reminded us that Portuguese pharmacies embraced the St. Vincent Declaration Action Program, a collaboration between the WHO Regional Office for Europe and the International Diabetes Federation Europe, as early as 1989 [27]. This initiative aimed at implementing a structured intervention plan for diabetes patients, comprising regular monitoring of blood glucose and blood pressure, as well as diabetes early detection, patient information, and education. In the following 25 years, several other interventions have been undertaken by pharmacists, with the National Association of Pharmacies (ANF) being the initiator or co-organizer of most of them. One of the most recent and notable ones led to the screening of 7007 patients in 225 pharmacies, with 24.05% being found to have a high or very high risk of diabetes, according to FINDRISK [28].

Although the contribution of Portuguese pharmacies to the objectives of the Portuguese National Health Service (P-NHS) led to the recognition of the Diabetes Management Program in 2003, being the first capitated payment for pharmacies to provide a full scope service, this payment has since been discontinued, and pharmacies continue to provide it with patients paying out-of-pocket, as is the case for blood pressure and cholesterol as well.

Arrhythmia

Atrial fibrillation (AF) is a cardiac arrhythmia responsible for one third of ischemic strokes. Early detection of AF plays an important role in preventing embolic stroke.

The contribution of pharmacists and pharmacies to the early identification of patients with arrhythmias is relatively new in Portugal. It was initiated in 2016 under an international collaboration led by the International Pharmacists for Anticoagulation Care Taskforce (iPACT), the Arrhythmia Alliance (A-A), and Atrial Fibrillation Association (AFA).

The first study involved only 5 countries, Portugal being one of them, and was later expanded in 2017 to a wider study involving 10 countries. In this larger study, pharmacists across 120 sites invited individuals (≥ 40 years; without anticoagulation therapy of AF) to participate in the awareness campaign. Participants agreeing were engaged in the early detection of AF (EDAF) using pulse palpation. Individuals with rhythm discrepancies were referred and prospectively assessed to gain information on the proportion of confirmed diagnosis, leading to estimate the detection rate. The country contributing the most valid data was Portugal, where a total of 958 were included. Overall, the study involved 4193 participants in the awareness campaign and 2762 in the EDAF event (mean age 65.3 ± 13.0), of whom 46.2% individuals were asymptomatic. The most common CHA2DS2-VASc risk factor was hypertension. Among 161 patients referred to a physician, feedback was obtained for 32 cases, of whom 12 new arrhythmia diagnoses were confirmed (five for AF, two for atrial flutter), all among elders (≥ 65 years) [29].

This study led to country-specific initiatives, which in some countries were more focused on community pharmacy, in other countries in hospital, community day-care centers, or in residential facilities.

The Portuguese experience resorted to three of these settings in the international study, although the largest contribution is unquestionably from community pharmacy. A research-led study was also conducted ad hoc in Portugal, aiming to identify not only the possibility to further expand the use of hand-held single lead electrocardiogram devices, and to evaluate their sensitivity and specificity, but also to study in-depth interprofessional collaboration and the referral pathways in place.

This study was initiated as an awareness campaign for 2 weeks, where individuals consenting to participation received a manual pulse check by the pharmacists, were clinically evaluated, and subsequently evaluated using AliveCor Kardia mobile. ECGs highlighted as possible AF were confirmed by the cardiologist and those signaled with abnormalities in cardiac rhythm were referred to their physician. The hand-held single lead electrocardiogram device's sensitivity and specificity was tested against the standard 12-lead ECG. This study included 205 individuals involved in the awareness and screening events. Mean age was 66 years (SD = 15) and hypertension was the most frequently reported condition ($n = 107$; 52.2%). Mean CHAD2DS2-VASc score was three (SD = 1.8). Cardiac irregularities were identified in 45 individuals, 14 confirmed to be new cases of AF (6.8%) by the cardiologist. The sensitivity and specificity were 90.9% and 97.4%, attesting to the use of this device (or any equivalent one) as a possible addition to ease the workflow and raise the pharmacists' confidence in referral. Data suggested that if interprofessional collaboration is ensured, suspect cases are adequately managed and in a timely way. Nonetheless, opportunities for improvement of the referral process were visible, particularly within primary care [30].

Addressing the major modifiable risk factors
Smoking

Smoking is a leading cause of cardiovascular disease morbidity and mortality, and has been shown to increase the risk of virtually all cardiovascular disease subtypes, at least doubling the risk of many, including acute myocardial infarction and heart failure [31]. What studies also show is that quitting smoking reduces the risk substantially, at least by 39% within 5 years [32]. The Canadian Agency for Drugs and Technologies in Health (CADTH) has recently published a report about pharmacist-led interventions for tobacco smoking cessation, in which it concluded that due to the limited availability and low quality of published evidence, their clinical effectiveness and cost-effectiveness remain uncertain [33]. However, another systematic review of community pharmacy-delivered smoking interventions, which included behavioral support and/or nicotine replacement therapy, found them to be effective and cost-effective in helping adults to stop smoking, particularly when compared with the usual care, although it was unable to ascertain which specific types of smoking cessation interventions were the most effective [34].

Consequently, according to the PGEU annual report, 70% of countries provide smoking-cessation services to help people give up smoking at national, regional, and local levels [10]. In Portugal, preliminary results of a smoking cessation pharmaceutical program implemented in community pharmacies, using an external pharmacist, showed positive results, with 23.2% of patients remaining abstinent after 1 year [35]. Although it is recognized that an increasing number of pharmacies are providing brief interventions to full programs for tobacco cessation, the actual number of pharmacies and the results of these interventions are not known. Unfortunately, this is also the case for most complex pharmacist interventions in community pharmacies, apart from point-of-care measurements, which are usually registered in the pharmacy software system, as patients are paying for them out-of-pocket. This also reflects the fact that the existing software is not designed to provide patient follow-up, thus making it hard to evaluate success rates and follow up on clinical outcomes.

Sedentary behavior

Apart from the Healthy Generation project, which has already been described above, the role of community pharmacies in promoting physical activity has led to fewer publications. It is usually included as part of the nonpharmacological recommendations given in the context of cardiovascular diseases, but it is less structured and therefore very seldom recorded. In a recent survey aimed at ascertaining pharmacists' knowledge, attitudes, and behaviors, which obtained responses from about 5% of pharmacists, 80% of participants reported promoting physical activity in their daily routine [36]. The most frequent intervention was verbal counselling by 90% of participants, with walking being the most promoted activity, in 95% of cases. Lifestyle changes have been associated with a decreasing risk for cardiovascular events, and pharmacists' counselling has been found to result in significant lifestyle changes and weight loss in overweight individuals, particularly after screening for type 2 diabetes [37]. For Portuguese pharmacists to be better prepared to address this topic, further education, be it at under-graduate or post-graduate level, is necessary [38].

Overweight and obesity

According to the OECD's latest "Health at a Glance" report, life expectancy gains have slowed recently across most countries, with one of the causes being the rising levels of obesity and diabetes, which have made it difficult to maintain progress in decreasing cardiovascular mortality [39]. Portugal is in fifth place within the OECD countries with the highest prevalence of obesity, at 67.6% in the population over 15 years old with BMI ≥ 25, whereas the OECD average is at 55.6%. In terms of childhood obesity, between 2008 and 2019, Portugal showed an inverted trend in the prevalence of overweight and childhood obesity, with an 8.3% reduction in the prevalence of overweight children (37.9%–29.6%) and childhood obesity from 15.3% in 2008 to 12.0% (− 3.3%) in 2019 [40]. While these numbers are encouraging, still in 2018/2019, 15.3% of 8-year-old children were obese, including 5.4% with severe obesity. Therefore, initiatives like the Healthy Generation, described above, remain pertinent, but are most likely not to produce immediate results for individuals who already need to manage weight in order to prevent cardiovascular events.

International systematic reviews that have looked at pharmacy-based efforts for weight and lifestyle management, be it pharmacist-led or collaborative efforts, have shown promising results, although many have failed to provide significant evidence of the pharmacist providing these services [34, 41, 42]. When addressed specifically to persons at risk of diabetes, following a screening intervention in pharmacies, participants showed significant weight loss 3 months after screening, with a further weight reduction observed at 1 year follow up [37]. These results are informative, as they may imply that counselling is most effective when done immediately after risk factors are identified.

In Portugal, there is legislation that allows nutritionists to provide services in community pharmacies, which has led to a significant (although empirical) number of pharmacies providing dietary interventions. Results are still limited, but one study that involved 2047 patients, 88.3% of which were overweight, showed that after a dietary intervention provided by nutritionists in 140 pharmacies around Portugal, 21.9% had reduced their initial body weight by more than 5% after 6 months [43].

Harmful use of alcohol

Among the modifiable risk factors, this is probably the area where pharmacists have been least engaged. A recent systematic review identified the effectiveness of community pharmacy interventions to manage alcohol misuse, smoking cessation, and weight loss. Results from 24 studies show that only two were specifically targeted at harmful alcohol use. In addition to the small number, it was also reported that the evidence of community-pharmacy short and brief interventions (SBI) for alcohol was considered insufficient at the time.

Probably the most relevant aspect mentioned for alcohol in this review is the suggestion that the characteristics of people likely to access such services in pharmacies are different from those searching other settings for alcohol management. Frequently, the participants were found to have low socioeconomic status and belong to an ethnic minority [34]. In both referred studies, the identification of individuals that could benefit from a pharmacist's intervention was made using a standardized questionnaire leading to a score indicating possible harmful alcohol use but not dependence. The study by Watson and Stewart resorted to FAST and was focused on delivering SBI for a period of 6 months [44]. A study by Dhital et al. used the AUDIT tool to identify individuals and then also developed SBI, but only for 3 months [45]. Because many of the possible effective interventions to be delivered in pharmacy practice require the institution of prescription medication, more commonly in the setting the term "screening, brief intervention, and referral to treatment" (SBIRT) has been used [46].

To our knowledge, there is no published research in Portugal focusing on pharmacists' interventions in this area. Most initiatives have been politically led, inclusive of all professions, and perhaps for all these reasons, have failed to achieve any practical implementation. The truth is that pharmacists are not sufficiently trained to deal with harmful alcohol use and would benefit from additional education for successful interventions. This could ideally take a bottom-up approach and involve functional referral systems through which the pharmacists can intervene in specific areas (e.g., early identification and medicines management) and liaise with their counterparts in other areas (e.g., physicians for confirmation of diagnosis and treatment institution; social care for homeless and other identical needs that may hinder full success of the intervention).

Interventions focusing on medicines optimization, including the management of medication adherence

Pharmaceutical care involves patient-centered pharmacist activity to improve medicines management by patients and encompasses a variety of specific services that may be delivered at one point in time or, ideally, throughout time. Previous studies have shown that the implementation of pharmaceutical care in Europe is suboptimal, although increasing in more recent years [47, 48]. A specific study conducted in Portugal demonstrated an evolution in the provision of pharmaceutical care between 2006 and 2012, as could be expected by the legal recognition of the service and its essence. [49–51]. One of the services that is very much centered on medicines optimization, and which falls under the broad scope of pharmaceutical care, is medication review. According to the PGEU, 53% of countries provide medication review type 2 in pharmacies [10]. Supplementary research data suggests that 55.9% of the countries provide at least one type of medication review, although this number decreases as the complexity of the service increases. Specifically, out of the 44 countries assessed, medication review type 1 and type 2A were reported, respectively, by 13 and 14 countries, and going down to two and four countries, respectively, for types 2B and 3 [52]. Even though all these types are valuable, if one is to work directly with the patient, type 2A is the most relevant as it provides the pharmacist with the opportunity to interact directly with the patient (type 3 is also applicable). This is most important when focusing on medication adherence and on enabling interventions.

Medication adherence has been one of the services where pharmacists have been strongly investing by developing tailor-made solutions and by engaging in different sorts of programs. According to the PGEU, 37% of countries have manual preparation of personalized dosage systems in pharmacies [10]. Already 6 years ago, individual Portuguese community pharmacists were publishing results of programs resorting to multicompartment adherence aids to optimize medication for the elderly [53]. Much earlier than that, innovative technologies to support medication adherence among hypertensive patients had also been tested in community pharmacies and demonstrated differences between intervention and control groups [54]. With the boom of smartphones also reaching older people, such technologies are no longer innovative, as their sole benefit was reminding patients about the time of intake. Beyond cardiovascular diseases, other technologies have been tested in Portuguese community pharmacies, including the use of medication event monitoring systems (MEMs) [55], showing that such a device, in addition to being an accurate measure of adherence, is also an intervention in itself, as a result of the Hawthorne effect, particularly in the first phases of use.

Medication nonadherence has been demonstrated to be a reason for concern worldwide, with various consequences at the clinical, humanistic, and economic level. Portugal is no exception and previous studies undertaken in community pharmacy, focusing on chronic medication users, highlighted 22.8% as being primary nonadherers, i.e., those that do not even fill or refill their prescription. However, when considering various forms of nonadherence, more than 50% of all patients reported engaging in some sort of change to the prescribed regimen [56]. Similar research undertaken some years later and focusing on the elderly additionally showed that almost 30% of patients stopped purchasing treatments for financial reasons and adopted alternatives to reduce costs, including generic substitution, but also ceasing therapy and increasing the interdose interval [57].

Being aware that there is a need, as shown by different studies, the government announced in 2018 the intention to reinforce medication adherence as an area for privileged pharmacist's intervention. This has been published in a legal decree, updating the previous one issued in 2007, where it states as one of the possible services to be provided in community pharmacy "Adherence programmes, medicines reconciliation, services making use of multicompartment aids, health education programmes for the use of medical devices." [58] These appear in addition to "pharmaceutical care programmes," which obviously also contribute to optimizing medication therapy and may contain aspects of direct patient education to improve medication use.

Working collaboratively to achieve optimal therapy

A systematic review investigating the effectiveness of screening for cardiovascular disease risk factors in a community pharmacy setting, which included 16 studies, concluded that a significant number of previously unknown cases were identified, but that a significant number of referred high-risk participants did not visit their physician for follow up [26]. This compromises one of the objectives of the intervention, which is to reduce time between symptom/risk onset and diagnosis. This attrition is particularly relevant in the Portuguese context, where the electronic health record (EHR) is not available for community pharmacists to read and write, and communication with the physician is not facilitated by electronic means. There have been a few pilot projects that tested communication between community pharmacies and healthcare centers, but these have not been rolled out to all community pharmacies yet [15, 59]. However, the Portuguese Pharmaceutical Society has been advocating for access to the Portuguese Patient Health Data Platform, and it seems likely that this will occur in the future, facilitating referrals after screening interventions. In any case, even if (or when) information obtained at the pharmacy is made more easily accessible to the physician, interprofessional work implies the establishment of a trusting relationship, which can be facilitated by the implementation of multimodal strategies that address facilitators, i.e., joint training [60, 61].

The private nature of community pharmacies has also been depicted as a challenge in considering these structures as part of the P-NHS, requiring a paradigm change by the government to regard private providers as a supplementary or complementary source of healthcare [62]. Ribeiro et al. argue that an ongoing pilot service directed at people living with multimorbidity, involving co-located primary care pharmacists, general practitioners, and nurses, represents an opportunity to foster the integration of community pharmacies in the P-NHS. In this service, after being signaled by primary care pharmacists, patients can be referred to their community pharmacist for follow-up and continuity of care. There are still no results from this intervention, but a previous study on a collaborative pharmacotherapy follow-up service in primary care showed a significant clinical improvement in patients receiving the service, when compared to a control group [13].

Legislation in Portugal allows community pharmacies to integrate other healthcare professionals, such as nurses and nutritionists, in the pharmacy team, to provide direct patient services. A qualitative study performed at two community pharmacies showed a high degree of patient satisfaction about the availability of nutrition consultations in pharmacies, particularly considering the pharmacies' accessibility and proximity [63]. In addition, having these services in the pharmacy allows for internal referrals, which has a positive impact on the patient pathway [64, 65]. To ensure seamless care in community pharmacies within this multidisciplinary approach, the Nutrition Society, which is the regulatory organization for nutritionists in Portugal, has produced a professional orientation guideline that describes how these professionals should collaborate with the pharmacy team, as well as the responsibilities of each professional [66].

Liaising with social care in special population groups

Some of the barriers identified in medication use when the pharmacist works closely with patients may benefit from referral to social care. These include those situations where patients cannot afford the co-payment of their medications or even the payment of a service currently not remunerated by the government. This support may also be beneficial in other more extreme situations, where patients for instance do not even have a refrigerator to store their insulin, or when their mental state does not allow them to know which day of the week it is. There is no structured national procedure for referring these cases to social care. However, there are many local agreements made between community pharmacies and the town hall that, depending on the municipalities, may have different arrangements in place. One example occurs in Cascais where the town hall signals cases of extreme poverty that are chronic medication users, referring the person to the local pharmacy[a]. The person is identified by presenting a special formulary, similar to a prescription but issued by the town hall, where all the medications and products needed are listed (it may include, for instance, newborns feeding milk) and given for free to the person. At the end of the month, the pharmacy issues a bill to the town hall and periodic payments are made, which also benefit from a reduction in the pharmacy's profit margin.

Conclusion

Portuguese pharmacists have long been active in health promotion, disease prevention, and in medicines management for cardiovascular health. Their interventions are extensive, both in scope and in population reached. The main drawback seems to be a limited culture for documenting interventions and results, mostly in the scientific and international literature, often limiting themselves to showcase their good practices in conferences. This chapter has summarized some of the most relevant areas where pharmacists have been active; some of these found in the grey literature. Naturally, some individual and valuable interventions developed in local contexts will have been missed. Notwithstanding, the road is long, and this is a mere contribution to demonstrate the value of Portuguese pharmacists in the fight against cardiovascular ill-health (Table 1).

---

[a] https://www.cascais.pt/projeto/protocolo-farmacias-do-concelho-de-cascais.

Table 1 Summary of studies undertaken in Portugal demonstrating impact of pharmacists' interventions.

Author	Objectives	Design	Sample	Country	Summary of results
Garção et al. [11]	To evaluate the impact of a pharmaceutical care program on the results of antihypertensive drug therapy	Randomized, controlled study, 6-month follow-up	100 Hypertensive patients (50 in the intervention —IG —and 50 in the control group—CG) in one community pharmacy	Portugal	Prevalence of uncontrolled blood pressure decreased by 77.4% in the IG ($P < .0001$) and by 10.3% in the CG ($P = .48$). 24 out of 29 (83%) DRPs were resolved. Around 40% of potential DRPs were prevented
Morgado et al. [12]	To evaluate if a pharmaceutical care program could improve antihypertensive medication adherence and blood pressure control	Randomized, controlled study	197 Hypertensive patients (99 in the CG and 98 in the IG) visiting a secondary care hypertension/ dyslipidemia outpatient clinic	Portugal	Blood pressure control was higher in the IG ($P = .005$) at the end of the study. Medication adherence was also significantly higher in the IG at the end of the study (74.5% vs 57.6%, $P = .012$)

| Condinho et al. [13] | To underline the clinical added value for hypertensive patients that results from pharmacist–physician collaborations | Randomized, controlled study | 34 Hypertensive patients from a family health unit (17 in the IG and 17 in the GC) | Portugal | The IG achieved mean reductions of 28.85±5.90 mmHg (P<.0005) and 11.23±2.75 mmHg (P<.005) in their systolic and diastolic blood pressure, respectively. The CG had improvements of 18.63±6.44 mmHg (P=.011) in systolic blood pressure and 9.03±2.63 mmHg (P<.005) in diastolic blood pressure. The therapeutic goals were achieved for 11 of the 13 initially uncontrolled patients in IG and for eight of the 13 patients in the GC |
| Condinho et al. [35] | To assess the effectiveness of implementing pharmaceutical care services in Portuguese community pharmacies using an outsourcing-based regimen | Longitudinal retrospective analysis of patient records | 510 Patients enrolled in 20 community pharmacies | Portugal | There was an increase in the percentage of patients achieving therapeutic goals: for cholesterol (54.3% at baseline to 71.3% after follow-up); hypertension (44.8%–84.3%); diabetes (from 26.2% to 54.5%). All clinical parameter differences were significant (P<.001) |

Continued

Table 1 Summary of studies undertaken in Portugal demonstrating impact of pharmacists' interventions—cont'd

Author	Objectives	Design	Sample	Country	Summary of results
Costa et al. [15, 27]	To assess the effectiveness, process, and patient experience/satisfaction of a collaborative care pilot between community pharmacies and a healthcare center; to test the feasibility of collecting a standard set of indicators in real world patients	Multicenter quasiexperimental controlled trial	P-NHS Primary Care Unit patients ≥18 years on medication for hypertension and/or hyperlipidemia	Portugal	In progress
de Oliveira Martins et al. [18]	To estimate the 10-year risk of fatal CVD in Portuguese adults; to assess the prevalence of major cardiovascular risk factors, according to the SCORE risk prediction system	Cross-sectional survey	1043 Individuals (≥40 and ≤65 years old) from 60 community pharmacies	Portugal	About 20% of the studied adults were at high risk, of which 39.4% were asymptomatic. The prevalence of main CV risk factors were: hypertension—54.8%; hypercholesterolemia—63.1%, diabetes—13.4%; smoking—10.4%; and obesity—29.0%

Study	Aim	Study design	Participants	Country	Results
Rosa et al. [19]	To describe and assess the capacity of a group of pharmacies in organizing campaigns on CV risk assessment; to characterize participants according to their CV risk factors	Cross-sectional survey	1268 Individuals from 120 community pharmacies; 634 ($\geq$40 and $\leq$65 years old) for which SCORE risk prediction system was used	Portugal	Among participants, 12.0% were smokers, 48.0% and 45.0% had, respectively; total cholesterol and systolic blood pressure values above reference values; 73.0% an increased BMI. For individuals assessed by SCORE, 59.0% had moderate risk; 4.0% high risk; and 12.4% very high risk for CVD
Jacinto et al. [28]	To identify people at risk of diabetes	Cross-sectional survey	7007 Participants from 295 community pharmacies	Portugal	24.0% of participants had high or very high risk of developing diabetes type 2 within the next 10 years
Costa et al. [29]	To test a model for raising awareness of atrial fibrillation (AF) involving pharmacists globally; and to identify barriers and enablers to its implementation	Prospective study, 3-month follow-up	4193 Participants in the awareness campaign; 2762 participants in AF screening event, from 120 sites in 10 different countries	10 Countries, including Portugal	Among 161 patients referred to physician, feedback was obtained for 32 cases, of which 12 new arrhythmia diagnoses were confirmed (5 for AF; 2 for atrial flutter). Qualitative data suggested a local champion to enable pharmacists' success; technology-enhanced engagement amongst patients; increased pharmacists' confidence in referring to physicians; and interprofessional collaboration

Continued

Table 1 Summary of studies undertaken in Portugal demonstrating impact of pharmacists' interventions—cont'd

Author	Objectives	Design	Sample	Country	Summary of results
Cunha et al. [30]	To test the feasibility of an awareness event including opportunistic screening for atrial fibrillation; to test the reliability of the innovative portable electrocardiogram (ECG) device used	Prospective study, 3-month follow-up	223 Participants, of which 205 were screened in a community pharmacy	Portugal	Cardiac irregularities were identified in 45 individuals, 14 confirmed to be new cases of AF (6.8%) by the cardiologist. The sensitivity and specificity of the device used were 90.9% and 97.4%, respectively (against 12-lead ECG)
Condinho et al. [35]	To report the preliminary results of a study to assess the effectiveness of a smoking cessation program delivered in Portuguese community pharmacies using an outsourcing-based regimen	Longitudinal, retrospective study	69 Smokers (among which 17 dropped out in the first consultation and were excluded)	Portugal	At 1 month after the quit date, 37 patients were abstinent (53.6%); at 6 months, 24 (34.8%); and at 1 year, 16 patients (23.2%)

Custódio et al. [36]	To characterize physical activity promotion actions of pharmacists taking place in Portuguese pharmacies; and to explore barriers for implementation	Cross-sectional survey	396 Community pharmacists	Portugal	80% of pharmacists promote physical activity in their daily routine, most frequently through verbal counselling (90%), walking being the most advised activity (95%). More than 90% of pharmacists believe this activity is important or very important. Main barriers were lack of time, resources or interest by costumers
Ramos et al. [43]	To evaluate the prevalence of overweight and obesity in Portuguese adults and their correlation with comorbidities; to verify the impact of a dietary intervention, conducted by nutritionists in community pharmacies, on overweight and obesity	Before and after study, with 6-month follow-up	2047 Patients	Portugal	After dietary intervention, 21.9% of patients reduced more than 5% their initial weight; prevalence of normal weight increased from 10.1% to 32.9%

Continued

Table 1 Summary of studies undertaken in Portugal demonstrating impact of pharmacists' interventions—cont'd

Author	Objectives	Design	Sample	Country	Summary of results
Costa et al. [48]	To assess the evolution of pharmaceutical care provision within community pharmacy in Europe	Cross-sectional study resorting to the Behavioral Pharmaceutical Care Scale (BPCS), with repeated measures in 2006 and 2012	5208 Community pharmacists from 16 countries (2012)	16 Countries involved, where 8 answered both assessments, including Portugal	The provision of comprehensive pharmaceutical care has slightly improved in all European countries that participated in both editions of the study. There was also a wider country uptake, indicating spread of the concept
Martins et al. [51]	To assess the level of implementation of pharmaceutical care services in Portugal; to characterize workforce, infrastructure, and type of services offered in Portuguese pharmacies; and to analyze the evolution of these between 2006 and 2012	Cross-sectional survey, using the Behavioral Pharmaceutical Care Scale (BPCS)	686 Community pharmacies	Portugal	Most prevalent services were measurement of blood pressure (99.9%) and blood glucose (99.0%). There was a significant increase in the provision of new services, including nutritional appointments (63.2%) and podiatry (40.7%). BPCS score increased from 76.5 to 86.3, indicating a greater offer of pharmaceutical care services

| Mosca et al. [53] | To assess the impact of using multicompartment compliance aids (MCAs) in self-reported adherence and clinical biomarkers of elderly patients followed in a community pharmacy | Prospective, nonrandomized, controlled study | 54 Patients aged between 65 and 90 years from one community pharmacy | Portugal | Significant improvements in the IG, but not in CG, for glycaemia ($P<.001$), HDL-c ($P=.018$), systolic ($P<.001$), and diastolic ($P=.012$) BP. All differences became nonsignificant when considering "time in follow-up," except for systolic BP |
| Costa et al. [54] | To evaluate the effect of reminder cards on medication adherence in people taking antihypertensives | Open label multipharmacy study, 4-month follow-up | Patients aged 30–74 prescribed angiotensin–converting enzyme inhibitor (ACEI) in monotherapy taken once daily were included IG: 35 patients; CG: 36 patients | Portugal; pharmacies from Lisbon and Porto | Adherence was higher in IG at end of study (97.3% IG vs 87.3% CG; $P<.011$) but no differences in blood pressure control were noted ($P>.05$) |

Continued

Table 1 Summary of studies undertaken in Portugal demonstrating impact of pharmacists' interventions—cont'd

Author	Objectives	Design	Sample	Country	Summary of results
Martins et al. [55]	To test a novel method of compliance measurement in Portuguese community pharmacy in *Helicobacter pylori* patients	Case series design with prospective measurements	23 Patients from 17 community pharmacies	Portugal	The use of electronic devices for measuring compliance to *H. pylori* eradication therapy was feasible, since no patient refused to participate; there were no patient drop-outs, and no patients damaging the devices during the study
Costa et al. [56]	To determine the prevalence of nonadherence in chronic medication users (primary and secondary)	Cross-sectional study	375 Patients recruited in 32 pharmacies. Primary nonadherence judged by prescription refill and secondary by questionnaire (MAT)	Portugal	Primary nonadherence identified in 22.8% of patients; most commonly reported reason was having "leftovers" or financial problems. Primary nonadherence was associated with low income ($P = .026$). Secondary nonadherence was detected in over 50% (reaching 65% in hypertension), with unintentional nonadherence higher

Costa et al. [57]	To evaluate the perceived effects of crises on elderly patients' access to medicines and medical care, and its implications on medicine-taking behavior	Cross-sectional study	Self-administered questionnaire applied to 1231 elderly chronic medication users	Portugal	27.3% of patients had stopped using treatments or health services in the previous year for financial motives. Almost 30% of patients stopped purchasing prescribed medicines. The most common strategy developed to cope with increasing costs of medicines was generic substitution, but around 15% of patients also stopped taking their medication or started saving by increasing the interdose interval

Continued

Table 1 Summary of studies undertaken in Portugal demonstrating impact of pharmacists' interventions—cont'd

Author	Objectives	Design	Sample	Country	Summary of results
Miranda et al. [59]	To provide an overview of pharmacy interventions (therapeutic notes–TN) using a direct communication channel between pharmacists and physicians, supported by a connection established between the dispensing and prescribing software systems	Prospective 4-month pilot-study	60 Pharmacies were invited to the pilot, out of which 23 sent TN	Portugal	34 pharmacists sent a total of 259 TN. 226 TN (87%) were related to nondispenses and 33 (13%) related to dispenses. 33% of TN obtained feedback from physician, and 39% were considered useful. The most frequent TN ($n = 83$) was "already had the medicine at home." Severe interactions were reported in 12 TN

| Paulino et al. [60] | To explore the opinions and experiences of a range of stakeholders on interprofessional working relationships between community pharmacists and physicians | Secondary analysis of qualitative datasets obtained for a PhD and an MSc program | 5 Qualitative studies included: (1) 17 community pharmacists; (2) 8 professional leaders; (3) 14 community pharmacists; (4) 21 patients; (5) 12 physicians | Portugal | Facilitators identified to establish a fruitful working relationship were increased role awareness; existence of formal agreements or protocols; and data sharing. Findings suggest that a multimodal strategy that addresses these factors, involving both top-down and bottom-up approaches, is needed |
| Borralho et al. [63] | To characterize the experience of people attending nutrition consultations provided by nutritionists at two different pharmacies and to understand their perception of the role community pharmacists may have in weight management | Cross-sectional | 10 Participants, users of nutrition services from two community pharmacies | Portugal | There is a general satisfaction with the service. The biggest advantages were accessibility and low cost. The biggest disadvantage was the price of nutritional supplements. Lack of motivation was seen as a major impediment to continue with the nutrition consultations. 50% of participants disagreed with the idea of pharmacists providing the service on their own |

Continued

Table 1 Summary of studies undertaken in Portugal demonstrating impact of pharmacists' interventions—cont'd

Author	Objectives	Design	Sample	Country	Summary of results
Paulino et al. [64]	To describe the implementation of a service that promotes early identification of people at risk of developing diabetes and provides patient follow-up for people with diabetes, in a group of community pharmacies; to assess the uptake of the service by community pharmacies	Observational retrospective study, through patient record analysis	Early identification of people at risk through FindRisk: 196 participants from 26 pharmacies Educational sessions: 851 participants Patient follow-up service for people with diabetes: 106 patients from 31 pharmacies	Portugal	Early identification of people at risk: 20.9% of participants had moderate risk, 23.0% high risk, and 5.6% very high risk to develop diabetes in 10 years. Patient follow-up service for people with diabetes: the most prevalent interventions were adherence promotion (75.0%), counselling on the correct use of medicines (72.4%) and healthy eating (70.7%). The most common referrals were for nutrition and diabetic foot consultations (29.3%) and for a subsequent follow-up in a pharmaceutical consultation (25.0%)
Pinto et al. [65]	To describe a Diabetic Foot Service in a group of community pharmacies and characterize the profile of service users	Observational retrospective study, through patient record analysis	1213 Patients with diabetes who used the Diabetic Foot Service in 115 community pharmacies	Portugal	More than a quarter of patients (28.5%, $n = 346$) had risk of ulceration and amputation (Grade 1: $n = 151$; Grade 2: $n = 173$; Grade 3: $n = 22$)

References

[1] World Health Organization. Noncommunicable diseases global monitoring framework: indicator definitions and specifications. Geneva: World Health Organization; 2014.

[2] International Pharmaceutical Federation (FIP). Beating non-communicable diseases in the community—the contribution of pharmacists. The Hague: FIP; 2019.

[3] Peterson GM, Fitzmaurice KD, Kruup H, et al. Cardiovascular risk screening program in Australian community pharmacies. Pharm World Sci 2010;32. 373e80.

[4] Krass I, Mitchell B, Song YJ, et al. Diabetes medication assistance service stage 1: impact and sustainability of glycaemic and lipids control in patients with type 2 diabetes. Diabet Med 2011;28:987e93.

[5] Martins S, van Mil JWF, Costa FA. The organizational framework of community pharmacies in Europe. Int J Clin Pharm 2015;37(5):896–905.

[6] Soares IB, Imfeld-Isenegger TL, Makovec UN, Horvat N, Kos M, Arnet I, Hersberger KE, Costa FA. A survey to assess the availability, implementation rate and remuneration of pharmacist-led cognitive services in Europe. Res Social Adm Pharm 2020;16:41–7.

[7] Lim SS, Vos T, Flaxman AD, et al. A comparative risk assessment of burden of disease and injury attributable to 67 risk factors and risk factor clusters in 21 regions, 1990-2010: a systematic analysis for the Global Burden of Disease Study 2010. Lancet 2012;380(9859):2224–60.

[8] Rodrigues AP, Gaio V, Kislaya I, Graff-Iversen S, Cordeiro E, Silva AC, Namorado S, Barreto M, Gil AP, Antunes L, Santos A. Prevalência de hipertensão arterial em Portugal: resultados do Primeiro Inquérito Nacional com Exame Físico (INSEF 2015). Observações_Boletim Epidemiológico. vol. 2nd series, esp. 9, (2015) pp. 11-14.

[9] World Health Organization. Pharmacy-based hypertension management model: protocol and guidelines: a joint CINDI/EuroPharm Forum project. Copenhagen: WHO Regional Office for Europe; 2005.

[10] Pharmaceutical Group of the European Union. Guaranteeing continued access to medicines [annual report]. Brussels: s.n; 2018.

[11] Garção JA, Cabrita J. Evaluation of a pharmaceutical care program for hypertensive patients in rural Portugal. J Am Pharm Assoc (1996) 2002;42(6):858–64.

[12] Morgado M, Rolo S, Castelo-Branco M. Pharmacist intervention program to enhance hypertension control: a randomised controlled trial. Int J Clin Pharm 2011;33(1):132–40.

[13] Condinho M, Sá J, Eliseu A, Figueiredo IV, Sinogas C. Clinical impact of a pharmaceutical care programme developed in a family health unit: results of a pharmacist-physician collaboration in the treatment of hypertensive patients. Rev Port Farmacoter 2016;8:164–71.

[14] Atención Farmacéutica, Lda. Assessing the effects on clinical outcomes of an outsourced pharmaceutical care service in Portuguese community pharmacies. Latin Am J Pharm 2015;34(4):782–9.

[15] Costa S, Rodrigues AT, Biscaia JS, Romano S, Guerreiro JP, Heudtlass P, Cary M, Romão M, Miranda AC, Martins AP, Bento AS. Effectiveness of a collaborative care intervention between pharmacies and primary care targeting hypertension and hyperlipidemia: a multicentre quasi-experimental controlled trial (USFarmácia). Revista Portuguesa de Farmacoterapia 2019;11(Suppl 1). S33-4.

[16] Haggerty L, Tran D. Cholesterol point-of-care testing for community pharmacies: a review of the current literature. J Pharm Pract 2017;30(4):451–8.

[17] Direção Geral da Saúde. Norma n° 005/2013 de 19/03/2013, atualizada a 21/01/2015: Avaliação do Risco Cardiovascular SCORE [Systematic Coronary Risk Evaluation]. Lisboa : s.n., 2015. 005/2013.

[18] de Oliveira Martins S, e Silva PS, Papoila AL, Caramona M, van Mil JW, Cabrita J. Assessment of global cardiovascular risk and risk factors in Portugal according to the SCORE® model. J Public Health 2008;16(5):361–7.

[19] Rosa M, Pinto AL, Teixeira ML, Maximiano S, Soares P, Noronha M, Paulino E. Pharmacists' interventions in cardiovascular disease awareness and assessment. Stockholm: FIP PSWC; 2017.

[20] Pousinho S, Morgado M, Falcão A, Alves G. Pharmacist interventions in the management of type 2 diabetes mellitus: a systematic review of randomized controlled trials. J Manag Care Spec Pharm 2016;22(5):493–515.[21]Australian and Portuguese pharmacy initiatives win international awards. Available at. Pharm J 2016.Australian and Portuguese pharmacy initiatives win international awards. Available at. Pharm J 2016.

[22] OECD/European Union. Diabetes prevalence. In: Health at a glance: Europe 2018: State of health in the EU cycle. Paris/European Union, Brussels: OECD Publishing; 2018.

[23] The Emerging Risk Factors Collaboration. Diabetes mellitus, fasting blood glucose concentration, and risk of vascular disease: a collaborative meta-analysis of 102 prospective studies. The Lancet 2010;375(9733):2215–22.[24]Programa Nacional para a diabetes 2018.Programa Nacional para a diabetes 2018.

[25] Sociedade Portuguesa de Diabetologia. Diabetes: Factos e Números–O Ano de 2015. – Relatório Anual do Observatório Nacional da Diabetes. Lisboa: Sociedade Portuguesa de Diabetologia; 2016.

[26] Willis A, Rivers P, Gray LJ, Davies M, Khunti K. The effectiveness of screening for diabetes and cardiovascular disease risk factors in a community pharmacy setting. PLoS One 2014;9(4). e91157.

[27] Costa S, Horta MR, Santos R, Mendes Z, Jacinto I, Guerreiro J, Cary M, Miranda A, Helling DK, Martins AP. Diabetes policies and pharmacy-based diabetes interventions in Portugal: a comprehensive review. 2019. J Pharm Policy Pract 2019;12(1):5.

[28] Jacinto I, Horta R, Santos R, Cary M, Guerreiro JP, Torre C, Costa S, editors. World diabetes month campaign in Portuguese pharmacies. Poster presented at the 76th Annual Congress of FIP, Buenos Aires; 2016.

[29] Costa FA, Lee V, Tous S, Papastergiou J, Griffiths D, Chaumais M-C, Hersberger KE, Viola R, Mala-Ladova K, Paulino E, Lobban T, Neubeck L, Freedman B, Antoniou S. Awareness campaigns of atrial fibrillation as an opportunity for early detection by pharmacists- an international cross-sectional study. J Thromb Thrombolysis 2020;49:606–17.

[30] Cunha S, Antunes E, Antoniou S, Fernandez-Llimós F, Relvas R, Tiago S, et al. Raising awareness and early detection of atrial fibrillation, an experience resorting to innovative technology and interprofessional collaboration. Res Social Adm Pharm 2020;16(6):787–92.

[31] Banks E, Joshy G, Korda RJ, Stavreski B, Soga K, Egger S, Day C, Clarke NE, Lewington S, Lopez AD. Tobacco smoking and risk of 36 cardiovascular disease subtypes: fatal and non-fatal outcomes in a large prospective Australian study. BMC Med 2019;17(1):128.

[32] Duncan MS, Freiberg MS, Greevy RA, Kundu S, Vasan RS, Tindle HA. Association of smoking cessation with subsequent risk of cardiovascular disease. JAMA 2019;322(7):642–50.

[33] Brett K, Yeung SS, Ford C. Pharmacist-led interventions for tobacco smoking cessation: a review of clinical effectiveness and cost-effectiveness. [Internet]. Ottawa, ON: Canadian Agency for Drugs and Technologies in Health; 2019.

[34] Brown TJ, Todd A, O'Malley CL, et al. Community pharmacy interventions for public health priorities: a systematic review of community pharmacy-delivered smoking, alcohol and weight management interventions. Southampton, United Kingdom: NIHR Journals Library; 2016.

[35] Condinho M, Fernandez-Llimos F, Figueiredo IV, Sinogas C. Smoking cessation in a community pharmacy: preliminary results of a pharmaceutical care programme. Vitae 2015;22(1):42–6.

[36] Custódio RE. Physical activity promotion in the Portuguese pharmacies: a survey of knowledge, attitudes and behaviours of pharmacists. MSc Dissertation in Exercise and Health, Lisboa: University of Lisbon; 2019.

[37] Botomino A, Bruppacher R, Krähenbühl S, Hersberger KE. Change of body weight and lifestyle of persons at risk for diabetes after screening and counselling in pharmacies. Pharm World Sci 2008;30(3):222–6.

[38] Kotecki JE, Clayton BD. Educating pharmacy students about nutrition and physical activity counseling. Am J Health Educ 2003;34(1):34–40.

[39] OECD. Health at a glance 2019: OECD indicators. Paris: OECD Publishing; 2019.[40]Childhood Obesity Surveillance Initiative: COSI Portugal—Factsheet 2019.Childhood Obesity Surveillance Initiative: COSI Portugal—Factsheet 2019.

[41] O'Neal KS, Crosby KM. What is the role of the pharmacist in obesity management? Current Obesity Reports 2014;3(3):298–306.

[42] Jordan MA, Harmon J. Pharmacist interventions for obesity: improving treatment adherence and patient outcomes. Integr Pharm Res Prac 2015;4:79.

[43] Ramos D, Oliveira L, Pinheiro R, Barreirinhas S, Rosa M, Paulino E. Dietary intervention for overweight and obese patients followed in Portuguese community pharmacies. Clin Nutr 2018;37:S144.

[44] Watson MC, Stewart D. Screening and brief interventions for alcohol misuse delivered in the community pharmacy setting: a pilot study. Aberdeen: Chief Scientist Office; 2011.

[45] Dhital R, Norman I, Whittlesea C, Murrells T, McCambridge J. The effectiveness of brief alcohol interventions delivered by community pharmacists: randomised controlled trial. Addiction 2015;110:1586–94.

[46] Newhouse R, Janney M, Gilbert A, et al. Study protocol testing toolkit versus usual care for implementation of screening, brief intervention, referral to treatment in hospitals: a phased cluster randomized approach. Addict Sci Clin Pract 2018;13(1):28.

[47] Hughes CM, Hawwa AF, Scullin C, Anderson C, Bernsten CB, Bjornsdóttir I, Cordina MA, Costa FA, et al. Provision of pharmaceutical care by community pharmacists: a comparison across Europe. Pharm World Sci 2010;32(4):472–87.

[48] Costa F, et al. Provision of pharmaceutical care by community pharmacists across Europe: is it developing and spreading? J Eval Clin Prac 2017;23(6):1336–47.

[49] Ministério da Saúde. Decreto-Lei nº 307/2007. [Diário da República] Lisboa: s.n. 2007.

[50] Ministério da Saúde. Portaria n.º 1429/2007. [Diário da República] Lisboa : s.n. 2007.

[51] Martins S, Costa FA, Caramona M. Implementação de Cuidados Farmacêuticos em Portugal, 6 anos depois. Revista Portuguesa de Farmacoterapia 2013;5(4):255–63.

[52] Imfeld-Isenegger TL, Soares IB, Makovec UN, Horvat N, Kos M, van Mil JWF, et al. Pharmacist-led medication review procedures: a survey across Europe. Res Social Adm Pharm 2020;16(8):1057–66.

[53] Mosca C, Castel-Branco MM, Ribeiro-Rama AC, Caramona MM, Fernandez-Llimos F, Figueiredo IV. Assessing the impact of multi-compartment compliance aids on clinical outcomes in the elderly: a pilot study. Int J Clin Pharm 2014;36:98–104.

[54] Costa F, Guerreiro JP, Melo M, Miranda AC, Martins AP, Garção J, Madureira B. Effect or reminder cards on compliance with antihypertensive medication. Int J Pharm Pract 2005;3:205–11.

[55] Martins AP, Ferreira AF, Costa FA, Cabrita J. How to measure (or not) compliance to eradication therapy? Pharm Pract 2006;4(2):88–94.

[56] Costa FA, Pedro AR, Teixeira I, Bragança F, Silva JA, Cabrita J. Primary non-adherence in Portugal: findings and implications. Int J Clin Pharm 2015;37(4):626–35.

[57] Costa FA, Teixeira I, Duarte-Ramos F, Proença L, Pedro AR, Furtado C, Silva JA, Cabrita J. Effects of economic recession on elderly patients' perceptions of access to health care and implications on their medicines-taking behaviour in Portugal, 2013. Int J Clin Pharm 2016;39(1):104–12.

[58] Ministério da Saúde. Portaria nº 97/2018: First modification to the document defining services provided by pharmacies. [Diário da República] Lisboa: s.n, 2018.

[59] Miranda I, Jacinto I, Horta R, Salvador A, Guerreiro J, Romano S, Costa S. Therapeutic Notes (TN)—a tool for reinforcing interaction between Portuguese pharmacists and doctors. The Hague: International Pharmaceutical Federation (FIP); 2018.

[60] Paulino E, Guerreiro MP, Cantrill JÁ, Martins AP, Costa FA, Benrimoj SI. Community pharmacists' and physicians' interprofessional work: insights from qualitative studies with multiple stakeholders. Rev Port Clin Geral 2010;26:590–606.

[61] Calouste Gulbenkian Foundation. The future for health—working group 3: staffing the services. s.l. : Calouste Gulbenkian Foundation; 2015, ISBN:978-989-8807-13-7.

[62] Ribeiro N, Mota-Filipe H, Guerreiro MP, Costa FA. Primary health care policy and vision for community pharmacy and pharmacists in Portugal. Pharm Pract 2020;18(3):2043.

[63] Borralho J, Gregório J. "Each one has their own role": Exploratory study on consumers' perceptions about nutritionists services provided in community pharmacies. Res Social Adm Pharm 2020. https://doi.org/10.1016/j.sapharm.2020.04.008. S1551-7411(20)30331-4.

[64] Paulino E, Rosa M, Pinto AL, Maximiano S, Teixeira ML, Soares P, et al. The contribution of community pharmacies to diabetes control: a multidisciplinary approach. Seoul: s.n.: International Pharmaceutical Federation (FIP) Congress; 2017.

[65] Pinto AL, Monteiro L, Carvalho T, Moreira M, Parrinha P, Soares P, et al. Serviço do Pé Diabético em farmácias comunitárias: um contributo multidisciplinar. Rev Port Diabetes 2017;12(Suppl 1):42.[66]Ordem dos Nutricionistas. Norma Orientação Profissional nº 001/2019, Versão 1. *Atuação do Nutricionista na Farmácia Comunitária*. Porto : s.n., 2019.Ordem dos Nutricionistas. Norma Orientação Profissional nº 001/2019, Versão 1. *Atuação do Nutricionista na Farmácia Comunitária*. Porto : s.n., 2019.

CHAPTER 9

Pharmacy practice and continuing professional development in low and middle income countries (LMICs)

Amy Chan[a], Rula Darwish[b], Saba Shamim[c], and Zaheer-Ud-Din Babar[c]
[a]School of Pharmacy, University of Auckland, Auckland, New Zealand
[b]Department of Pharmaceutics and Pharmaceutical Technology, Faculty of Pharmacy, University of Jordan, Amman, Jordan
[c]Centre for Pharmaceutical Policy and Practice Research, Department of Pharmacy, University of Huddersfield, Huddersfield, United Kingdom

Introduction

Globally, there is an increasing burden from both communicable and non-communicable diseases (NCDs). The effects of these disproportionately impact low and middle income countries (LMICs) where health systems struggle to meet the demands brought about from NCDs. These long-term health conditions have increased rapidly over the last decade, leading to a double burden of disease from both NCDs and communicable diseases [1]. LMICs also face an increasing rise in the use of antimicrobials, and the presence of substandard and falsified medicines [1], which further contributes to antimicrobial resistance, and affects health outcomes in LMICs [2, 3]. This increasing prevalence of health conditions requires management with complex medication regimens. Pharmacists are well-placed to provide medicines expertise to manage these needs and regimens. Having a pharmacy workforce that is able to provide clinical support for patients has also been shown to improve health outcomes [4, 5]. However, to achieve this, there is a need to ensure that pharmacists have access to appropriate, up-to-date education and training to support the delivery of evidence-based pharmaceutical care. The need for diversified, advanced pharmacy education is recognized internationally [6–8], yet in many LMICs there is limited capacity and experience to develop such training.

Continuing professional development (CPD) has the potential to provide pharmacists with the skills they require to meet the health needs of

Pharmacy Practice Research Case Studies
https://doi.org/10.1016/B978-0-12-819378-5.00007-6
187

their local population, and to ensure that key learning needs of pharmacists are met. In many countries, the ongoing maintenance of pharmacist registration requires participation in some sort of pharmacy learning or education through lifelong learning frameworks, of which CPD is a widely adopted framework. CPD essentially involves a cycle in which individual practitioners reflect on their practice and assess their knowledge and skills, identify learning needs, create a personal learning plan, implement the plan, and evaluate the effectiveness of the educational interventions and the plan in relation to their practice [2]. The International Pharmaceutical Federation (FIP) defines CPD as the "responsibility of individual pharmacists for systemic maintenance, development and broadening of knowledge, skills and attitudes." This is to ensure continuing competence as a professional, throughout the pharmacist's career. CPD enables a pharmacist to assess their learning gaps to devise a plan, execute their planned strategy and then evaluate the success of their implemented intervention [3]. Closely related to this is continuing education (CE), which is an integral part of a health professional's CPD [6] and entails traditional delivery of learning materials such as lectures and workshops [3]. CPD does not replace CE, but rather offers a systematic approach to documenting the practitioner's learning, which leads to quality assurance and quality improvement of CE [2]. In contrast, CPD can draw on multiple educational approaches and strategies to provide the necessary skills and knowledge that are important to enhance the pharmacy workforce, and to improve practice and ultimate patient outcomes [9]. The studies have demonstrated CPD can improve clinical knowledge [10, 11] and improve pharmacists' perceptions of their practice [12].

How CPD is currently delivered varies significantly depending on the country, the health system, and how the pharmacy workforce regulates the profession locally. The health needs of people also differ depending on the income, geographical location, urban and rural setting, and healthcare infrastructures and governance of the region [13]. This will impact the learning and skill development needs of pharmacists that enable them to best support their patients. Understanding local healthcare needs is crucial to ensure that the CPD training that is provided is tailored to the local health needs and to improve patients' health outcomes. For CPD to be effective, the learning of pharmacists that it supports must also be aligned with local, regional, and national practice, and pharmaceutical policies.

There is currently little data on the CPD systems in LMICs and how these are presently being delivered. In particular, the health needs of LMICs are unique and special considerations need to be made in terms of their healthcare resourcing, evolving health needs of the local population, cultural and geographic diversity, and accessibility. Previous reviews of CPD frameworks have been conducted; for example, Tran et al. and Karas et al. have reported on CPD frameworks in Australia, Canada, the United Kingdom, and New Zealand [6, 7]. However, these comparisons of CPD frameworks have not included information from LMICs. Additionally, Tran et al. reported that not only the terms and definitions of lifelong learning frameworks varied tremendously from country to country, but also that the CPD requirements were not uniform [6]. How these findings apply to LMICs is currently unknown.

This chapter presents a focused review of the literature on the role of pharmacists in CPD, with examples and experiences from two ethnically and culturally diverse countries—first from Pakistan, classed as a lower-middle income economy, and second from Jordan, recently reclassified from lower-middle to upper-middle income economy. The chapter covers the barriers and facilitators to CPD, and provides recommendations for countries to consider when implementing their own CPD models and frameworks.

Evidence for CPD

Research on CPD of pharmacists is relatively limited and has to date focused on higher-income and developed countries; a focused review of studies and methodologies used, and considerations for each, are shown in Table 1. The approaches that these studies have adopted provide a useful starting point for LMICs to explore and gather evidence on CPD. This is also helpful to define the role of the pharmacists in CPD.

Most of the research on CPD of pharmacists relates to the views and barriers of pharmacists toward CPD programs. This is a key first step in understanding the opportunities for CPD and the barriers to implementation. Power et al. conducted a questionnaire-based survey of pharmacists' CPD activity, views, and attitudes in 543 pharmacists in Scotland, and identified that a small but significant proportion of pharmacists (~ 10%) do not engage with CPD [8]. This was similar to the reported findings from a qualitative study of 21 pharmacists from Nottingham, United Kingdom, which found that few pharmacists understood and practiced the principles of CPD [4]; similarly a survey of pharmacist attitudes toward CPD in Texas, United States, reported that more than half of respondents were unsure of the benefits of CPD and nearly one-third felt that a change to CPD would be beneficial to their professional development [5]. These views and barriers

Table 1 Summary of studies on CPD in pharmacy.

Study	Participants	Aim/scope	Study design	Considerations
Power et al. [8]	Royal Pharmaceutical Society of Great Britain registered Scottish pharmacists	To summarize Scottish pharmacists' views and attitudes toward CPD	Postal questionnaire of pharmacists' CPD activity, views, and attitudes	– Cross-sectional study design – Based on self-report – Low response rate – Response bias from pharmacists who had an interest in CPD – Questionnaire not validated
Attewell et al. [4]	Community pharmacists in Nottingham, United Kingdom	To investigate community pharmacists' perceptions and ideas about what constitutes CPD and to establish the types and amounts of CPD undertaken	Qualitative semistructured interviews covering pharmacists' understanding, attitudes, and behavior in relation to CPD and CE	– In-depth evaluation of CPD attitudes – Focused, narrow sample – Content analysis approach of interviews used – Broad interview schedule
Bellanger et al. [5]	Registered pharmacists from two large pharmacy organizations in Texas	To assess the knowledge and attitudes of Texas pharmacists regarding continuing professional development (CPD)	Email survey incorporating demographic and informational questions about CPD	– Cross-sectional online survey – 9.5% response rate
Haughey et al. [9]	Registered pharmacists in Northern Ireland	To determine the extent of pharmacists' understanding of continuing professional development (CPD) prior to the implementation of a mandatory CPD system and the level of implementation of CPD, and to gain insight into pharmacists' attitudes toward the concept and the introduction of a mandatory CPD system	Postal questionnaire to determine pharmacists' attitudes toward CPD, their understanding and experience of CPD and their attitudes toward sanctions and portfolio review	– High response rate (41%) – Piloted questionnaire but not validated – Comparison of 2001 and 2004 responses to evaluate impact of mandatory CPD on attitudes

Study	Population	Objective	Method	Notes
Thompson et al. [14]	Registered pharmacists with Pharmacy Board of Australia	To explore Australian pharmacists' understanding and engagement with the CPD requirements for renewal of registration	Online survey to explore the level of understanding and engagement Australian pharmacists have with the CPD framework	– Low response rate (only 1% of registered pharmacists) – Response bias
Gelayee et al. [10]	Community pharmacies in Gondar Town, northwest Ethiopia	To identify the pattern of CPD practice, attitude, preferences, and barriers to engagement on CPD of community pharmacists in Gondar town, northwest Ethiopia	Structured interviewing questionnaire, cross-sectional study	– Pretested questionnaire on pharmacy technicians – Data collection instrument based on literature reviews – Likert-type scale questions on CPD concept, attitude, practice, type of CPD preferences, barriers to CPD – Face validity and internal reliability assessments conducted – Small sample size
Austin et al. [13]	Pharmacists participating in the Ontario College of Pharmacists' Quality Assurance and Peer Review Process Leaning Portfolio session	To examine pharmacists' attitudes, behaviors, and preferences toward continuous professional development in Ontario, Canada	11 Focus group sessions; qualitative thematic analysis	– Structured focus group sessions – In-depth qualitative approach – Limited generalizability

Continued

Table 1 Summary of studies on CPD in pharmacy—cont'd

Study	Participants	Aim/scope	Study design	Considerations
Tsoi et al. [11]	Dutch pharmacists	To explore what factors influence pharmacists' participation in CE with a focus on motivation	Questionnaire-based online survey	– Informed by a theoretical framework on behavior (self-determination theory) – Focus on CE rather than CPD
McConnell et al. [15]	Licensed pharmacists employed at a health maintenance organization in the United States	To assess the effect of CPD, compared with that of traditional continuing pharmacy education (CPE), on perceptions of factors related to pharmacy practice	Nonblinded, randomized controlled study	– Randomized study design to compare effects of CPD versus CE – Evaluated effects on perceptions of pharmacy practice – Follow-up over 10 months
Aziz et al. [12]	Government pharmacists in Malaysia	To examine the pharmacists' preferred CPD activities and barriers to CPD participation	Survey based study on pharmacists' views and barriers toward CPD participation	– Low response rate – Response bias – Reasons for nonresponse not able to be identified
Wilbur et al. [16]	Pharmacists in Qatar	To determine their specific continuing education (CE) needs, preferences and attitudes	Survey of pharmacist demographics, internet access, frequency, and characteristics of past CE activity, preferences for delivery and content, barriers to participation, and plans for future CE activities	– Lack of formal national pharmacist registry—incomplete sampling – Internet based questionnaire—so pharmacists with no internet access excluded – Nonresponse error/bias

| Dopp et al. [17] | Pharmacists from the National Association of Boards of Pharmacy and Accreditation Council for Pharmacy Education in the United States | To determine whether pharmacists who adopted a CPD approach were more or less likely to assess and identify their professional needs, develop and implement a personal learning plan, evaluate their learning outcomes, and document each of these elements compared to pharmacists who utilized a traditional approach to CE without a structured intervention | Prospective, randomized, observational case-control study | – Small sample size
– Significant participant attrition, possibly due to personal and professional constraints
– Difficulties in follow-up of participants |

are supported by other studies in this field that have evaluated pharmacist attitudes on mandatory CPD [9, 10], and explored factors that influence participation in CE [11] and CPD [12–14] (Table 1). Commonly cited barriers to CPD include time, job constraints, cost, and accessibility [16].

Other studies have compared the effects of CPD programs on outcomes, such as learning activities and pharmacy practice. Dopp et al. evaluated the effects of a CPD program versus control (no CPD) on learning behaviors, and found that pharmacists in the intervention group were more likely to review and reconsider their learning objectives and personal learning plan compared to controls [17]. Intervention participants were also more likely to maintain a record of their professional practice activities and review their learning needs and opportunities. McConnell et al. conducted a randomized, controlled study comparing the effect of CPD versus traditional CE and impact on perceptions of factors related to pharmacy practice [15]. Pharmacists who participated in CPD reported that their perceptions of pharmacy practice improved as a result of their education activities compared to those who participated in traditional CE—for example, improvements in patient care changes, professional knowledge/skills, and attitudes and values. However those in the CPD group reported more often that time was a barrier to complete educational activities.

These findings are supported by those reported by Micallef et al., who completed a systematic review of literature on CPD models used and the preferences for CE and CPD. The review reported that whilst there are positive attitudes toward CPD from the profession, consideration of barriers such as innovative approaches to support ongoing motivation and engagement, and delivery models such as online versus face-to-face, language and technology is needed. [18]

Translating evidence into practice—Country experiences
Experiences from Pakistan

Pakistan is a low middle-income country and is the world's sixth most populous nation [19]. The pharmacy education system in Pakistan is currently undergoing continuous improvement in the curriculum that is being taught in pharmacy schools to train future pharmacists, with a focus on improving patient-centered practice and to help develop essential skills to provide optimum pharmaceutical services to the population [20]. Pharmacists in Pakistan are struggling in terms of unattractive salary packages, weak health and pharmacy support infrastructure, and little recognition of their role as a patient-centered practitioner [21]. Table 2 shows information regarding the

Table 2 Status of pharmacy education and practice development in Pakistan.

Country	Requirement of accredited degree for licensing	Regulatory authority for licensing pharmacists	Formal system for licensing of pharmacist	National licensing exam	Requirements to maintain licensure	Competency framework for foundation level practice	Competency framework for advanced practice
Pakistan	Yes	Pharmacy Council of Pakistan	Yes	No	No	Yes	In development

Data from International Pharmaceutical Federation (FIP). Global report of international pharmaceutical federation (FIP) on continuing professional development/continuing education in pharmacy. The Hague: International Pharmaceutical Federation; 2014.

current status of pharmacy education and practice. Some of this information has been extracted from the Global report of International Pharmaceutical Federation on Continuing Professional Development in Pharmacy [22–24].

Limited data, however, exists on CPD models in Pakistan—particularly what the facilitators, barriers, and opportunities are for CPD. There is no compulsory CPD program in Pakistan at present.

Pharmacists in Pakistan only need to pay a fee for the renewal of their practicing licenses and it is not compulsory for them to carry out CPD as there is no established system of CPD in the country [24].

Barriers to the development of such a CPD model include issues of finances, system constraints, and pharmacist attitudes toward participating in CPD programs. Financially, it is perceived that a large amount of revenue is required to bring such a CPD model into practice and the government is perceived as being unable to spare funds to take up such a big project for pharmacists. The findings are similar to what is reported in the literature for other countries, as financial barriers to the development and implementation of advanced pharmacy practice techniques and interventions in LMICs are also identified as a key barrier to implementation [25]. There is an appetite for the design and implementation of CPD for pharmacists, but in Pakistan, the responsible authorities do not have sufficient funds to do so. Financial support is needed to hire experts who will design a CPD model for the country's needs, then the next step is perhaps training sessions and training of the trainers. For a system be successful, it was also recognized that local regulatory and professional bodies, such as the Pharmacy Council of Pakistan (PCP) and Pakistan Pharmacists Association (PPA), need to work together to establish CPD for pharmacist practitioners. Confusion about where the lines of responsibility lie in terms of which professional body should lead this work further impedes the progression of CPD. The profession feels that development of a CPD model should be the joint responsibility of the National Ministry of Health, Pharmacy Council of Pakistan (PCP), and the Pakistan Pharmacists Association. From the literature, it is also evident that the national pharmacy associations also need to respect their mandates and work hard to develop pharmacy practice as per the global standards [26].

How CPD is defined is also a barrier to CPD uptake—differences exist between how CPD and CE are understood by the pharmacy profession. Whilst most are aware of the terms continuing professional development (CPD) and continuing education (CE), and recognize that CPD is important to maintain professional competence, the interpretation and understanding of these terms differs between individuals. Many recognize that, with the rapid change in knowledge and evidence, CPD is inevitable and will need to be implemented to support ongoing professional learning. Furthermore, many consider CPD to be paramount for pharmacists as it will help the pharmacists on the ground to assess and improve their abilities and update their knowledge. This is to overcome gaps in their skills, and most importantly, focus on advancement of patient care. The regulators also feel that CPD needs to be made mandatory if pharmacists are to engage with CPD events. Building registration or pharmacist license to practice into CPD courses, as well as having support from the employers for pharmacists to attend CPD events, would help facilitate uptake. If CPD was to be made mandatory, however, there can be expectations that national universities would be involved in offering and designing a CPD program for pharmacists [27]. Pharmacy councils in respective countries could approach academics, and work and collaborate with them to organize joint CPD events at universities. The role of academics to promote CPD is also supported from the literature [28], which shows that pharmacy academia can add their valuable knowledge in updating the current curriculum and training students [28]. CPD should also be embedded within the pharmacy curriculum so graduates can be well aware about the CPD practice when embarking on their careers.

When considering CPD course content, the health indicators of the community need to be considered, and the delivery of the CPD model should be carefully designed to motivate and facilitate pharmacist uptake. In Pakistan, a focus on leadership and management skills was highlighted as an important part of CPD. These and other priority health areas need to be identified and mapped as part of the design and delivery strategy of CPD models in Pakistan and beyond [21, 29].

Experiences from Jordan

The Hashemite Kingdom of Jordan is an Arab country located in the Middle East [30]. It occupies an area of about 92,000 km^2, with an estimated total population of about 9.5 million, most of whom reside in the capital [30, 31]. Jordan is renowned for its high-quality healthcare services and is considered one of the major destinations for medical tourism in the Middle East and North Africa region [32]. Pharmacists comprise 16% of the health workforce in Jordan with more than two-thirds of pharmacists being female. For every 10,000 Jordanians, there are 17.8 pharmacists. [33, 34] These per-population rates are considered among the highest in the

Middle East. However, there are major geographical disparities in the distribution of pharmacists among the major cities and the rural governorate in the Kingdom. In addition, the country in recent times received about 1.4 million Syrian refugees, which has resulted in an unplanned increase in the population and is putting pressure on pharmacists and other healthcare providers. [33, 35, 36]

To practice as a pharmacist in Jordan, a qualified pharmacist must be registered with the Jordan Pharmacists Association (JPA) and licensed by the Ministry of Health. Registration with the JPA requires completion of a pharmacy degree (Bachelor of Science [BSc] in pharmacy or Doctor of Pharmacy [Pharm D]) from an accredited school of pharmacy and completion of 1440 h of professional training. Pharmacists with pharmacy degrees from non-Jordanian universities are required to pass a pharmacy license examination by JPA. To maintain registration with the JPA, annual license renewal is required. This license renewal would need completion of CPD or education (e.g., credit hours of continuing pharmacy education) as approved by the High Health Council and Jordan Medical Council (JMC) [36].

CE programs are managed and supervised by the JPA and the JMC. A plan to introduce internship and residency programs for pharmacists is ongoing, similar to that for physicians and dentists, which is implemented in both the public and private sectors. The CE programs are not provided on a regular or compulsory basis. They are provided optionally by educational institutions, hospitals, and professional associations, and as activities provided by some individuals. Most of these programs are provided in the form of on-the-job training, seminars, workshops, and conferences. It is worth mentioning that one of the strategic objectives of the national strategy for the health sector in Jordan is development and training of healthcare providers with anticipated outcomes that include trained, qualified, and sufficient health human resources. [33] In fact, developing the workforce has become a critical issue on the global health agenda. [37] The importance of advancing the workforce is recognized by the United Nations Sustainable Development Goals (SDG) through the inclusion of a target focused on the health workforce [38]. This would require all public and private health sectors to apply continuous learning and training programs for all health professions.

The JPA, in collaboration with the FIP, is working on a project that aims to identify the existing workforce and analyze the current state of the pharmacy workforce against internationally set goals or standards. The FIP has developed Pharmaceutical Workforce Development Goals

(PWDGs), which aim at facilitating the development of the workforce [39]. The JPA proposed that pharmacists should be able to upgrade themselves into different levels, which depends not only on years of experience but also on CPD.

In 2018, CPD instructions were issued in the official newspaper through the prime minister in Jordan. This document states that CPD is mandatory and that relicensing will be conducted every 5 years for every healthcare provider and should include the required number of accredited CPD hours. Pharmacists should complete 50 CPD hours in 5 years with an average of 10 CPD hours per year. The CPD hours are distributed across those activities related to the profession and those related to personal development.

There is no doubt that the public expect that health practitioners, including pharmacists, will remain competent to practice throughout their professional life (not just at the time of initial graduation and registration). This is also in the interests of public safety and quality of healthcare. As mentioned earlier, this has been facilitated through fulfilling requirements set out by the JMC where all health practitioners are obligated to undertake CPD and to inform the JPA when applying for the renewal of registration that the CPD requirements have been met. The JPA are currently exploring the CPD culture among pharmacists in Jordan, to improve the uptake of CPD among Jordanian pharmacists, and to enhance pharmacists' career progression. The CPD committee has been restructured with the aim to fulfil these objectives. The reformed CPD committee focus is on supervising and delivering the activities needed to improve pharmacists' competencies. The committee consists of sixteen dedicated members who work voluntarily to improve pharmacists' performance among health providers; they meet regularly every 2 weeks, or more frequently if there is a need.

As professional practice and competencies change and evolve, so too do pharmacists and, therefore, the requirement for on-going CPD. In Jordan, there has been a change in the focus of pharmacy practice, from one dominated by a product supply process to one incorporating professional services—a trend that is mirrored globally in other countries. As such, the recognition of advanced pharmacy practice, pharmacist prescribing, and other expansions of practice will require changes in CPD requirements. Documentation is an integral aspect of CPD and a personal portfolio is used for this purpose. The JPA hold workshops for pharmacy practitioners to introduce them to the CPD plan and how to document their achievements in their personal portfolio. The five-step cycle was used in a statement on CPD adopted by the International Pharmaceutical Federation [22] in 2014 [24], including an adaptation of that five-step cycle with the modification provided by Rouse [2], in which documentation is shown as a central component and not a separate stage of the cycle. The CPD committee in JPA structured some local guidelines to control different activities related to CPD to ensure quality and assess development of competencies; guidelines that should help in regulating and evaluating the process of training. This training and activities should be of a need-based type. Moreover, the committee designed forms for training bodies and trainers, and material to be given in order to ensure quality.

One successful training program that was provided through a CPD program in Jordan was the SMART Pharmacist Program, initiated by the Accreditation Council for Pharmacy Education (ACPE) and Pharma Expert, in 2014. This was designed to introduce a new continuing education model for pharmacists under the subtitle "Learn Today—Apply Tomorrow". Following the full CPD cycle, it starts with reflection (pharmacists' learning portfolio), learning (developing SMART learning objectives), followed by application of learning in practice. It includes competency assessment and development, as well as new approaches to patient care. Pharmacists evaluate the appropriateness, process, and outcomes of their learning, as well as changes made and their impact. It is worth mentioning that the program spread to 16 more countries under the leadership of national host organizations, after successful implementation in Turkey. Respecting the national context, globally adopted and validated tools were used and new services for chronic patients implemented. In several countries, the program showed an impact on the patient level, especially those with asthma and COPD, hypertension and dyslipidemia, diabetes, and the patient care process in general. Changes are visible at the individual (pharmacists) and organizational levels. In some countries, the program is recognized as one of the most important initiatives in pharmacy education and practice, with visible support of national medicines agencies, academia, government, and WHO regional offices.

After initiating the program in Amman, Jordan, two more training activities followed to cover more participants in different geographic areas of Jordan and to ensure the competencies were achieved. Another important workshop was the Medication Therapy Management (MTM) and Patient Education workshop, which focused on important competencies that pharmacists in different disciplines should have. This was followed by another workshop to assure that pharmacists in different geographic areas in Jordan would benefit. The CPD committee, in collaboration with the immunization committee, studied the competencies needed for the community pharmacies to become immunizers.

The CPD committee seeks to collaborate with national and international bodies, with the aims of improving the role of pharmacists and developing competencies. In this context, the CPD committee had two meetings with FIP representatives in an attempt to align the local competencies with the international ones. The committee is in the process of adopting and adapting the global competency framework from the FIP [24], which is in use in many international settings to guide practitioner professional development. The CPD committee collaborated with the USAID in delivering several successful workshops entitled "Consult your Pharmacist," which focuses on the role of pharmacists as a counselor in family planning, and includes several soft skills sessions in addition to roleplaying models. Another collaboration with the King Hussain Cancer Centre was initiated on smoking cessation—a training workshop entitled "An Introduction to Tobacco Dependence Treatment (TDT)," which focused on the role of pharmacists in smoking cessation and the competency needed to become a counselor for patients. It included hands-on activities and case studies together with roleplaying.

In terms of engaging the local workforce, two workshops on wound management were delivered aiming to improve pharmacists' competencies in managing patients suffering from wounds or burns. It is worth mentioning that most of the activities were delivered by pharmacists and other healthcare workers in an attempt to improve interprofessional relationship among the healthcare team and to cover different subject from all disciplines.

Recently, with the COVID 19 pandemic, online training is being assessed and guidelines are being formulated and made ready to be approved. The emphasis was on the importance of social distancing, decreased exposure to COVID 19, increasing awareness of this pandemic in addition to dealing with possible cases of the disease. Furthermore, work needs to be done to link competency standards, pharmacist learning plans, and competency mapping of CPD activities, and raise awareness of pharmacists on CPD. All pharmaceutical sectors should be considered when making the plan to ensure workforce development.

Recommendations for countries to establish local CPD models

These two country case studies from Pakistan and Jordan highlight several common themes with regards to the design, development, implementation, and uptake of CPD. These steps and recommendations are outlined below:

(1) The state of CPD in each country needs to be scoped out and mapped. There are differences in how individuals and stakeholder interpret and define CPD, which needs to be the starting point prior to the design of any CPD models.

(2) Key stakeholders need to be identified. In both Pakistan and Jordan, the views, perceptions, and practices relating to CPD needed to be identified from key stakeholders from academic sectors, pharmacy practitioners, regulators, pharmacy associations, and government bodies (e.g., Ministry of Health). Involving global organizations such as the Commonwealth Pharmacists' Association (CPA) and FIP can also be key facilitators in developing a CPD model [24, 40]. This step is pivotal to identifying the barriers and facilitators to uptake and implementation of CPD. This is also in line with the earlier challenges identified in the literature with regards to pharmacy education and practice [41].

(3) The health needs of the local population and learning needs of the pharmacy workforce need to be defined. CPD needs to be designed to cover all aspects involved that relate to day-to-day pharmacy practice. Along with relevance to the present need of the health sector and the local population, CPD should also address the technicalities involved in administering patient care as well as patient-pharmacist communication [29].

An example CPD model could include the following components:

(1) Managerial and leadership skills
(2) Pharmacotherapy and pharmacy management CPD courses
(3) Updated knowledge on diseases and public health
(4) Local needs of the country and the regions
(5) Support from pharmacists' employers
(6) Links with international organizations
(7) Efficiency in renewal and registration of the pharmacists

The model shown in Fig. 1 is an example of factors to consider, drawn from the experiences in Pakistan, which highlights these components.

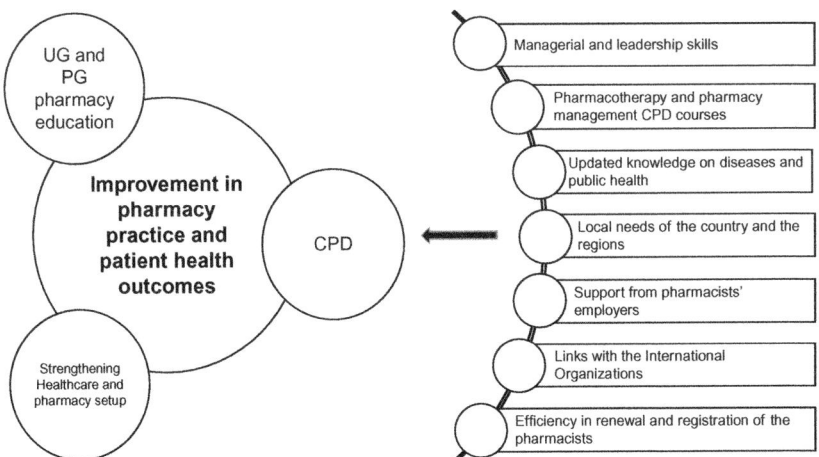

Fig. 1 An example CPD model for pharmacists based on experiences from Pakistan—produced by Saba Shamim and Zaheer-Ud-Din Babar.

Conclusion

With the increasing and evolving health needs of the global population, and the rapid rate of change of health-related information and evidence, ensuring currency of the pharmacy profession is vital. Having access to a dynamic CPD model that can adapt to the changing needs of the profession and of local populations, whilst ensuring a robust, reliable infrastructure to ensure sustainable and equitable CPD delivery to all members of the pharmacy workforce, should be a key priority for all countries. Stakeholders from professional organizations and government bodies need to be involved to ensure system barriers such as finance, cost, and regulation are identified and overcome.

References

[1] Almuzaini T, Choonara I, Sammons H. Substandard and counterfeit medicines: a systematic review of the literature. BMJ Open 2013;3(8), e002923.

[2] Rouse MJ. Continuing professional development in pharmacy. J Pharm Technol 2004;20(5):303–6.

[3] Driesen A, Verbeke K, Simoens S, Laekeman G. International trends in lifelong learning for pharmacists. Am J Pharm Educ 2007;71(3).

[4] Attewell J, Blenkinsopp A, Black P. Community pharmacists and continuing professional development—a qualitative study of perceptions and current involvement. Pharm J 2005;274(519):524.

[5] Bellanger RA, Shank TC. Continuing professional development in Texas: survey of pharmacists' knowledge and attitudes: 2008. J Am Pharm Assoc (2003) 2010;50(3):368–74.

[6] Tran D, Tofade T, Thakkar N, Rouse M. US and international health professions' requirements for continuing professional development. Am J Pharm Educ 2014;78(6).

[7] Karas M, Sheen NJ, North RV, Ryan B, Bullock A. Continuing professional development requirements for UK health professionals: a scoping review. BMJ Open 2020;10(3), e032781.

[8] Power A, Johnson BJ, Diack HL, McKellar S, Stewart D, Hudson SA. Scottish pharmacists' views and attitudes towards continuing professional development. Pharm World Sci 2008;30(1):136–43.

[9] Haughey SL, Hughes CM, Adair CG, Bell HM. Introducing a mandatory continuing professional development system: an evaluation of pharmacists' attitudes and experiences in Northern Ireland. Int J Pharm Pract 2007;15(3):243–9.

[10] Gelayee DA, Mekonnen GB, Birarra MK. Involvement of community pharmacists in continuing professional development (CPD): a baseline survey in Gondar, Northwest Ethiopia. Glob Health 2018;14(1):1–6.

[11] Tjin A, Tsoi SLNM, de Boer A, Croiset G, Koster AS, Kusurkar RA. Factors influencing participation in continuing professional development: a focus on motivation among pharmacists. J Contin Educ Health Prof 2016;36(3):144–50.

[12] Aziz Z, Jet CN, Rahman SSA. Continuing professional development: views and barriers toward participation among Malaysian pharmacists. Eur J Social Behav Sci 2013;4(1):713.

[13] Austin Z, Marini A, Croteau D. Continuous professional development: a qualitative study of pharmacists' attitudes, behaviors, and preferences in Ontario, Canada. Am J Pharm Educ 2005;69(1).

[14] Thompson W, Nissen LM. Australian pharmacists' understanding of their continuing professional development obligations. J Pharm Pract Res 2013;43(3):213–7.

[15] McConnell KJ, Newlon CL, Delate T. The impact of continuing professional development versus traditional continuing pharmacy education on pharmacy practice. Ann Pharmacother 2010;44(10):1585–95.

[16] Wilbur K. Continuing professional pharmacy development needs assessment of Qatar pharmacists. Int J Pharm Pract 2010;18(4):236–41.

[17] Dopp AL, Moulton JR, Rouse MJ, Trewet CB. A five-state continuing professional development pilot program for practicing pharmacists. Am J Pharm Educ 2010;74(2).

[18] Micallef R, Kayyali R. A systematic review of models used and preferences for continuing education and continuing professional development of pharmacists. Pharmacy 2019;7(4):154.

[19] Farrukh MJ, Ming LC, Zaidi ST, Khan TM. Barriers and strategies to improve influenza vaccination in Pakistan. J Infect Public Heal 2017;10(6):881–3.

[20] Hashmi FK, Hassali MA, Khalid A, Saleem F, Aljadhey H, Babar Z, Bashaar M. A qualitative study exploring perceptions and attitudes of community pharmacists about extended pharmacy services in Lahore, Pakistan. BMC Health Serv Res 2017;17(1):500. https://doi.org/10.1186/s12913-017-2442-6.

[21] Malik I, Atif M, Scahill SL, ZUD B. Pharmacy practice and policy research in Pakistan: a review of literature between 2014 and 2019. In: Global pharmaceutical policy. Springer; 2020. p. 139–75.

[22] International Pharmaceutical Federation (FIP). FIP statement of professional standards continuing professional development. The Hague: International Pharmaceutical Federation; 2002.

[23] Anderson C, Bates I, Beck D, et al. The WHO UNESCO FIP pharmacy education taskforce. Hum Resour Health 2009;7(1):1–8.

[24] International Pharmaceutical Federation (FIP). Global report of international pharmaceutical federation (FIP) on continuing professional development/continuing education in pharmacy. The Hague: International Pharmaceutical Federation; 2014.

[25] Rasheed H, Ibrahim MIM, Babar ZUD. Evidence-based pharmacy practice research in low-and middle-income countries: issues, challenges and synthesis. Encyclopedia Pharm Pract Clin Pharm 2019;94.

[26] Donyai P, Denicolo P, Alexander A. Continuing professional development for pharmacy professionals' revalidation: results of an experimental study. Int J Pharm Pract 2011;19(S1):37.

[27] Babar Z-U-D. Pakistan's National University of Pharmaceutical Sciences. Am J Pharm Educ 2006;70(5):123.

[28] McLaughlin JE, Dean MJ, Mumper RJ, Blouin RA, Roth MT. A roadmap for educational research in pharmacy. Am J Pharm Educ 2013;77(10).

[29] Jamshed S, Babar ZUD. Social pharmacy strengthening clinical pharmacy: why pharmaceutical policy research is needed in Pakistan? Pharm World Sci 2008;30(5):617–9.

[30] About Jordan. Facs about Jordan. Amman (Jordan): Government of Jordan, www.jordangovjo; 2016.

[31] Population and housing census 2015. Amman (Jordan): Department of Statistics, http://censusdosgovjo/; 2016.

[32] Medical tourism and health care status from around the world. Medical Tourism Association, www.medicaltourismassociationcom/en/research-and-surveyshtml; 2016.

[33] Barkhof E, Meijer CJ, de Sonneville LMJ, Linszen DH, de Haan L. Interventions to improve adherence to antipsychotic medication in patients with schizophrenia–A review of the past decade. Eur Psychiatry 2012;27(1):9–18.

[34] Haddad PM, Brain C, Scott J. Nonadherence with antipsychotic medication in schizophrenia: challenges and management strategies. Patient Relat Outcome Meas 2014;5:43–62.

[35] Murshidi MM, Hijjawi MQB, Jeriesat S, Eltom A. Syrian refugees and Jordan's health sector. Lancet 2013;382(9888):206–7.

[36] Nose M, Barbui C, Tansella M. How often do patients with psychosis fail to adhere to treatment programmes? A systematic review. Psychol Med 2003;33(07):1149–60.

[37] Hawthorne N, Anderson C. The global pharmacy workforce: a systematic review of the literature. Hum Res Health 2009;7(1):48.

[38] United Nations. Transforming our world: the 2030 agenda for sustainable development. Division for sustainable development goals: New York, NY; 2015.

[39] Law M, Bader L, Uzman N, Williams A, Bates I. The FIP nanjing statements: shaping global pharmacy and pharmaceutical sciences education. Res Social Adm Pharm 2019;15(12):1472–5.

[40] Chan AHY, Rutter V, Ashiru-Oredope D, Tuck C, Babar ZUD. Together we unite: the role of the COMMONWEALTH in achieving universal health coverage through pharmaceutical care amidst the COVID-19 pandemic. J Pharm Policy Pract 2020;13:1–7.

[41] Babar ZUD, Scahill SL, Akhlaq M, et al. A bibliometric review of pharmacy education literature in the context of low-to middle-income countries. Curr Pharm Teach Learn 2013;5(3):218–32.

CHAPTER 10

Personalizing patient care with medicines: Innovative models of care from the United Kingdom

Tania L. Jones[a,b], Wasim Baqir[c,d], and Fraser N. Birrell[b]
[a]Population Health Sciences Institute, Newcastle University, Newcastle-upon-Tyne, United Kingdom
[b]Northumbria Healthcare NHS Foundation Trust, Northumberland, United Kingdom
[c]Research and Development, Northumbria Healthcare NHS Foundation Trust, Northumberland, United Kingdom
[d]School of Healthcare, Faculty of Medicine and Health, The University of Leeds, Leeds, United Kingdom

Introduction

Concepts and models for personalization of care from the United Kingdom

Personalized care considers individuals as a whole; their physical, mental, and emotional needs. Personalization of care provides people with choice and control in decisions relating to their care, empowering them to be partners in health decision-making. To plan personalized care, a single or series of conversations between patient and clinician occur to tailor care strategies and agree action points or goal setting [1].

A variety of terminology is used, often interchangeably, under the "personalized healthcare" umbrella including "person-centered care, patient-centered care, personalization, patient-centric, relationship-centered care, or mutuality" [2]. However, there is no unifying definition of all of these aspects of personalized care.

The Health Foundation developed a framework for "person-centered" care for use in healthcare settings including the NHS (National Health Service). Within this framework, four core principles underpin the concept of "person-centered" care:

1. Affording people dignity, compassion, and respect.
2. Offering coordinated care, support, or treatment.
3. Offering personalized care, support, or treatment.
4. Supporting people to recognize and develop their own strengths and abilities to enable them to live an independent and fulfilling life.

Collins [3] for the Health Foundation recommended specific activities designed to implement the principles as demonstrated in Fig. 1.

Pharmacy Practice Research Case Studies
https://doi.org/10.1016/B978-0-12-819378-5.00001-5

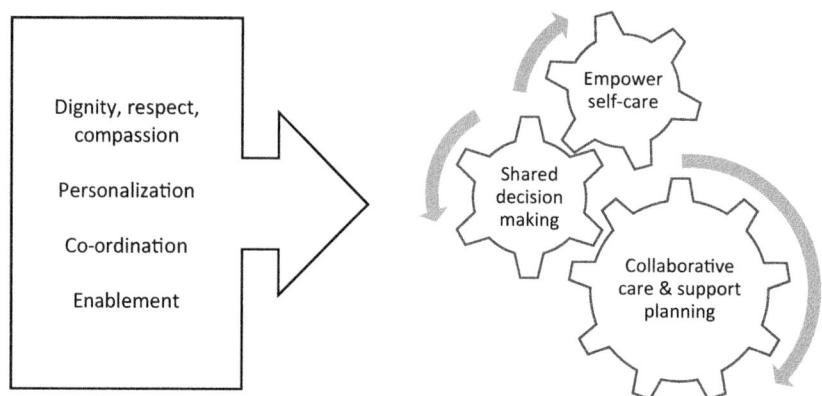

Fig. 1 Health Foundation person-centered care principles and activities. *(Modified with permission from Collins A. Measuring what really matters: towards a coherent measurement system to support person-centred care. The Health Foundation. Copyright (2014) The Health Foundation.)*

In Fig. 1, the arrow represents the principles of person-centered care and the cogs illustrate the activities required to deliver the core principles. The relationship between the principles and activities is complex and relies on the development of slightly different skill sets [3].

The House of Care Framework (HoC) for long-term conditions was developed by the Kings Fund for person-centered, coordinated care planning. The HoC Framework is based on the internationally recognized Chronic Care Model [4] and uses the metaphor of a house to outline components required to achieve successful personalized care delivery. The walls of the house represent the clinician who is prepared for collaborative care and the well-informed and engaged patient, the roof is built with organizational processes and systems (including evidence-based clinical guidance), and the floor represents the local, responsive commissioning plan that considers the needs of patients, carers, and clinicians. Commissioning may also include social prescribing to meet the needs of the service users. At the very heart is person-centered, coordinated care planning.

HoC was developed and tested by the Year of Care Program which was designed to assess whether personalized care planning could replace routine care in diabetes (and applicable now to any long-term condition). Findings were striking; in the program pilots, the Tower Hamlets region of London moved from being one of the worst areas in the United Kingdom for diabetes outcomes to one of the best [5].

The NHS Long-Term Plan outlines the intention to make personalized care "business as usual" within healthcare systems and the comprehensive model used within the plan documents six standard elements to deliver this. These are shared decision-making; personalized care and support planning; enabling choice; social prescribing and community-based support; supported self-management; and personal health budgets and integrated personal budgets [6].

Evidence for personalizing care with medicines

Personalized care by pharmacists has been shown to improve chronic disease control metrics as evidenced by an endocrinologist-pharmacist collaborative model. Pharmacist-led personalized care in the form of three 60-min visits over 6 months was compared to standard care with no pharmacist input. The pharmacist-led arm achieved significantly greater reductions in HbA1c, with fewer diabetes-related complications and a greater improvement in QALYs (quality-adjusted life years), at lower cost compared to usual care [7].

Another benefit is improved medicines adherence, as demonstrated in a prospective, randomized controlled trial in type 2 diabetes. The control group received usual care and the intervention arm delivered a personalized, pharmacotherapeutic plan and additional diabetes education led by pharmacists. Adherence to medication regimens increased from 9% at baseline to 61% at the 6-month point in contrast to 13%–30% increase in the usual care arm ($P<.01$). An additional advantage was a 51% reduction in hospital admissions ($P<.001$) with pharmacist-led medication therapy management [8].

Personalized medicines optimization also encompasses the review and cessation of unnecessary or harmful medicines in a process called deprescribing. A cluster randomized trial "D-PRESCRIBE" demonstrated that personalized medicines rationalization and deprescribing can be successfully achieved by community pharmacists using an educational intervention. 43% of patients receiving the personalized education intervention discontinued an inappropriately prescribed medicine versus 12% of patients in the usual care group (risk difference, 31% [95% CI: 23%, 38%]). No patients were admitted to hospital during this period due to cessation of a drug [9].

A deprescribing personalized care model: The SHINE project

Overview

Drug treatments remain the most common healthcare intervention in the National Health Service (NHS), accounting for 1.1 billion items, costing the NHS £8.8 billion in 2018 [10]. Older people are disproportionately prescribed more medicines, giving rise to polypharmacy; an individual using multiple medicines concurrently. It is now recognized that polypharmacy can be appropriate in some instances, e.g., for someone with multiple morbidities (myocardial infarction typically requires two antiplatelet agents, a beta-blocker, an angiotensin-converting enzyme inhibitor, and a statin). However, polypharmacy in care homes remains problematic, with up to two-thirds of patients taking 10 or more medicines [11–16]. Many of those medicines are unnecessary or inappropriate [17–19]. Older people in care homes are particularly at risk of harm from medicines nonadherence, interactions (drug-disease and drug-drug), side-effects, adverse events, hospitalization, and generally a poorer quality of life [13,16].

Care home residents presently have little control over which medicines are prescribed or administered [20]. The Care Home Use of Medicines Study (CHUMS) of 256 residents from 55 care homes reported that more than two-thirds of care home residents experienced at least one error with the prescribing, dispensing or administration of their medicines during the study period [21]. In England, of the estimated 237 million medicines errors, 44% are attributable to care home settings [22].

In recent years, the term "deprescribing" has emerged, to describe the act of stopping medicines that patients may no longer need or which may be causing harm [23]. First coined in an Australian paper by Woodward [24], deprescribing has captured the attention of the health sciences research community [25–29]. The main principles of deprescribing are to ascertain the indications for each medicine, identifying those that no longer have a valid indication or those that may be inappropriate because of the patient's social situation or comorbidities [30]. The process of stopping medicines can be perceived as problematic as there is less published guidance available in comparison to starting medicines. However, the limited evidence base does suggest that medicines can be withdrawn safely with benefits to patients [31,32].

Patients cite fear and appropriateness of cessation, previous experience of medicines, and influences from family and friends as concerns with deprescribing [33]. Using shared decision-making to tailor the medicines optimization process allows for both parties (patient and clinician) to put forward ideas on the choice of which medicines to stop, instilling confidence.

The impact of deprescribing: Benefits to patients, the multidisciplinary team and healthcare provision

Systematic reviews have demonstrated that safer and better-quality care can be achieved when medicines are stopped across a wide range of therapeutic areas [31,32]. The key benefits to patients when medicines are deprescribed are preventing falls [27,34–36], improvements in adherence [37] and cognitive function [32], and a reduction in either harmful or inappropriate medicines [38]. A current ongoing randomized study (CHIPPS) is investigating the impact of pharmacists deprescribing for care home residents, with falls being the primary outcome measure after analysis of early feasibility data [39].

Studies are beginning to suggest a net benefit to deprescribing [25,40,41] and that it may bring some real, tangible benefits for patients [31]. While this is encouraging, the evidence is not presently generalizable to all medicine classes and patient population groups. The risk of adverse events following deprescribing should be considered and minimized by taking a structured, tailored approach to medication review; understanding why the medicine was started, the current indication, and whether deprescribing has been attempted previously. Close surveillance of patients post deprescribing for any reemergence of symptoms or new onset of symptoms is of great importance. By working with residents in care homes, pharmacists and the wider multidisciplinary team are able to make complex, joint decisions to deprescribe medicines.

Findings from the SHINE project

The SHINE project was developed from the misconception that involving residents in decisions about medicines was difficult to do. Using robust quality improvement methodology, care home residents were offered medication reviews within a shared decision-making framework to personalize each review [42,43]. Clinical pharmacists were keen to understand the role of shared decision-making and outcomes when deprescribing medicines. Three questions were developed [42]:

1. Is there an indication for the medication (is the medicine neither treating nor preventing any disease nor alleviating symptoms)?
2. Is the indication appropriate when the current clinical situation is taken into consideration?
3. Is the medication safe and free from side-effects and adverse events?

This study was undertaken in 20 care homes in the North East of England. All care homes across two localities were invited to participate and of those consenting, 20 were selected. The project was funded by the Health Foundation as part of the SHINE 2012 program.

An initial review of clinical notes was undertaken, followed by a consultation with the resident and/or their family and carers. Other members of the multidisciplinary team were invited to join the meeting. The answers to the above questions were then discussed and residents were supported to make a decision about stopping, changing, or continuing medicines. The individual's personal circumstances, symptoms, medicine history, social history, and diagnoses were factored into the decision-making process. The risks and benefits were discussed with the resident. All interventions were recorded on a database and every resident followed up after 1 month for any adverse events. Care home staff were encouraged to proactively report any adverse events following deprescribing.

422 residents were reviewed by the clinical pharmacists; they made 1346 interventions. Deprescribing was the most common intervention with 704 medicines stopped in 298 (70.6%) residents. For each intervention, the reason, cost, and outcomes were recorded. Descriptive analysis was undertaken. Savings for medicines deprescribed were annualized.

Two models of deprescribing were tested: pharmacists working independently (all clinical pharmacists were independent prescribers) or working in collaboration with general medical practitioners (GPs).

IBM SPSS Statistics (V.21) was used to determine statistical differences between the two models (t-test) and to ascertain any relationship between the original number of medicines prescribed to the patient and level of deprescribing undertaken (Pearson's correlation).

422 residents were reviewed; 77.7% were female and the average age was 85.5 years. These 422 residents were taking 3602 medicines prior to the review of which 704 (19.5%) were deprescribed in 298 residents. The medicines deprescribed accounted for 52.3% of the 1346 medicines that were being taken before the reviews. The mean number of medicines stopped was 2.36 (SD 1.53) per resident, ranging from 0 to 9. There was no statistical difference between numbers of medicines stopped by pharmacist prescribers (53.4% stopped) and numbers stopped (51.9%) where GPs and pharmacists worked collaboratively ($P = .9702$; 95% CI: -0.39 to 0.38).

The relationship between the number of medicines originally prescribed and number deprescribed was tested using Pearson's correlation. There was a weak positive relationship with number of original medicines and level of deprescribing ($r = .333$), which tailed off at 15 medicines originally prescribed.

Of all medicines deprescribed, 142 were acute medicines and 562 were repeat medicines. The main reason for deprescribing medicines was no current indication ($n = 400$; 56.8%) with 15.9%, 8.7%, and 6.5% of deprescribing being accounted for by patient choice, inappropriate indication, and medicines safety, respectively.

Medicines were stopped from all therapeutic areas, with the most common group being laxatives (14.5%), skin products (8.4%), bone protection drugs (7%), acid-regulating medicines (5.4%), antidepressants (4.7%), anti-hypertensives (4.3%), and lipid-regulating medicines (4.3%).

Residents were reviewed and monitored in the period following any deprescribing and any adverse events documented. Each resident was actively reviewed 1 month after the intervention. Only seven adverse events (1%) were identified with all being minor and reversible. In one case, the resident saw reemergence of depression symptoms when an antidepressant was deprescribed. In four situations, another medicine was started, and for the remaining two cases, the original medicine was restarted at a lower dose and further monitoring initiated. The 704 medicines deprescribed accounted for £64,471 per annum in prescribing costs.

This study has demonstrated that a personalized approach to medicines optimization can lead to a reduction in polypharmacy without putting residents at risk of harm. It also highlights the important role of the pharmacist in optimizing care through shared decision-making, as highlighted by [3].

This example also illustrates cost-effective prescribing using a one-to-one consultation between clinician and patient (plus family/carers) for medicines review. However, when treating patients with similar medical conditions or where resources are limited, a group consultation can be considered in any setting. The question commonly raised by those without experience in running a group clinic is; "how can we deliver personalized care in a group setting?" It is a good question and we explain in the following section how this novel model of care can serve patients as well as (or typically, better) than a one-to-one consultation.

Personalized care in groups: A randomized controlled trial of a pharmacist-led group clinic for osteoporosis

Group consultations: What are they?

It may seem counterintuitive to use group settings to deliver personalized care. However, it is important to fully understand the nature of group consultations and how they can feed into the personalized medicine agenda. There are a variety of group care models used around the world, but they can generally be grouped into three main types: the access model, the chronic care model, and a hybrid version of both. Fig. 2 illustrates the variety of model designs and terminology used. Generally, a type A access model allows for urgent care or unplanned appointments to improve access to medical care where there is increasing need/demand; type C are typically used to ensure continuity of care in long-term illnesses; and type B are a mixture of the

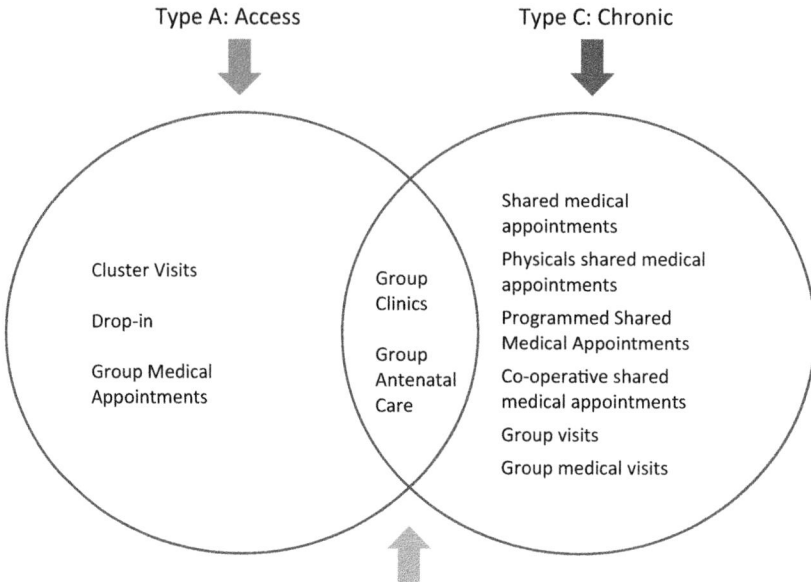

Fig. 2 Types of group consultation. *(Modified with permission from Jones T, Darzi A, Egger G, Ickovics J, Noffsinger E, Ramdas K, Stevens J, Sumego M, Birrell F. A systems approach to embedding group consultations in the NHS. Future Healthc J 2019. Copyright (2019) Royal College of Physicians.)*

two, where newly diagnosed patients may be seen in the same setting as repeat attenders. Further explanation of group definitions and examples can be found in our systems approach review article [44].

Group consultations are different to traditional models of care such as one-to-one appointments, education-only groups/support groups, or round-robin annual review clinics with serial one-to-one consultation. Group consultations should deliver all the usual clinical elements of care that would normally be available in a traditional one-to-one appointment with the added benefit of group support, with education to facilitate self-care (as described by Collins [3]). Although the interactions occur in a group, personalization is possible through shared decision-making (with peer-support) and tailor-made clinical/pharmaceutical plans. Confidentiality has to be agreed by all parties on arrival; in the UK model, written agreement is desirable, but in other countries such as the United States, written agreement by all parties is often required.

Group consultations usually require a facilitator (typically not the clinician) and a medical practitioner or clinically qualified healthcare professional to deliver any necessary medical treatment or answer questions arising from the group discussion. In some models, a clinician may also be the facilitator; for example, the Northumbria Healthcare design uses a healthcare professional in rotation to encourage a holistic approach. The facilitator team consists of pharmacists, occupational therapists, physiotherapists, specialist nurses, and podiatrists, sharing expertise from their specialist viewpoint while directing the flow of the clinic. The clinic is also attended by a consultant rheumatologist plus support staff to allow for administration of medicines and blood taking.

The facilitator role is to manage the delivery of the event, coordinate patient questions, encourage participation, organize the flow of the clinic/appointments, and prepare any clinical information to be shared within the group. This might be a results board of laboratory investigations such as glycosylated hemoglobin for diabetes or inflammatory markers for rheumatoid arthritis. This allows the patient to "benchmark" their disease control with others and spark debate on how to manage their condition. A group discussion or education session continues "in the round" while patients are clinically assessed individually by the clinician in a "micro-consult." The micro-consult is conducted using a separate room or bay, allowing further personalization of care to support physical examination, sharing of decision-making on treatment choice, and formulation of individual management plans. Each patient is assessed and, in partnership with the clinician, agrees a care plan tailored to their needs. They then return to the group to continue to share experiences and ideas, discuss their results, raise any questions/worries, and receive any necessary interventions such as injections or receive prescriptions.

How can group consultations deliver personalized care? Pharmacist perspective

Going back to the actions required to deliver personalized care as recommended by the Health Foundation; empowering people to engage in self-care, shared-decision making, collaborative care, and support planning, it becomes more obvious how a group setting can nurture personalized care. Group consultation delivery is usually by iterative codesign and learning from patients is key to what works. Having patients help to codesign group consultations from the outset allows for a patient-centered and patient-led format. Support from peers can also help in decision-making about aspects of care. The facilitator's role is not to dictate the content of the conversation, but to encourage questions from patients themselves to start the conversation in a two-way flow.

The starting point is addressing questions raised by patients, ensuring the focus is patient-centered. Alternatively, the results board can prompt those with good control of their disease to share tactics used to optimize outcomes or share tips on how to deal with exacerbations of the condition. The role of the pharmacist in the group consultation can be to offer evidence-based recommendations for treatment of the condition, suggest adjustment to regimens in light of the laboratory results, and to tailor pharmaceutical or medical care plans as needed.

In addition, problems arising from treatment can be dealt with, and patients may like to share experiences on how to manage these best, considering they are the experts in their own disease. An example of this would be when a newly diagnosed lady with rheumatoid arthritis struggled with feeling sick when starting to take sulfasalazine. The others in the group offered suggestions to help that had worked for them; taking the dose at night-time, taking it as a single-dose rather than a split dose, understanding that the effect is commonly transient. The pharmacist can listen to the discussions and support the individual through sharing knowledge or signposting to evidence-based guidance. Equally, there is an important role in dealing with queries in relation to emerging/novel or untested therapies, with patients commonly bringing in newspaper cuttings of "magic cures" for their disease, turning the conversation to the evidence-base.

As highlighted in the NHS England definition of personalized care, social prescribing is also an important element of holistic care, where medicines are not always considered to be the solution in long-term conditions. In the group consultation setting, there is an excellent opportunity to discuss healthy lifestyles, promote smoking cessation, discuss sensible alcohol intake, learn about diet and exercise, and share nondrug strategies such as TENS machines for pain. In the Northumbria model, we have even conducted a Tai Chi session during the clinic. Embedding holistic care in a group setting comes naturally.

The evidence for pharmacist-led groups

There is widespread use of multidisciplinary teams incorporating pharmacists in group consultations and several examples of pharmacist-led models of group care. Examples of the former include shared medical appointments for gynecological chemotherapy [45], weight loss [46], and heart failure [47]. Several distinct pharmacist-led models have also been developed for diabetes [48], specifically for cardiovascular risk reduction [49], and diabetes with depression [50], with evidence of cost reduction compared to usual care [51]. Other pharmacist-led models include anticoagulant clinics [52], heart failure, including warfarin management in those with cardiac transplant and left ventricular assist devices [53], and erectile dysfunction [54]. The simplest summary of this is that group models, like one-to-one models, can be equally well delivered by any trained clinician, and the choice of clinician will often be driven by clinician availability, expertise on drug and other interventions, and cost-effectiveness. Pharmacists are often the best choice by these criteria.

Non-inferiority randomized controlled trial (RCT): Pharmacist-led group clinics for osteoporosis

After a positive experience of codesigning rheumatology group consultations with inflammatory arthritis patients including pharmacy input in community hospitals [55], we wanted to test this approach in primary care for osteoporosis. National Osteoporosis Society funding to address the high rates of untreated osteoporosis shown by regional audits and hip fracture rates in the top 10% nationally allowed us to set up an equivalence trial adopted by the National Institute for Health Research network. Pilot work had shown that a doctor, nurse, or pharmacist was equally capable of leading this novel form of group consultation. The choice to use a pharmacist for the trial was based on the criteria mentioned above. We knew there were thousands of untreated people in the highest risk group (red zone using the 10-year fracture risk with FRAX/NOGG). However, having calculated FRAX scores using data held on the practice registers, many of those who needed treatment were not aware of it. That educational need made the group consultation approach especially important. However, it also meant that we were inviting patients for a treatment they didn't know they needed as part of a trial for a novel model of care they hadn't previously encountered. This big ask did result in reasonable participation rates, with 18% consenting; but this is low for an RCT, which definitely made it harder to get the paper published in a high impact journal, despite robust methodology [56]. Designing a trial now, we would likely use a stepped wedge design.

We invited all high-risk patients at three Northumberland practices to take part, randomizing them in equal proportions to a single pharmacist-led group consultation or 15-min one-to-one appointment with the same pharmacist. Single-blinding of the teams analyzing the data was ensured. High-risk patients were offered treatment with alendronate 70 mg weekly with a calcium and vitamin D3 supplement to be taken daily. The study aimed to determine whether group clinics were noninferior to traditional one-to-one appointments for the primary outcome of medication possession ratio for bisphosphonates. Non-inferiority was acceptable if greater efficiency could be achieved using groups. Persistence with bisphosphonate therapy (months after treatment initiation), patient satisfaction, and cost differences between study arms formed the secondary outcome measures. Persistence with treatment was calculated by the number of months the drug was taken before cessation.

Participants were included if aged 50 years or older, at high-risk of fracture, ambulatory, with no previous osteoporosis treatment used, and who were happy to consent. Exclusions included those unable or too unwell to attend in person, those not consenting to participate, contra-indications to bisphosphonate therapy (severe renal impairment with glomerular filtration rate of < 35 mL/min, or upper gastrointestinal problems).

There was no statistical difference between the group and one-to-one clinic attenders in terms of age, sex, and FRAX score. From the 178 consented, there was no differential drop out and medication possession ratio (MPR) was equivalent at all time points (see Fig. 3) and for the 12-month

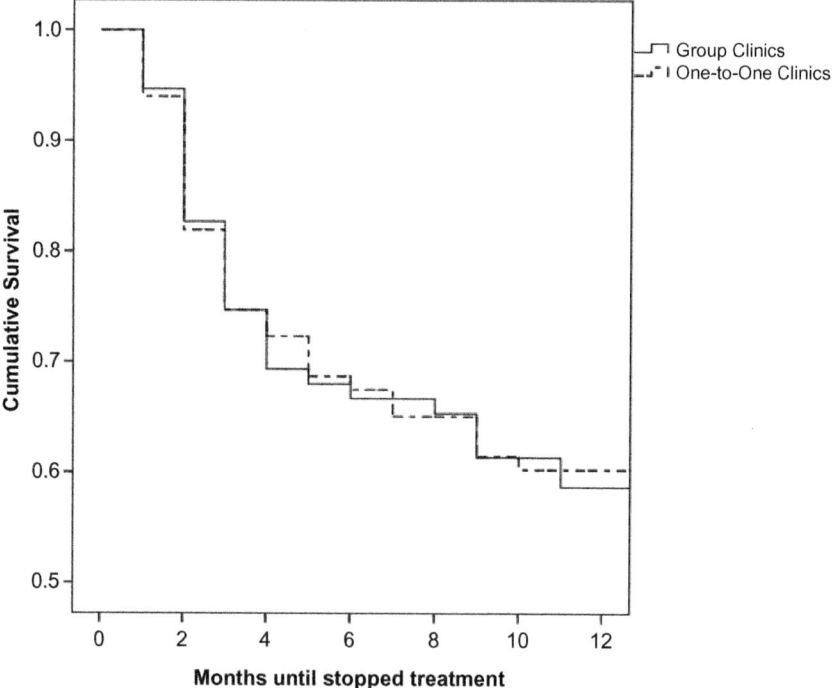

Fig. 3 Survival curve by treatment group. *(Used with permission from Birrell F; Osteoporosis group consultations are as effective as usual care: Results from a non-inferiority randomized controlled trial. Lifestyle Medicine, Wiley. Copyright (2020) John Wiley & Sons Inc.)*

primary endpoint (MPR group 0.62 vs. usual care 0.54). The median MPR was 0.62 (IQR 0.23–0.92, range 0–1.08) over 12 months for the group attenders and 0.54 (IQR 0.15–0.92, range 0–1.08) for one-to-one attenders. In univariate Cox regression analysis, one-to-one or group clinic attendance was not a significant predictor of outcome (OR = 1.038, 95% CI 0.636–1.694). This remained the case after adjustment for age, sex, FRAX hip score, and FRAX score for all major osteoporotic fractures (adjusted OR = 0.92, 95% CI 0.55–1.53). The medication possession ratio is a method of measuring medicines adherence; calculated by the proportion of time with adequate medication supply (i.e., prescriptions requested from their family doctor) divided by the number of doses that they should have had during 1 year from the point of starting treatment.

Treatment was shown to be noninferior, but the big advantage was that groups with a mean of 19 attendees took one-third of the time (4.8 min vs. 15 min). Therefore, this intervention was equally effective to usual care, but more cost-effective. Given that the patients received more time with the clinician (90-min clinic vs. 15-min one-to-one appointment), were able to ask and get more questions answered, and feel supported by others with the same condition, there is a compelling case for using this approach more widely. Within the group, the discussion led by the pharmacist covered FRAX-risk scoring, lifestyle advice including exercise, diet, smoking/alcohol reduction or cessation, and the rationale for weekly bisphosphonate treatment, while also offering opportunities to identify adverse drug reactions, side effects, and other drug-related concerns.

Patient satisfaction was high in both arms of the trial and equivalent with both approaches.

In clinical practice, if a patient stopped picking up their bisphosphonate prescription, this could trigger an invitation to the regular osteoporosis group consultation (or at scale, a dedicated shorter reinforcement group consultation, where those who had a fracture could share their experience to motivate others).

The key features of the osteoporosis group model are that it is codesigned, self-facilitated by the pharmacist who leads it (unlike most other models, which require a facilitator), and can be implemented quickly with minimal training. Many view big groups as being undesirable, believing "small is beautiful." In group consultation practice, big is beautiful: more questions, more answers, greater shared experience. The higher efficiency can come without a loss of quality, contrary to expectations of those unfamiliar with group models of care.

Both approaches allow for the personalization of care. With a one-to-one clinic, it is possible to tailor care individually but it is time-limited (15 min). With a group, greater efficiency is a major benefit, however, with the extended time available (90 min) in the group, extra opportunities for personalized care can be offered; social prescribing including lifestyle and general health advice, individual questions posed with answers shared with peers, responsive clinic design, tailoring of drug regimens, and sharing of experiences with medication between patients. The opportunities for empowering self-care are not limited by a 15-min appointment.

In the time of the coronavirus (COVID-19) pandemic, new ways of delivering group consultations have had to be imagined. The use of virtual group consultations provides an elegant solution and studies have shown that virtual groups are well received by patients and healthcare providers alike and are perceived as culturally sensitive and effective in reaching geographically and socially isolated patients [57,58].

Learning points for pharmacists

The key learning points from this chapter are as follows:
- Personalized care is important; patients are our partners.
- Shared decision-making improves deprescribing decisions.
- Polypharmacy is a worldwide problem and deprescribing medicines can help tackle its impact on welfare and health of the patients.
- Further robust studies are needed to support the development of multimorbidity guidelines for deprescribing.
- Group consultations can deliver high-quality, personalized care at scale
- Bigger is usually better in group consultations.
- Pharmacists can lead or be part of the multidisciplinary team in group consultations.
- Virtual group consultations are a key solution to delivering personalized care and scaling is being accelerated by the pandemic.

Recommendations

Pharmacists can lead the way when it comes to personalizing care in medicines optimization, deprescribing, and delivering group consultations. With many pharmacists now being independent prescribers, there should be little stopping us from innovating new ways of looking after our patients; the COVID-19 pandemic has also been a major catalyst for change. If you are a pharmacist looking to inspire change and wish to learn more about group consultations, consider downloading the group consultations app for free resources designed by our team or contact Alison@groupconsultations.com.

References

[1]   Coulter A, Roberts S, Dixon A. Delivering better services for people with long-term conditions: building the house of care. London: King's Fund; 2013.

[2]   The Health Foundation. Person-centred care made simple: What everyone should know about person-centred care. Available online at: https://www.health.org.uk/publications/person-centred-care-made-simple; 2016. [Accessed June 2020].

[3]   Collins A. Measuring what really matters: Towards a coherent measurement system to support person-centred care. The Health Foundation; 2014.

[4]   Wagner EH. Chronic disease management: what will it take to improve care for chronic illness? Eff Clin Pract 1998;1(1):2–4.

[5]   The Year of Care Partnerships. Care planning: impacts and benefits. Available at: www.yearofcare.co.uk/impact-and-benefits; 2014. [Accessed June 2020].

[6]   NHS England. Universal personalised care: implementing the comprehensive model. Personalised care guidance. Available online at: https://www.england.nhs.uk/publication/universal-personalised-care-implementing-the-comprehensive-model/; 2019. [Accessed June 2020].

[7]   Hirsch J, Bounthavong M, Arjmand A, Ha DR, Cadiz CL, Zimmerman A, Ourth H, Morreale AP, Edelman SV, Morello CM. Estimated cost-effectiveness, cost benefit, and risk reduction associated with an endocrinologist-pharmacist Diabetes Intense Medical Management "Tune-Up" clinic. J Manag Care Spec Pharm 2017;23(3):318–26.

[8]   Erku DA, Ayele AA, Mekuria AB, Belachew SA, Hailemeskel B, Tegegn HG. The impact of pharmacist-led medication therapy management on medication adherence in patients with type 2 diabetes mellitus: a randomized controlled study. Pharm Pract (Granada) 2017;15(3). https://doi.org/10.18549/pharmpract.2017.03.1026. Redondela Jul./Sep.

[9]   Martin P, Tamblyn R, Benedetti A, Ahmed S, Tannenbaum C. Effect of a pharmacist-led educational intervention on inappropriate medication prescriptions in older adults: the D-PRESCRIBE randomized clinical trial. JAMA 2018;320(18):1889–98. https://doi.org/10.1001/jama.2018.16131.

[10] NHS Digital. Prescription cost analysis - England. Published 2019 https://digital.nhs.uk/data-and-information/publications/statistical/prescription-cost-analysis/2018; 2018. [Accessed 27 June 2020].

[11] Bronskill SE, Gill SS, Paterson JM, Bell CM, Anderson GM, Rochon PA. Exploring variation in rates of polypharmacy across long term care homes. J Am Med Dir Assoc 2012;13(3):309.e15–21.

[12] Dwyer LL, Han B, Woodwell DA, Rechtsteiner EA. Polypharmacy in nursing home residents in the United States: results of the 2004 national nursing home survey. Am J Geriatr Pharmacother 2010;8(1):63–72.

[13] Flaherty JH, Perry III HM, Lynchard GS, Morley JE. Polypharmacy and hospitalization among older home care patients. J Gerontol Ser A 2000;55(10):M554–9.

[14] Fulton MM, Allen ER. Polypharmacy in the elderly: a literature review. J Am Acad Nurse Pract 2005;17(4):123–32.

[15] Jokanovic N, Tan EC, Dooley MJ, Kirkpatrick CM, Bell JS. Prevalence and factors associated with polypharmacy in long-term care facilities: a systematic review. J Am Med Dir Assoc 2015;16(6):535.e1–535.e12.

[16] Shah BM, Hajjar ER. Polypharmacy, adverse drug reactions, and geriatric syndromes. Clin Geriatr Med 2012;28(2):173–86.

[17] Gallagher P, O'Mahony D. STOPP (screening tool of older persons' potentially inappropriate prescriptions): application to acutely ill elderly patients and comparison with Beers' criteria. Age Ageing 2008;37(6):673–9.

[18] Gallagher PF, O'Connor MN, O'Mahony D. Prevention of potentially inappropriate prescribing for elderly patients: a randomized controlled trial using STOPP/START criteria. Clin Pharmacol Ther 2011;89(6):845–54.

[19] Parsons C, Johnston S, Mathie E. Potentially inappropriate prescribing in older people with dementia in care homes: a retrospective analysis. Drugs Aging 2012;29(2):143–55.

[20] Age UK. Making care safer. Improving medication safety for people in care homes: thoughts and experiences from carers and relatives. London: The Health Foundation; 2011. http://www.health.org.uk/publications/making-care-safer. [Last accessed 21 September 2014].

[21] Barber ND, Alldred DP, Raynor DK, et al. Care homes' use of medicines study: prevalence, causes and potential harm of medication errors in care homes for older people. Qual Saf Health Care 2009;18(5):341–6.

[22] Elliott RA, Camacho E, Campbell F, et al. Prevalence and economic burden of medication errors in the NHS in England. Policy Research Unit in Economic Evaluation of Health and Care Interventions (EEPRU); 2018.

[23] Reeve E, Gnjidic D, Long J. A systematic review of the emerging definition of 'deprescribing' with network analysis: implications for future research and clinical practice. Br J Clin Pharmacol 2015;20:1254–68.

[24] Woodward MC. Deprescribing: achieving better health outcomes for older people through reducing medications. J Pharm Pract Res 2003;33:323–8.

[25] Barnett N, Garfinkel D. Deprescribing one year on: challenging the first iatrogenic epidemic. Eur J Hosp Pharm 2018;25:63–4.

[26] Gillespie RJ, Harrison L, Mullan J. Deprescribing medications for older adults in the primary care context: a mixed studies review. Health Sci Rep 2018;1:e45. https://doi.org/10.1002/hsr2.45.

[27] Marvin V, Ward E, Poots AJ, Heard K, Rajagopalan A, Jubraj B. Deprescribing medicines in the acute setting to reduce the risk of falls. Eur J Hosp Pharm Sci Pract 2017;24(1):10–5.

[28] Naughton C, Hayes N. Deprescribing in older adults: a new concept for nurses in administering medicines and as prescribers of medicine. Eur J Hosp Pharm 2017;24(1):47–50.

[29] Todd A, Holmes HM. Recommendations to support deprescribing medications late in life. Int J Clin Pharm 2015;37(5):678–81.

[30] Scott IA, Hilmer SN, Reeve E, et al. Reducing inappropriate polypharmacy: the process of deprescribing. JAMA Intern Med 2015;175(5):827–34.

[31] Iyer S, Naganathan V, McLachlan AJ, Le Couteur DG. Medication withdrawal trials in people aged 65 years and older: a systematic review. Drugs Aging 2008;25(12):1021–31.

[32] van der Cammen TJ, Rajkumar C, Onder G, Sterke CS, Petrovic M. Drug cessation in complex older adults: time for action. Age Ageing 2014;43(1):20–5.

[33] Reeve E, Shakib S, Hendrix I, et al. The benefits and harms of deprescribing. Med J Aust 2014;201(7):386–9.

[34] Frankenthal D, Lerman Y, Kalendaryev E, Lerman Y. Intervention with the screening tool of older persons potentially inappropriate prescriptions/screening tool to alert doctors to right treatment criteria in elderly residents of a chronic geriatric facility: a randomized clinical trial. J Am Geriatr Soc 2014;62(9):1658–65.

[35] Park H, Satoh H, Miki A, Urushihara H, Sawada Y. Medications associated with falls in older people: systematic review of publications from a recent 5-year period. Eur J Clin Pharmacol 2015;71(12):1429–40.

[36] Zermansky A, Alldred D, DR P, et al. Clinical medication review by a pharmacist of elderly people living in care homes—randomised controlled trial. Age Ageing 2006;35:586–91.

[37] Ulley J, Harrop D, Ali A, Alton S, Davis SF. Deprescribing interventions and their impact on medication adherence in community-dwelling older adults with polypharmacy: a systematic review. BMC Geriatr 2019;19(1):15.

[38] Shrestha S, Poudel A, Steadman K, Nissen L. Outcomes of deprescribing interventions in older patients with life-limiting illness and limited life expectancy: a systematic review. Br J Clin Pharmacol 2020;86(10):1931–45. https://doi.org/10.1111/bcp.14113.

[39] Inch J, Notman F, Bond CM, et al. The Care Home Independent Prescribing Pharmacist Study (CHIPPS)-a non-randomised feasibility study of independent pharmacist prescribing in care homes. Pilot Feasibility Stud 2019;5:89.

[40] Garfinkel D, Mangin D. Feasibility study of a systematic approach for discontinuation of multiple medications in older adults: addressing polypharmacy. Arch Intern Med 2010;170(18):1648–54.

[41] Garfinkel D. Poly-de-prescribing to treat polypharmacy: efficacy and safety. Ther Adv Drug Saf 2018;9(1):25–43.

[42] Baqir W, Barrett S, Desai N, Copeland R, Hughes J. A clinico-ethical framework for multidisciplinary review of medication in nursing homes. BMJ Qual Improv Rep 2014;3(1). u203261.w202538.

[43] Baqir W, Hughes J, Jones T, et al. Impact of medication review, within a shared decision-making framework, on deprescribing in people living in care homes. Eur J Hosp Pharm 2017;24(1):30–3.

[44] Jones T, Darzi A, Egger G, Ickovics J, Noffsinger E, Ramdas K, Stevens J, Sumego M, Birrell F. A systems approach to embedding group consultations in the NHS. Future Healthc J 2019;6(1):8–16.

[45] Prescott LS, Dickens AS, Guerra SL, et al. Fighting cancer together: development and implementation of shared medical appointments to standardize and improve chemotherapy education. Gynecol Oncol 2016;140(1):114–9. https://doi.org/10.1016/j.ygyno.2015.11.006.

[46] Yager S, Parker M, Luxenburg J, Varghai NH. Evaluation of multidisciplinary weight loss shared medical appointments. J Am Pharm Assoc (2003) 2020;60(1):93–9. https://doi.org/10.1016/j.japh.2019.07.014.

[47] Singrey AM, Mehta BH, Casper KA. Management of heart failure patients through integrative medical group visits. Am J Health Syst Pharm 2015;72(5):349–51. https://doi.org/10.2146/ajhp140294.

[48] Taveira TH, Friedmann PD, Cohen LB, Dooley AG, Khatana SA, Pirraglia PA, et al. Pharmacist-led group medical appointment model in type 2 diabetes. Diabetes Educ 2010;36(1):109–17. https://doi.org/10.1177/0145721709352383.

[49] Cohen LB, Taveira TH, Khatana SA, Dooley AG, Pirraglia PA, Wu WC. Pharmacist-led shared medical appointments for multiple cardiovascular risk reduction in patients with type 2 diabetes. Diabetes Educ 2011;37(6):801–12. https://doi.org/10.1177/0145721711423980.

[50] Taveira TH, Dooley AG, Cohen LB, Khatana SA, Wu WC. Pharmacist-led group medical appointments for the management of type 2 diabetes with comorbid depression in older adults. Ann Pharmacother 2011;45(11):1346–55. https://doi.org/10.1345/aph.1Q212.

[51] Wu WC, Taveira TH, Jeffery S, et al. Costs and effectiveness of pharmacist-led group medical visits for type-2 diabetes: A multi-center randomized controlled trial. PLoS One 2018;13(4):e0195898. Published 2018 Apr 19 https://doi.org/10.1371/journal.pone.0195898.

[52] Griffin BL, Burkiewicz JS, Peppers LR, Warholak TL. International normalized ratio values in group versus individual appointments in a pharmacist-managed anticoagulation clinic. Am J Health Syst Pharm 2009;66(13):1218–23. https://doi.org/10.2146/ajhp080278.

[53] West LM, Williams JB, Faulkenberg KD. The impact of pharmacist-based services across the spectrum of outpatient heart failure therapy. Curr Treat Options Cardiovasc Med 2019;21(10):59. Published 2019 Sep 10 https://doi.org/10.1007/s11936-019-0750-3.

[54] Oehlke KJ, Whitehill DM. Shared medical appointments in a pharmacy-based erectile dysfunction clinic. Am J Health Syst Pharm 2006;63(12):1165–6. https://doi.org/10.2146/ajhp050497.

[55] Russell-Westhead M, O'Brien N, Goff I, Coulson E, Pape J, Birrell F. Mixed methods study of a new model of care for chronic disease: co-design and sustainable implementation of group consultations into clinical practice. Rheumatol Adv Pract 2020;4(1). https://doi.org/10.1093/rap/rkaa003. rkaa003. Published 2020 Jan 28.

[56] Baqir W, Gray WK, Blair A, Haining S, Birrell F. Osteoporosis group consultations are as effective as usual care: results from a non-inferiority randomized trial. Lifestyle Med 2020;1:e3. https://doi.org/10.1002/lim2.3.

[57] Shibuya K, Pantalone KM, Burguera B. Virtual shared medical appointments: a novel tool to treat obesity. Endocr Pract 2018;24:1108–9.

[58] Tokuda L, et al. The utilization of video-conference shared medical appointments in rural diabetes care. Int J Med Inform 2016;93:34–41. https://doi.org/10.1016/j.ijmedinf.2016.05.007.

CHAPTER 11

Pharmacy services for safe parenteral nutrition

Teresa Isichei Pounds[a,b] and Gil Hardy[c]
[a]PGY1 Pharmacy Residency Program, Pharmacy Clinical Services at the Atlanta Medical Center, Atlanta, GA, United States
[b]Experiential Education of South University School of Pharmacy, Savannah, GA, United States
[c]Ipanema Research Trust, Auckland, New Zealand

Introduction

It is well established that at least one-third of all adult patients admitted to hospital are either malnourished or at significant risk of disease-related malnutrition (DRM) [1, 2]. An estimated 33% of US patients are malnourished upon hospital admission with many remaining undiagnosed, leading to a rapid decline in their nutritional status during hospitalization [3]. Likewise, in Australia/New Zealand, it is estimated that 30%–40% of hospital patients are malnourished [4]. Adult DRM is a significant contributor to increased morbidity and mortality, poor quality of life, and longer hospital stays with higher healthcare costs. Pediatric malnutrition is estimated to contribute to approximately 45% of all child deaths, globally.

Suboptimal nutritional status can negatively impact patient outcomes. In the intensive care unit (ICU), poor outcomes have been associated with inflammation generated by critical illness that leads to deterioration of nutrition status and malnutrition [5]. If the patient's nutritional status is not addressed early enough and improved, this can lead to several negative outcomes that will affect not only the patient but also costs for the institution. Inaction can lead to increased length of stay, readmission rate, morbidity rate, clinical complications and infection rates, as well as higher costs of care.

Through evolution of specialized nutrition support, procedures in clinical nutrition have become efficacious but have gained in invasiveness as well as complexity. Therefore, nutrition support therapy is best performed as a collaborative effort among clinicians with specialized training and experience. In order to improve patient nutrition status, clinical outcomes, and reduce costs associated with inappropriate management of patients, many healthcare facilities have implemented a nutrition support team (NST) in lieu of individual caregivers [6]. NSTs became commonplace in the United

States, United Kingdom, and Taiwan in the 1990s [7, 8], but have been less widely adopted in other countries.

In the early days, an NST comprised a physician, a pharmacist, and preferably a specialist nurse, with dietitians playing a minor role, if any. Over the years, NSTs have become more multidisciplinary, with increasing responsibility taken by dietitians to assess nutrition status, determine the nutrition needs of patients, and in some countries, prescribe the nutrition regimen. This has sometimes meant less involvement from other clinicians and pharmacists; in particular, with advances in technology, it is now possible to purchase a range of standard parenteral nutrition (PN) regimens in multichamber bags (MCB), eliminating the need for "in-house" compounding. Consequently, some pharmacists have become "semidetached" from the NST, institutions in some countries have made NST redundant, and some countries have not adopted a team approach. A summary of the evolution of NST over the past 3–4 decades is included in Table 1 [9–16, 18].

PN is an important therapeutic modality that is used in adults, children, and infants for a variety of indications. Appropriate use of this complex therapy aims to maximize clinical benefit while minimizing the potential risk of adverse events. Despite being classified as a high-alert medication [19], only 58% of US organizations have precautions in place to prevent errors and patient harm associated with PN [20]. Complications can occur during the therapy and as the result of the PN process. In every clinical setting, it is the responsibility of the prescriber, whether it be a physician, pharmacist, nurse, or dietitian in the NST, to recognize and report all PN-related medication errors, whether or not they reach the patient [21].

Pharmacists have diverse roles when it comes to nutrition support, which can include: the assessment of patients' nutritional needs; the formulation, compounding, interventions on drug/nutrient interactions (DNI), dispensing, and quality management of EN/PN formulations; monitoring patients' response to nutrition therapy; education of patients, caregivers, and other health care professionals (HP) on long term/home nutrition support; and conducting EN/PN-related research and quality improvement activities [22].

Medications, such as antibiotics or chemotherapy, can sometimes contribute to secondary malnutrition, especially when they induce nausea, vomiting, diarrhea, constipation, or loss of appetite. PN and EN patients may also be receiving complex drug therapies, so having a medication expert on the NST is crucial. Pharmacists' in-depth knowledge of PN com-

Table 1 The evolution of nutrition support teams (NST).

Author (year published)	Year(s) study conducted and location	Study design (number of participants and primary diagnosis)	Pharmacy involvement	Follow up duration	Outcome measures	Summary of results	Conclusion
Dalton et al. J Parenter Enteral Nutr (1984) [9]	1982 United States	Prospective investigation into effect of NST on PN complications in cancer, Crohns, and G.I patients. Group A 28 patients: No NST Group B 32 patients: with NST	Clinical pharmacist collated and analyzed data	9 months	Incidence of PN mechanical, metabolic, and infectious complications	35% Mechanical (CVC related) 58% metabolic complications 5% infections NST improved PN monitoring	
Maurer et al. J Parenter Enteral Nutr (1996) [10]	1992 USA	Prospective review of PN prescribing. 50 patients Mixed surgical and medical	Assessment of PN appropriateness, follow up physician education	12 months	Proportion of appropriate PN prescriptions	22% PN inappropriate (43% medical, 2% surgical) Poor physician knowledge of PN indications Decision to establish a PNAG	Establishing a PNAG (NST) and improved physician education significantly reduced inappropriate PN ($P<.0005$)

Continued

Table 1 The evolution of nutrition support teams (NST)—cont'd

Author (year published)	Year(s) study conducted and location	Study design (number of participants and primary diagnosis)	Pharmacy involvement	Follow up duration	Outcome measures	Summary of results	Conclusion
Chris Anderson et al. J Parenter Enteral Nutr (1996) [11]	1979 and 1992 United States	Retrospective comparison of experience with NST involvement in PN prescribing and management 2×100 adult surgical and medical patients	Coauthor. Routinely involved in PN management	2×12 month periods separated by 13 years	Metabolic complications and costs	Decreased metabolic complications with NST. Specifically: hyperglycemia, hypokalemia, hypophosphatemia Only 2/3 patients referred to NST	No significant cost savings. Effectiveness could be improved with standard order forms and improved PN monitoring
Naylor et al. J Parenter Enteral Nutr (2004) [12]	1982–2001 Australia	Systematic review of 11 studies	Data analyzed by 2 reviewers and 2 independent assessors	6 months	Nutritional, metabolic, CVC–related complications, costs	NST reduced mechanical complications. 5/7 reported decreased CRS, only 2 studies reported lower costs with NST	Most studies small and underpowered. Patients with NST received energy requirements at lower cost. Other outcomes influenced by NST disciplines

Kennedy and Nightingale Nutrition (2005) [13]	1999–2001 United Kingdom	Hospital audit of PN episodes pre- and post-NST	NST includes a pharmacist	2 years: 1st year no NST 2nd year with NST	Cost Savings. Quality of care. CRS rates. Duration of PN. Mortality	CRS reduced from 71% to 29% with NST. Mortality reduced 43%–24%	Improved outcomes and tangible cost savings justified salaries of NST nurse and dietitian
Winkler Nutr Clin Pract (2005) [14]	2003 United States	Editorial review	All NST included a pharmacist	ASPEN safe practices survey in 2003	Patient safety and quality of care of PN/EN patients	54% had a performance improvement Program to monitor PN management	ASPEN must promote the interdisciplinary NST as a solution for patient safety quality care and controlled costs
Schneider Nutr Clin Pract (2006) [15]		Evidence-based review	Pharmacist author	1995–2004	Evidence for standardization and measurement of performance	Nutrition support is expensive and risky. The evidence-based standard is the interdisciplinary team approach	Nutrition support administered by a NST is superior to that provided by individual clinicians

Continued

Table 1 The evolution of nutrition support teams (NST)—cont'd

Author (year published)	Year(s) study conducted and location	Study design (number of participants and primary diagnosis)	Pharmacy involvement	Follow up duration	Outcome measures	Summary of results	Conclusion
DeLegge et al. Nutr Clin Pract (2010) [16]	2008 United States	ASPEN e-survey of 698 members on NST	15.2% of respondents were pharmacists	12 months	70 Questions on NST. Some open-ended. 8 questions on team effectiveness	42% Hospitals have NST of which 54% include a pharmacist. 23% had disbanded NST due to lack of physician interest (23%) or finances (17%)	Patient outcomes adversely affected in institutions that formerly had an NST [17]. Safety and efficacy of care are enhanced in a team that includes a pharmacist
DeLegge and Kelly Nutr Clin Pract (2013) [18]	2012 United States	Systematic literature review	Potential role for pharmacist in NST defined	12 months	NST costs training and implementation Future directions	NST increasing in Europe but decreasing in United States	NST dwindling in United States mostly for cost reasons Propose NST for more complex PN

CRS, catheter related sepsis; CVC, central venous catheter; EN, enteral nutrition; NST, nutrition support team; PN, parenteral nutrition; PNAG, parenteral nutrition advisory group.

pounding processes, ingredient stability/compatibility, and sterility, positions them as the ideal HP to offer suggestions on final product stability, storage, and administration hang times.

When we also consider the severity of drug shortages facing healthcare providers (e.g., potassium phosphate, atropine sulfate, dextrose, and intravenous multivitamins), involving a pharmacist will help the NST select alternative options without compromising overall patient care. This can help mitigate any potential complications along the way and shorten the recovery time. The multiple DNI associated with EN (fluoroquinolone binding, liquid phenytoin bioavailability, warfarin therapeutic levels, etc.), can be avoided or minimized, and other priority interactions, such as drug/nutrient or drug/drug compatibility, can also be identified and avoided. These are very important issues that can be improved and limited with the involvement of a pharmacist in the NST. Keeping pharmacists, nurses, and all other disciplines actively involved in the nutrition care plan of the patient will significantly improve the patient outcome and likely reduce preventable expenses [17].

An internal study conducted at WellStar Atlanta Medical Center reviewed patients with a discharge diagnosis of pneumonia, acute myocardial infarction, stroke, or heart failure. Using nutrition subcommittee-approved criteria derived from the American Society for Parenteral and Enteral Nutrition (ASPEN) and Academy Consensus Statement on Malnutrition evaluated outcomes between malnourished and nonmalnourished patients within each disease group, the study concluded that there was a trend of increased length of hospital stay in malnourished patients with pneumonia and stroke, a higher rate of hospital readmission for malnourished patients with pneumonia, acute myocardial infarction, stroke, and heart failure (HF), and higher average variable costs for malnourished patients with pneumonia, acute myocardial infarction, and heart failure [23].

Methods

Purpose

The purpose of this study was to show return on investment of having a transdisciplinary NST with a pharmacist specialized in nutrition support at Atlanta Medical Center (AMC) in Atlanta, Georgia. As a team, we hope to decrease inappropriate utilization of PN, decrease duration of therapy, and increase compliance of screening by nurses, assessment of nutritional status and severity of malnutrition by dietitians, proper diagnosis and documentation of malnutrition by clinicians, and appropriate coding for reimbursement.

Study design

This study was conducted retrospectively at Atlanta Medical Center (AMC) in Atlanta, Georgia from March to April 2014. Differences between current nutrition support practice at AMC and ASPEN recommendations were assessed via a gap analysis, including a staff survey. Participants in the survey included physicians, pharmacists, clinical dietitians, and registered staff nurses.

Subject population
- Inclusion criteria:
  - Aged ≥ 18 years
  - Discharge diagnosis of acute myocardial infarction and stroke
  - Pneumonia
  - Diagnosed with HF
- Exclusion criteria:
  - Age < 18 years
  - Pregnancy
  - Trauma patients
  - Liver disease
  - Infection
  - Postop state
  - Nephrotic syndrome
  - Fluid Imbalance

Sample
Patients included in the data analysis ($n = 30$) were those who had been on EN or PN therapy, with records retrievable through the institution's electronic health records.

Outcome measures

The quality of an NST, performance of an NST, effectiveness of an NST, process of nutrition assessment, appropriateness of EN and PN therapies, and management of nutrition support.

Definitions

Patients eligible for nutrition support (with DRM) in this project are defined (ICD9 Code 263) as when two or more of the following criteria are met:
- Albumin < 3.5 g/dL★
- Current weight is ≤89% of ideal body weight

- Current weight is $\leq 95\%$ of usual weight

or

- Prealbumin $< 21\,mg/L$

  Multidisciplinary Nutrition Support P&T Subcommittee: a team comprised of dietitians, nurses, pharmacists, physicians, and respiratory therapists that support the implementation of nutritional and metabolic services

  *Serum albumin at AMC is measured by Bromocresol Green reagent methodology: Normal $\geq 3.5–5.0\,g/dL$

  The roles played:

- *Pharmacist*: The role of the pharmacist was to gather the necessary information to assess the appropriateness of PN indications and determine if the duration of PN therapy could be impacted by interdisciplinary collaboration within a NST. The pharmacist performed medication reconciliation; evaluated medication–nutrition and medication–medication interactions; advised on appropriate feeding regimen; compounded parenteral and other prescribed nutrition formulation and ensured solution stability. They assessed patients' nutritional needs and the formulation; intervened on DNI; dispensed, and ensured quality management of EN/PN formulations; and monitored patients' response to nutrition therapy. The pharmacoeconomic impact of inappropriate PN was also impacted as were the potential cost savings/avoidance if the PN was never initiated.
- *Nurse*: timely screening of all patients
- *Dietitian*: perform and properly document assessment of patient's nutritional status
- *Physician*: appropriate diagnosis and documentation of patient's nutritional status based on dietitian's recommendation
- *Documentation specialist*: determine if patients with documented malnourishment were appropriately coded with malnourishment as a comorbidity upon discharge. Documentation of malnutrition with severity by a physician in the progress notes

Results

A case study conducted by the NST revealed:

- 80% of the patients sampled were on PN
- 42% of patients on PN were found to have inappropriate or questionable indications for the PN
- 96.7% of patients were screened by nursing

- 96.7% of patients had a nutrition assessment by a dietitian
- 40% of patients were found to be malnourished
- 8.3% of the patients found to be malnourished were appropriately documented by the dietitian
- 50% of the patients found to be malnourished were appropriately documented by the physician in the progress notes
- Patients appropriately documented: 66.7% of the patients were missed by coder but it did not impact DRG code; 33.3% of the patients were appropriately coded
- Patients not documented: 33.3% of the patients were missed by coder but it did not impact DRG code; 50% already had the highest DRG code due to comorbidities; 16.7% of patients could increase revenue by up to $6000 if coded for appropriately
- Length of therapy:
  - Average number of days on PN: 19
- Appropriateness of therapy:
  - 42% of patients were found to have questionable or inappropriate PN
  - This would decrease the number of inappropriate PN regimens by approximately 3–5 patients.
- Cost savings/avoidance
  - Cost per day: $273–$455 (if we were to decrease the number of inappropriate PNs by approximately 3–5 patients, this would result in a cost savings/avoidance of $273–$455 per day)
- Total Potential cost: $5187–$8645
- An NST could decrease this number of PN prescriptions by approximately 15%–20%
- 96.7% compliant with nursing screening and nutrition assessments
- ~8.3% compliance of malnutrition (and severity) documentation by the dietitians
- 50% compliance of the physicians documenting malnutrition (and severity) as a comorbidity
  - Appropriate documentation of malnutrition (and severity) diagnosis by primary medicine team
- Length of therapy
  - Transition from PN to either PO eating or EN

Discussion

In our case study, compliance with nursing screening and nutrition assessments was high, at 96.7%. There was a 50% compliance of the physicians documenting malnutrition (and severity) as a comorbidity, but documentation of malnutrition (and severity) by the dietitians had poor compliance (~8.3%). There is a need for appropriate documentation of DNI (and severity) diagnosis by the primary medical team. Additionally, we found that the transition from PN to either PO eating or EN was not effective and timely enough.

Our data reflects shortcomings in other countries and other institutions in the United States. A pilot survey of experts working in 10 countries on 5 continents, conducted by the international clinical nutrition section (ICNS) of ASPEN, revealed several differences in nutrition therapy practices. Only 40% of PN was prescribed by a full NST, 20% of institutions had no pharmacist reviewing PN orders and 50% had no quality management procedures in place [24]. In a recent metaanalysis that audited nine published studies on the benefits of NST between 2004 and 2019 [25], only one NST received a positive rating against a quality criteria checklist. The analysis revealed that inappropriate PN use varied from 4.3% to 18%. Overall, NSTs were associated with decreased incidence of inappropriate PN use.

We have seen over time that the gaps in therapy, lack of communication between HPs, lack of and clarity of roles lead to less than optimal patient outcome and this adversely affects hospital costs. Patients end up staying longer, being readmitted more often, and in many cases, their conditions worsen. From an institution's perspective, trying to provide the best patient care while limiting costs, it is important to reevaluate the roles of each healthcare worker involved in the nutrition care plan of the patient and bring them together to achieve the best outcome for each patient. With the implementation of a multidisciplinary NST, we will have increased opportunities to be more aggressive in transitioning from PN to either PO eating or EN. This can decrease the duration of PN for those patients, thus resulting in increased cost avoidance per day until the patient comes off PN [26].

As pharmacists, our expertise, knowledge, and skillset are invaluable when it comes to offering optimal nutrition support for patients. In particular, regarding safety and efficacy of the products or contents of the nutrition formulations, including the medications, pharmacists help with adjustments, alternatives, and interventions, and ensure maintenance of quality standards. Pharmacists can play the integral role of bridging the gap between dietitians, nurses, and physicians. Therefore, the multidisciplinary nutrition team with pharmacists playing a leading role is crucial to achieving the goal of optimal patient outcomes while reducing costs for the institution.

Conclusion

A multidisciplinary NST provides a system that allows healthcare professionals from different disciplines to work together using a shared conceptual framework to provide timely, cost-effective, safe, and appropriate nutrition therapy. Its main functions include full collaboration between all members to maximize patient therapeutic outcomes through provision of nutrition assessment, determination of micro/macronutrient needs, recommendations for appropriate enteral/parenteral nutrition therapy, and nutrition support management. A unified team approach ultimately leads to cost-effective and safe nutrition therapy.

References

[1] Barker LA, et al. Hospital malnutrition: prevalence, identification and impact on patients and the healthcare system. Int J Environ Res Public Health 2011;8:514–27.

[2] Jensen GL, et al. Adult starvation and disease-related malnutrition: a proposal for etiology-based diagnosis in the clinical practice setting from the international consensus guideline committee. J Parenter Enteral Nutr 2010;34:156–9.

[3] Tappenden KA, et al. Critical role of nutrition in improving quality of care: an interdisciplinary call to action to address adult hospital malnutrition. J Parenter Enteral Nutr 2013;37:482–97.

[4] Agarwal E, et al. Nutrition care practices in hospital wards: results from the nutrition care day survey 2010. Clin Nutr 2012;31:995–1001.

[5] McClave SA, Taylor BE, Martindale RG, et al. Guidelines for the provision and assessment of nutrition support therapy in the adult critically ill patient. J Parenter Enteral Nutr 2016;40(2):159–211.

[6] Munger NM. Parenteral nutrition: a time for interdisciplinary cooperation. J Parenter Enteral Nutr 1987;11:599.

[7] Allwood M, Hardy G, Sizer T. Roles and functions of the pharmacists in the nutrition support team. Nutrition 1996;12:63.

[8] Lee H-S. Roles and functions of the pharmacists in the nutrition support team. Nutrition 1996;12:65.

[9] Dalton MJ, Schepers G, Gee JP, Alberts CC, Eckhauser FE, Kirking DM. Consultative total parenteral nutrition teams: effect on the incidence of total parenteral nutrition-related complications. J Parenter Enteral Nutr 1984;8(2):146–52.

[10] Maurer J, Weinbaum F, Turner J, et al. Reducing the inappropriate use of parenteral nutrition in an acute care teaching hospital. J Parenter Enteral Nutr 1996;20(4):272–4.

[11] ChrisAnderson D, Heimburger DC, Morgan SL, et al. Metabolic complications of total parenteral nutrition: effects of a nutrition support service. J Parenter Enteral Nutr 1996;20(3):206–10.

[12] Naylor CJ, Griffiths RD, Fernandez RS. Does a multidisciplinary total parenteral nutrition team improve patient outcomes? A systematic review. J Parenter Enteral Nutr 2004;28(4):251–8.

[13] Kennedy JF, Nightingale JM. Cost savings of an adult hospital nutrition support team. Nutrition 2005;21(2):1127–33.

[14] Winkler MF. Improving safety and reducing harm associated with specialized nutrition support. Nutr Clin Pract 2005;20(6):595–6.

[15] Schneider PJ. Nutrition support teams: an evidence-based practice. Nutr Clin Pract 2006;21(1):62–7.

[16] A.S.P.E.N. Practice Management Task Force, De Legge M, Wooley JA, Guenter P, et al. The state of nutrition support teams and update on current models for providing nutrition support therapy to patients. Nutr Clin Pract 2010;25(1):76–84.

[17] Jacobsson A. Malnutrition in patients suffering from chronic heart failure; the nurse's care. Eur J Heart Fail 2001;3(4):449–56.

[18] DeLegge MH, Kelly AT. The state of nutrition support teams. Nutr Clin Pract 2013;28(6):691–7.

[19] Ayers P, et al. ASPEN PN safety consensus recommendations. J Parenter Enteral Nutr 2014;38:296.

[20] Boullata J, Guenter P, Mirtallo J. A parenteral nutrition survey with gap analysis. J Parenter Enteral Nutr 2013;37(2):212–22.

[21] Sacks GS. Safety surrounding parenteral nutrition systems. J Parenter Enteral Nutr 2012;36:20S–2S.

[22] Katoue MG, Al-Taweel D. Role of the pharmacist in parenteral nutrition therapy: challenges and opportunities to implement pharmaceutical care in Kuwait. Pharm Pract 2016;14(2):680.

[23] Moye PM, PharmD, BCPS, AAHIVP, William Qian, PharmD Candidate. Impact of malnutrition in patients with heart failure on hospital length of stay and readmission rate. Atlanta Medical Center. Institutional Review Board; 2015.

[24] Hardy G, et al. Are international best PN practices being met? ASPEN; 2019.

[25] Stidham MA, Douglas JW. Nutrition support team oversight and appropriateness of parenteral nutrition in hospitalized adults: a systematic review. J Parenter Enteral Nutr 2020. https://doi.org/10.1002/jpen.1864.

[26] Guenter P, et al. Standardised competencies for PN: the ASPEN model. NCP 2018;33:295–304.

CHAPTER 12

Community pharmacists and pharmacovigilance: Global overview and a case study

Rabia Hussain[a,b]
[a]Commonwealth Pharmacists Association, London, United Kingdom
[b]Faculty of Pharmacy, The University of Lahore, Lahore, Pakistan

Introduction

Globally, patient safety is considered as a major public concern in any healthcare system. Drug-related morbidity and mortality is recognized as a major health problem by the public and healthcare professionals [1]. A drug-related adverse reaction can be defined as a response to a drug that is unintended, and which occurs at doses normally used. Adverse drug reactions (ADRs) are responsible for about 10% of hospital admissions and cause enormous fiscal burden on the healthcare systems [2, 3].

Medicine safety is a key issue within the broader prospect of patient safety [4–6]. A community pharmacist (CP) knows a drug product, and it's manufacturing, storage, and distribution, as well as its use. Additionally, a pharmacist's knowledge in pharmacology equip them well with regards to adverse drug events, thus, preparing them to design appropriate interventions to avoid the possible risk to patients' health [7]. In a community pharmacy, the pharmacist monitors the prescription, as well as the medicines for any possible side effects [8]. In this context, community pharmacists can play a vital role in the ongoing safety evaluation of medicines [9, 10].

The global landscape of community pharmacy

In England, there are 11,700 community pharmacies with a daily visit of more than 1.6 million individuals. In most areas, a pharmacy is located within a 20-min walk of about 89.2% of the population [11]. As pharmacists in a community environment can be consulted without an appointment, they claim the most considerable impact on the provision of healthcare services in England. This includes their role in ensuring the safe use of medicines among chronic patients, including through medicine reviews as well as screening services [11, 12].

Australia has 5700 community pharmacies and about two-thirds of 30,000 registered pharmacists work in those community pharmacies. On average, in Australia, an individual visits a pharmacy 14 times a year, making a total of 350 million visits by patients [13].

In New Zealand, there are more than 900 pharmacies, being visited by thousands of patients on a daily basis [14]. Canada has about 10,682 community pharmacies with more than 27,000 community pharmacists serving the community [15]. Similarly, Germany has approximately 21,400 community pharmacies accommodating 46,000 pharmacists, with each pharmacy serving on average 3900 inhabitants [16]. France has almost the same number of pharmacies as Germany, covering the whole nation, with 22,561 pharmacies, representing one per 2500 or 3000 inhabitants [17]. Having a population of 47 million people, Spain has approximately 22,000 community pharmacies and 52,000 community pharmacists [18].

In the United States (US), the number of community pharmacies is 67,753 with a total number of 186,000 individuals working as community pharmacists [19]. Thus, providing access to more than 90% of the population, who live within 2-miles of a community pharmacy, and fulfilling the needs of people including dispensing, health screening, preventive care, as well as medication therapy management [20, 21].

Table 1 shows the number of pharmacies available per 100,000 inhabitants in several countries [22].

Table 1 Number of pharmacies available per 100,000 inhabitants.

Country	Pharmacies per 100,000 population
Canada	27.0
Germany	25.9
Netherlands	11.6
New Zealand	20.8
United Kingdom	17.6
United States	17.2

Role of the community pharmacist in pharmacovigilance

Over the years, the scope of pharmacovigilance (PV) has evolved, and according to the World Health Organization (WHO), the activities pertaining to pharmacovigilance include detection, assessment, and understanding and prevention of adverse effects [10]. Hence, a pharmacovigilance (PV) system is not only meant for risk identification and collection of data but, it also involves risk minimization and communication to protect the public from harm related to medicines' adverse effects [23].

As part of the healthcare team, the pharmacist has a crucial role in serving as a source of information, early detection and monitoring of adverse drug reactions (ADRs) and other drug-related problems [24]. A pharmacist can educate and train fellow pharmacists and staff, as well as the other healthcare team members including physicians and nurses, about the importance of pharmacovigilance. They can educate their patients and can encourage them to report to the pharmacist, or any other healthcare professionals, if they ever encounter an adverse drug event.

Throughout the globe, many patients prefer visiting pharmacies to treat their minor ailments and to get advice from the community pharmacists. Hence community pharmacists have a distinct role to offer, as they are involved not only in the treatment process but also for the education of the patient. Thus, in such a scenario, the pharmacovigilance system, managed by pharmacists, can easily identify adverse drug reactions [25, 26], and drug regulatory authorities and other government bodies can improve the ADR monitoring system by providing necessary resources and incentives. In addition, awareness about ADRs, particularly their significance, management, prevention of ADRs, and availability of a concise and efficient reporting system is needed to achieve successful pharmacovigilance in a community pharmacy setting [27].

During the past few decades, the healthcare system has seen a major shift in the role of the pharmacist from a drug dispenser to a patient-focused healthcare provider in almost every part of the world [28, 29]. The community pharmacist is identified as the most accessible healthcare professional, who can optimize and facilitate rational use of medicines as well as improve patients' self-care [29, 30].

The role and contribution of community pharmacists differ from country to country. However, medicine safety issues remain the same [31]. Community pharmacists can monitor and report adverse drug reactions based on their clinical expertise as they interact with their patients regarding medicine management [3]. In addition, community pharmacists can serve as a bridge between patients and physicians and can counsel the patients to prevent an ADR by providing drug safety information [31, 32].

A schematic diagram of the role of the pharmacist in pharmacovigilance is given in Fig. 1.

In the United States, pharmacists were listed as one of the most important healthcare professionals in reporting. This is also the case in many European countries, including the Netherlands, Portugal, and Spain, where community pharmacists have played an important role in ADR reporting [33]. The ADR reporting rate from around the globe for community pharmacists ranged from 2.3% to 41% [34, 35]. Table 2 further elaborates this global data.

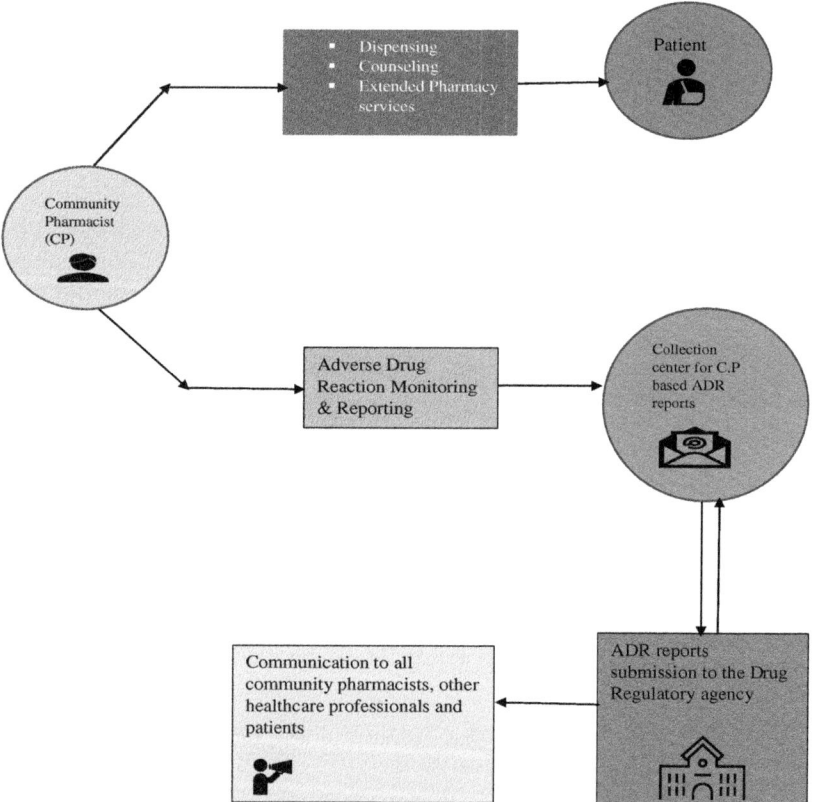

Fig. 1 Schematic diagram showing community pharmacy services and pharmacovigilance.

Table 2 Countries where community pharmacists submit ADR reports.

Country	Reporting from community pharmacists	Percentage of ADR reports
Australia	Yes	6%
Japan	Yes	39%
New Zealand	Yes	2.3%
Netherlands	Yes	40.2%
Spain	Yes	25.9%

Community pharmacy and pharmacovigilance: A case study from Pakistan

Aim of the study

The objectives of this study were to explore the knowledge and perceptions of community pharmacist about medicine safety and pharmacovigilance. It also aimed to assess the attitudes and preparedness of community pharmacists toward ADR reporting. The objectives of the study also included exploring the experiences of community pharmacists related to pharmacovigilance activities.

Methods
Study setting
Pakistan is a lower-middle-income country with a population of 207.8 million and is ranked as the fifth most populous country in the world [36]. Punjab is the most populous province of the country, comprising half of the country's population and Lahore is the provincial capital (of the Punjab province) and has a population of over 12 million people [37]. It was reported that there were 80,000 community pharmacies functioning in Pakistan, though this data still needs to be updated [38]. In Pakistan, the out of pocket expenditure on health care is more than 80%. In this context, having an ADR can severely impact the health of a patient [38].

The community pharmacist is an important component of any healthcare system. Similarly, their role and their participation in medicine safety are crucial for the development of a country's healthcare system. The community pharmacy in Pakistan is still in the transition phase, and the pharmacist's role in the provision of pharmacovigilance is still evolving [39], thus, in this context, the present study was planned to explore more in detail.

Study design

A qualitative research approach was employed, as this method produces data which is contextually rich and is based on an individual's experiences. It also helps in the identification of the gaps that otherwise could not be spotted with a quantitative research design [40, 41].

Study sampling

A nonprobability sampling technique was chosen for the qualitative study, and the required sample size achieved through the process of saturation of data. Saturation is related to the building of the data within the process of inquiry, by attending to scope and replication. While the scope of data means the comprehensiveness and the depth of the topic covered in qualitative research, replication means data have common but essential characteristics from several participants [42, 43].

The targeted participants were recruited from community pharmacies in Lahore. The selected participants were registered pharmacists from Punjab Pharmacy Council, and they were working as full-time employees. They were purposively selected and their convenience as per time and place availability with prior experience and an understanding of the community pharmacy practice was considered as a factor to include them in the study [9, 44]. All participants voluntarily participated in this study, and no incentive was offered to them to participate in this study. The interviews were recorded and transcribed verbatim. The study was approved under reference no. HEC/PUCP/1943 by the Humans Ethics Committee (HEC), University College of Pharmacy, University of the Punjab, Lahore, Pakistan.

Data collection

Semistructured interviews were considered as appropriate to collect the data. Semistructured interviews are based on an interview guide, which has predetermined topics or questions. Semistructured interviews have a flexible structure and provide freedom to the researcher to interview several people in a systematic manner [45]. A semistructured interview guide was developed based on an in-depth review of the literature and by considering current practices of the community pharmacist regarding medicine safety and pharmacovigilance [46–51]. A summary of the topic guides for the semistructured interview is given in Fig. 2.

Fig. 2 Development and summary of the topic guide to conduct semistructured interviews.

Results

Demographics of the participants

There were seven male ($n=7$) and four female ($n=4$) participants, who took part in the interviews. The majority of the participants ($n=8$) were below 30 years of age and the majority ($n=7$) had completed the specialization as Masters/M.Phil degree. Eight participating pharmacists ($n=8$) had experience of up to 10 years of service, and three ($n=3$) had experience of more than 10 years. None of the participants had ever reported about ADR (either in verbal or in written form). The demographic distribution of the participants is given in Table 3.

Thematic analysis of the interviews

Five major themes resulted from thematic analysis of the interviews. They were: (1) familiarity with medicine safety and its counseling; (2) knowledge about Adverse Drug Reaction and it's reporting system; (3) attitudes about ADR reporting; (4) knowledge about pharmacovigilance; and (5) barriers and facilitators to ADR reporting.

Table 3 Demographic characteristics of the participants.

Characteristics	Frequency
Gender	
Male	7
Females	4
Age (years)	
21–30	8
31–40	3
Education	
Pharm-D	4
Specialization	7
Experience (years)	
1–5	2
6–10	6
> 10	3
ADR reporting	
Yes	0
No	11

The participants were interviewed regarding their knowledge and perceptions about medicine safety. All participants had a good understanding of medicine safety.

Medicine safety is an important aspect of our practice as a community pharmacist. We think that all the medicines which we give to our patients should be free of adverse effects or having least side effects and the patient, whoever is taking that medicines, may not be troubled after these medicines. (CP1, Male)

Medicine safety is anything we can prevent harm from. It is a key responsibility of all healthcare professional, pharmacist, physician and nurses, we all are responsible for that, we are present to prevent drug reaction and interaction, to prevent ADR. (CP4, Female)

Medicine safety is when a doctor prescribes a medicine to the patients, it should be safe for patients and only targeted to achieve therapeutic goals. (CP7, Male)

All community pharmacists defined an ADR. Some of the responses are given below:

Those reactions, which are untoward reactions and sometimes we are aware about those reactions and sometimes we cannot predict. (CP2, Male)

Any unintended, obnoxious response of a drug is an ADR. (CP4, Female)

Bearing in mind the safety of medicines, almost all community pharmacists provided counseling to their patients, and two-thirds of the participants stated counseling as an important part of their professional responsibility.

Counseling depends upon the type of medicines as well as the query, a patient is usually asking for. It lasts up to 3–10 minutes, again depends on question of patients. (CP7, Male)

Some pharmacists also spoke about counseling and the challenges of time constraints and increased workload.

During business hours, rush hours, we usually request our patients to wait for some time or we give them some appropriate time, so that we can counsel them properly. (CP1, Male)

On an average, it takes around 4 to 5 mins. Not more than that. I have enough time to counsel, as well as I am willing to answer the query. If there is a long queue. I ask them to wait for a while.

I don't feel this as burden, this all depends upon handling of patient flow. Being a pharmacist, it's my major responsibility to counsel about medicine safety in a right way. I feel very satisfied after counseling the patients. In fact, I enjoy counseling the patient. (CP9, Female)

It mostly takes 5–6 minutes if there are 4 or 5 medicines in a prescription. It's quite difficult to manage my practice as pharmacist, It has impact on my workload as well. I just loose, focus on other customers, may be someone who needs the help most. (CP11, Male)

The pharmacists had a positive attitude toward ADR reporting, and they were willing to report an ADR.

It's my responsibility as a professional and my patients are my priority. No pressure, this is my profession and it's my responsibility. (CP1, Male)

Pharmacists are life savers, If we are reporting an ADR, we are saving other people lives. (CP4, Female)

I feel it's my core responsibility to report an ADR. (CP7, Male)

About one-third of community pharmacists were aware about the pharmacovigilance system, its establishment, and functions in Pakistan.

Yes, we have DRAP (Drug Regulatory Authority of Pakistan) and which is under Ministry of Health. It should have the responsibility of gathering all data of ADR. Ministry is there, but this is not functional. (CP2, Male)

No idea, that DRAP is related to ADR reporting. I thought, its working with the import and export of medicines. (CP4, Female)

No, because nobody guided about this system, and may be due to personal lack of interest from my side. May be DRAP has not introduced the system and did not provide the information. (CP7, Male)

When asked about the possible factors that can impede the process of ADR reporting, all community pharmacists provided almost similar responses:

Our system is the major barrier. They should have strict policies; all HCP (healthcare professionals) must be trained and should understand the difference between ADR and disease process. Lack of knowledge, lack of professional attitude of HCP is the barrier. Reporting is a positive thing and it should be made clear to the reporter that reporting will not put him in trouble, rather it contributes to the improvement of the system. (CP3, Male)

Pharmacist should be trained enough so that they are not reluctant to report an ADR. Training is a must, ADR form, online system is a must.

Lack of communication and lack of online reporting system or even manual reporting are the barriers. How one can report an ADR, if they don't have a source. (CP5, Female)

Main motivation is if we have a system and if we consider this as an ethical responsibility. If community pharmacies include this as part of the SOPs (standard operating procedures), then it can be done efficiently.

Main barrier is system lacking, awareness about ADR reporting, gaps in our knowledge, lack of time, up to certain extent but education is the main factor. (CP7, Male)

Lack of time, lack of interest are main barriers. (CP11, Male)

Discussion

The current study has identified several issues in Pakistan's pharmacovigilance system from a community pharmacy perspective. The results of the study have shown that community pharmacists had a good understanding of medicine safety and adverse drug reaction. They were able to define medicine safety and ADR properly. They were also aware of the importance of proper counseling to patients regarding the medicines they were using. This is in line with a study by Hajj et al. [1] in which it was reported that community pharmacists had a good understanding of medicine safety and they were able to report ADRs [1]. Another study from Saudi Arabia has also shown that community pharmacists had good knowledge about ADR; although this is contrary to a study from the United Arab Emirates (UAE), where none of the participants were able to define an ADR correctly [52].

In the current study, the participants have expressed a very positive attitude toward counseling, considering it as a way to improve medicines safety. A study by Leguelinel-Blache et al. has concluded that counseling is not only crucial to improve medication adherence but to improve medicine safety as well [53]. Similarly, Sanii et al. [54] outlined that counseling by pharmacists can improve therapeutic outcomes [54].

Concerning the attitudes of the participants toward reporting an ADR in the present study, the majority of the participants agreed that it was their professional responsibility and a core duty. Many studies have corroborated our findings, that ADR reporting is the professional responsibility of the community pharmacist and if a reporting system is introduced, community pharmacists will report ADRs [9, 50, 55, 56]. Such as a study by Yu et al. [33] highlighted that about 95% of the participants considered ADR reporting as a professional obligation [33]. Similarly, in a study by Qassim et al. [52], about 89.2% pharmacists believed that ADR reporting is part of their professional responsibility [52]. However, in other studies, it was seen that participants considered ADR reporting as an additional responsibility to their everyday routine work [57, 58].

In Pakistan, the national pharmacovigilance system was established in 2017, and the Drug Regulatory Authority of Pakistan (DRAP) is continuously making efforts to improve medicine safety and reporting of issues related to the adverse effects of medicines [4, 5, 59]. The current study has revealed that the majority of the participants had no idea about the existence of a pharmacovigilance system in the country. It is observed in the majority of the studies, that lack of knowledge about the existence of pharmacovigilance systems was an important factor for nonreporting of adverse events. For example, a study from Saudi Arabia has concluded that about 56% of the community pharmacists were unaware of the existence of a pharmacovigilance system in the country and never reported [60].

Despite the willingness to report an ADR, a majority of participants in the present study confirmed that the main barrier that could hinder a community pharmacist from reporting is the absence of having an ADR reporting system. The lack of knowledge, workload, nonprofessional attitude, and lack of training were also highlighted by the participants as major barriers to reporting. Many studies from community settings have discussed the same barriers; in particular, a study from Lebanon listed the lack of an established system, lack of knowledge, and the workload as the factors linked to nonreporting of ADRs by community pharmacists [1, 49, 61, 62]. A study by Irujo et al. [63] has also identified lack of knowledge and lack of time as the main barriers to ADR reporting among Spanish community pharmacists [63].

The participants in our study have also provided suggestions to improve the situation of ADR reporting in community pharmacy setting. This includes the establishment of an ADR reporting system as well as continuous education and training of community pharmacists [60, 63, 64].

A study from Nigeria has also recommended including pharmacovigilance as a topic in continuing education programs to improve ADR reporting [65]. The participants has also emphasized that having an online system of ADR reporting would help facilitate ADR reporting and ultimately such a pharmacovigilance system could connect and disseminate the ADR reports to all community pharmacises throughout the country [4, 5].

Strengths and limitations

This is the first study done on Pakistan's community pharmacists regarding the understanding of medicine safety and pharmacovigilance from a qualitative perspective. It is possible that respondents may have given socially desirable responses during the interviews. However, the anonymity and confidentiality of the participants were maintained throughout the process so that participants could express their views freely. Another limitation could be that the data was collected from community pharmacies in a single city, and the data cannot be generalized to the whole country. However, Lahore is the second biggest city in Pakistan. Thus, it is expected that the situation of the provision of medicines safety and pharmacovigilance would not be very different in other parts of the country.

Conclusion

The case study has focused on community pharmacists from a qualitative perspective regarding their understanding, knowledge, attitude and perceptions about medicine safety and pharmacovigilance system in Pakistan. The findings have suggested that the respondents had good knowledge about medicines safety and ADRs. However, they were not aware of the existence of a pharmacovigilance system in the country. The key barriers related to nonreporting of an ADR included lack of an established ADR reporting system as well as lack of education and training among community pharmacists.

References

[1] Hajj A, Hallit S, Ramia E, Salameh P, Order of Pharmacists Scientific Committee—Medication Safety Subcommittee. Medication safety knowledge, attitudes and practices among community pharmacists in Lebanon. Curr Med Res Opin 2018;34:149–56.
[2] Kongkaew C, Hann M, Mandal J, Williams SD, Metcalfe D, Noyce PR, Ashcroft DM. Risk factors for hospital admissions associated with adverse drug events. Pharmacotherapy 2013;33:827–37.
[3] WHO. Safety of medicines: a guide to detecting and reporting adverse drug reactions: why health professionals need to take action. World Health Organization; 2002. [online]. Available from: https://apps.who.int/iris/handle/10665/67378. [Accessed 2 July 2020].

[4] Hussain R, Hassali MA, Babar Z. Medicines safety in the globalized context. In: Global pharmaceutical policy. Springer; 2020.

[5] Hussain R, Hassali MA, Muneswarao J, Hashmi F. Physicians' understanding and practices of pharmacovigilance: qualitative experience from a lower middle-income country. Int J Environ Res Public Health 2020;17:2209.

[6] Phipps DL, Noyce PR, Parker D, Ashcroft DM. Medication safety in community pharmacy: a qualitative study of the sociotechnical context. BMC Health Serv Res 2009;9:1–10.

[7] Alli D. A day in the life of a head of pharmacovigilance. Pharm J 2019. United Kingdom [online]. Available from: https://www.pharmaceutical-journal.com/careers-and-jobs/careers-and-jobs/career-profile/a-day-in-the-life-of-a-head-of-pharmacovigilance/20206211.article. [Accessed 10 June 2020].

[8] Spears T. Community pharmacists play key role in improving medication safety. Texas: Pharmacy Times; 2010. [online]. Available from: https://www.pharmacytimes.com/publications/issue/2010/November2010/CommunityPharmacists_MedSafety. [Accessed 24 July 2020].

[9] Hussain R, Hassali MA, Hashmi F, Farooqui M. A qualitative exploration of knowledge, attitudes and practices of hospital pharmacists towards adverse drug reaction reporting system in Lahore, Pakistan. J Pharm Policy Pract 2018;11:16.

[10] WHO. The importance of pharmacovigilance – safety monitoring of medicinal products. World Health Organization; 2002. [online]. Available from: http://archives.who.int/tbs/safety/s4893e.pdf. [Accessed 15 July 2020].

[11] Goundrey-Smith S. The connected community pharmacy: benefits for healthcare and implications for health policy. Front Pharmacol 2018;9:1352.

[12] Murray R. Community pharmacy clinical services review. London: NHS England; 2016. p. 16.

[13] The Pharmacy Guild of Australia. Vital facts on community pharmacy. Australia: The Pharmacy Guild of Australia; 2018. [online]. Available from: https://www.guild.org.au/__data/assets/pdf_file/0020/12908/Vital-facts-on-community-pharmacy.pdf. [Accessed 12 July 2020].

[14] PSNZ. Careers and qualifications in pharmacy. New Zealand: Pharmaceutical Society of New Zealand; 2020. [online]. Available from: https://www.psnz.org.nz/Category?Action=View&Category_id=223#:~:text=Community%20Pharmacy&text=There%20are%20over%20900%20pharmacies,the%20maintenance%20of%20good%20health. [Accessed 15 July 2020].

[15] CPA. Where Canada's pharmacists work. Canada: Canadian Pharmacists Association; 2020. [online]. Available from: https://rethinkpharmacists.ca/by-the-numbers/#:~:text=There%20are%20more%20than%2042%2C500,every%20community%20across%20the%20country. [Accessed 15 July 2020].

[16] Eickhoff C, Schulz M. Pharmaceutical care in community pharmacies: practice and research in Germany. Ann Pharmacother 2006;40:729–35.

[17] Bourdon O, Ekeland C, Brion F. Pharmacy education in France. Am J Pharm Educ 2008;72.

[18] Gastelurrutia MA, Faus MJ, Martinez-Martinez F. Primary health care policy and vision for community pharmacy and pharmacists in Spain. Pharm Pract 2020;18:1999.

[19] Goode J-V, Owen J, Page A, Gatewood S. Community-based pharmacy practice innovation and the role of the community-based pharmacist practitioner in the United States. Pharmacy 2019;7:106.

[20] Qato DM, Zenk S, Wilder J, Harrington R, Gaskin D, Alexander GC. The availability of pharmacies in the United States: 2007–2015. PLoS ONE 2017;12, e0183172.

[21] Rudavsky R, Pollack CE, Mehrotra A. The geographic distribution, ownership, prices, and scope of practice at retail clinics. Ann Intern Med 2009;151:315–20.

[22] NPA. The retail pharmacy business in Canada. Canada: Neighbourhood Pharmacy Association of Canada; 2016. [online]. Available from: https://s3.amazonaws.com/icmsmedia/mycacdslucee/Pharmacy360%20Summary%20Final.pdf?AWSAccessKey-Id=AKIAIGKPNO5F3LUVCLLA&Expires=1598478312&Signature=LC5d0Jjzsrw-FyEzLiHzd6zQGF%2B4%3D. [Accessed 15 July 2020].

[23] Abiri OT, Johnson WC. Pharmacovigilance systems in resource-limited settings: an evaluative case study of Sierra Leone. J Pharm Policy Pract 2019;12:1–8.

[24] Mekonnen AB, McLachlan AJ, Jo-Anne EB, Mekonnen D, Abay Z. Barriers and facilitators to hospital pharmacists' engagement in medication safety activities: a qualitative study using the theoretical domains framework. J Pharm Policy Pract 2018;11:2.

[25] Toklu HZ, Hussain A. The changing face of pharmacy practice and the need for a new model of pharmacy education. J Young Pharm 2013;5:38–40.

[26] Toklu HZ, Mensah E. Why do we need pharmacists in pharmacovigilance systems? Online J Public Health Inform 2016;8.

[27] FIP. FIP statement of policy-the role of the pharmacist in pharmacovigilance. Netherlands: International Pharmaceutical Federation; 2006. [online]. Available from: https://www.fip.org/file/1464. [Accessed 10 July 2020].

[28] Jesson JK, Langley CA, Wilson KA, Hatfield K. Science or practice? UK undergraduate experiences and attitudes to the MPharm degree. Pharm World Sci 2006;28:278–83.

[29] Rutter P, Brown D, Howard J, Randall C. Pharmacists in pharmacovigilance: can increased diagnostic opportunity in community settings translate to better vigilance? Drug Saf 2014;37:465–9.

[30] Paudyal V, Hansford D, Cunningham S, Stewart D. Pharmacy assisted patient self care of minor ailments: a chronological review of UK health policy documents and key events 1997–2010. Health Policy 2011;101:253–9.

[31] Farooq N, Amin F. Role of community pharmacist in pharmacovigilence. Khyber Med Univ J 2019;11:181–3.

[32] Rajanandh M, Praveen Kumar V, Yuvasakthi S. Roles of pharmacist in pharmacovigilance: a need of the hour. J Pharmacovigil 2016;4:221–2.

[33] Yu YM, Lee E, Koo BS, Jeong KH, Choi KH, Kang LK, Lee MS, Choi KH, Oh JM, Shin WG. Predictive factors of spontaneous reporting of adverse drug reactions among community pharmacists. PLoS ONE 2016;11, e0155517.

[34] TGA. Medicines and vaccines post-market vigilance - statistics for 2016. Australia: Australian Government; 2017. [online]. Available from: https://www.tga.gov.au/medicines-and-vaccines-post-market-vigilance-statistics-2016. [Accessed 10 July 2020].

[35] Van Grootheest A, De Jong-Van Den Berg L. The role of hospital and community pharmacists in pharmacovigilance. Res Soc Adm Pharm 2005;1:126–33.

[36] Hussain R, Hassali MA, Muneswarao J, Atif M, Babar Z-U-D. A qualitative evaluation of adverse drug reaction reporting system in Pakistan: findings from the nurses' perspective. Int J Environ Res Public Health 2020;17:3039.

[37] WPR. Lahore population 2020. World Population Review; 2020. [online]. Available from: https://worldpopulationreview.com/world-cities/lahore-population. [Accessed 5 July 2020].

[38] Rashid H. Impact of the drug regulatory authority Pakistan: an evaluation. New Visions Public Aff 2015;7:50–61.

[39] Atif M, Ahmad M, Saleem Q, Curley L, Qamar-Uz-Zaman M. Pharmaceutical policy in Pakistan. In: Pharmaceutical policy in countries with developing healthcare systems. Springer; 2017.

[40] Punch KF. Introduction to social research: quantitative and qualitative approaches. Sage; 2013.

[41] Yilmaz K. Comparison of quantitative and qualitative research traditions: epistemological, theoretical, and methodological differences. Eur J Educ 2013;48:311–25.

[42] Morse JM. Data were saturated. Los Angeles, CA: Sage Publications; 2015.

[43] Saunders B, Sim J, Kingstone T, Baker S, Waterfield J, Bartlam B, Burroughs H, Jinks C. Saturation in qualitative research: exploring its conceptualization and operationalization. Qual Quant 2018;52:1893–907.

[44] Cresswell J, Plano Clark V. Designing and conducting mixed method research. 2nd ed. Thousand Oaks, CA: Sage; 2011. 201.

[45] Patton MQ. Qualitative research. In: Encyclopedia of statistics in behavioral science. John Wiley & Sons, Ltd; 2005.

[46] Elkalmi RM, Hassali MA, Ibrahim MIM, Liau SY, Awaisu A. A qualitative study exploring barriers and facilitators for reporting of adverse drug reactions (ADRs) among community pharmacists in Malaysia. J Pharm Health Serv Res 2011;2:71–8.

[47] Hadi MA, Neoh CF, Zin RM, Elrggal ME, Cheema E. Pharmacovigilance: pharmacists' perspective on spontaneous adverse drug reaction reporting. Integr Pharm Res Pract 2017;6:91.

[48] Hazell L, Shakir SA. Under-reporting of adverse drug reactions. Drug Saf 2006;29:385–96.

[49] Herdeiro MT, Figueiras A, Polónia J, Gestal-Otero J. Influence of pharmacists' attitudes on adverse drug reaction reporting. Drug Saf 2006;29:331–40.

[50] Jose J, Jimmy B, Al-Ghailani ASH, Al Majali MA. A cross sectional pilot study on assessing the knowledge, attitude and behavior of community pharmacists to adverse drug reaction related aspects in the Sultanate of Oman. Saudi Pharm J 2014;22:163–9.

[51] Suyagh M, Farah D, Farha RA. Pharmacist's knowledge, practice and attitudes toward pharmacovigilance and adverse drug reactions reporting process. Saudi Pharm J 2015;23:147–53.

[52] Qassim S, Metwaly Z, Shamsain M, Al Hariri Y. Reporting adverse drug reactions: evaluation of knowledge, attitude and practice among community pharmacists in UAE. IOSR J Pharm 2014;22:31–40.

[53] Leguelinel-Blache G, Dubois F, Bouvet S, Roux-Marson C, Arnaud F, Castelli C, Ray V, Kinowski J-M, Sotto A. Improving patient's primary medication adherence. Medicine 2015;94:e1805.

[54] Sanii Y, Torkamandi H, Gholami K, Hadavand N, Javadi M. Role of pharmacist counseling in pharmacotherapy quality improvement. J Res Pharm Pract 2016;5:132.

[55] Bawazir SA. Attitude of community pharmacists in Saudi Arabia towards adverse drug reaction reporting. Saudi Pharm J 2006;14:75.

[56] Khalili H, Mohebbi N, Hendoiee N, Keshtkar A-A, Dashti-Khavidaki S. Improvement of knowledge, attitude and perception of healthcare workers about ADR, a pre- and post-clinical pharmacists' interventional study. BMJ Open 2012;2.

[57] Gavaza P, Brown CM, Lawson KA, Rascati KL, Wilson JP, Steinhardt M. Influence of attitudes on pharmacists' intention to report serious adverse drug events to the Food and Drug Administration. Br J Clin Pharmacol 2011;72:143–52.

[58] Sweis D, Wong IC. A survey on factors that could affect adverse drug reaction reporting according to hospital pharmacists in Great Britain. Drug Saf 2000;23:165–72.

[59] Hussain R, Hassali MA. Current status and future prospects of pharmacovigilance in Pakistan. J Pharm Policy Pract 2019;12:1–3.

[60] Al-Hazmi NN, Naylor I. A study of community pharmacists' awareness and contributions to adverse drug reactions (ADRs) reporting systems in the Makkah, Kingdom of Saudi Arabia (KSA). J Clin Trials 2013;3:1–5.

[61] Ribeiro-Vaz I, Herdeiro MT, Polónia J, Figueiras A. Strategies to increase the sensitivity of pharmacovigilance in Portugal. Rev Saude Publica 2010;45:129–35.

[62] Toklu HZ, Uysal MK. The knowledge and attitude of the Turkish community pharmacists toward pharmacovigilance in the Kadikoy district of Istanbul. Pharm World Sci 2008;30:556–62.

[63] Irujo M, Beitia G, Bes-Rastrollo M, Figueiras A, Hernandez-Diaz S, Lasheras B. Factors that influence under-reporting of suspected adverse drug reactions among community pharmacists in a Spanish region. Drug Saf 2007;30:1073–82.

[64] Saygi S, Alkas FB, Etikan I, Gelisen I, Sardas S. Pharmacovigilance awareness among the community pharmacists and pharmacy students in the Turkish Republic of Northern Cyprus. J Pharmacovigil 2016;4(2), 1000204.

[65] Oshikoya KA, Awobusuyi JO. Perceptions of doctors to adverse drug reaction reporting in a teaching hospital in Lagos, Nigeria. BMC Clin Pharmacol 2009;9:14.

Index

Note: Page numbers followed by *f* indicate figures, *t* indicate tables, and *b* indicate boxes.

CPI Antony Rowe
Eastbourne, UK
May 13, 2021